154677

LAKE BLACKSHEAR LIBRARY

3 4710 42940286 4

D0843413

629.28822   154677
Chilton Book Company.   Automotive
guide for the SAAB
    Chilton's repair and tune-up
guide for the SAAB

LAKE BLACKSHEAR REGIONAL LIBRARY
307 EAST LAMAR STREET
AMERICUS, GEORGIA 31709

Chilton's

Repair and Tune-Up Guide

for the

SAAB

Illustrated

PRODUCED BY THE AUTOMOTIVE BOOK DEPARTMENT

Managing Editor: JOHN MILTON

Technical Writer: RICHARD ALTMAN

Technical Editor: JEFFREY HALLINGER

CHILTON BOOK COMPANY

PHILADELPHIA   NEW YORK   LONDON

Copyright © 1970 by Chilton Book Company.
Published in Philadelphia by Chilton Book Company,
and simultaneously in Ontario, Canada,
by Thomas Nelson & Sons, Ltd.
All rights reserved.
Manufactured in the United States of America by
Alpine Press, Inc.

ISBN 0-8019-5541-6

Library of Congress Catalog Card Number 70-133032

Chilton Book Company expresses appreciation to SAAB Motors, Inc., New Haven, Conn., and The Free Library
of Philadelphia, Pa., for supplying most of the illustrations used in this book, and for their generous assistance
in obtaining technical information.

LAKE BLACKSHEAR REGIONAL LIBRARY
AMERICUS, GEORGIA

154677

Contents

Chapter 1

Identification, Maintenance and Troubleshooting

Introduction

The SAAB, a product of the Swedish aircraft firm SAAB Aktiebolag, was first introduced in 1949 to meet the demand for economical, dependable automobiles in the immediate post-war period. Designated the Model 92, the original design proved so sound that it has lasted to this day in the form of the Model 96, and its station wagon version the Model 95. The Sonett, SAAB's sport car, shares many components with the Monte Carlo 850 and V4 models and is covered in this book along with those models.

Identification

The chassis number is found stamped on a plate attached to the firewall under the hood, as well as on the left-hand side of the support member underneath the front edge of the back seat. On 1969–70 models, however, the number is embossed on a tab visible through the driver's side windshield. The chart shows the cut-off chassis numbers for the different models.

Location of Chassis number on models up to 1969

Location of Chassis number on 1969-70 models

Maintenance

Two-Stroke Models

Engine oil requirements basically are the same for all models. Self-mixing two-stroke

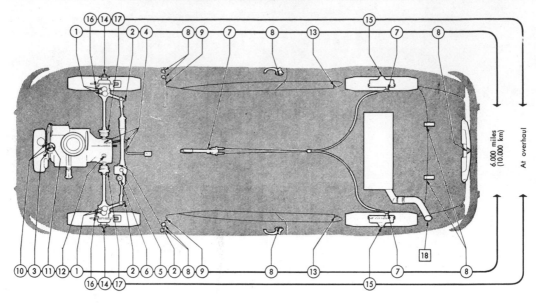

Lubrication table—two-stroke models

3,000 MILES (5,000 KM) OR TWICE A YEAR

Index	Lubrication points	Number	Lubricant	Instructions
1	Upper & lower ball joints, L & R	4	SAAB Special Chassis grease	Grease gun
2	Steering gear with ball joints	3	SAAB Special Chassis grease	Grease gun. Steering wheel turned fully to the left
3	Distributor gear	1	SAAB Special Chassis grease	Grease gun
4	Accelerator	4	SAE 40 Oil	Oil can
5	Hydraulic brake system	1	Brake fluid SAE 70 R 3	Check, intervals of max. 3 months*
6	Hydraulically operated clutch	1	Brake fluid SAE 70 R 3	Check, intervals of max. 3 months*
7	Handbrake links	3	SAE 40 Oil	Oil can
8	Hinges and locks	9	SAE 40 Oil	Oil can
9	Distributor shaft	2	Vaseline	Grease
10	Door stops	2	SAE 40 Oil	Oil can
11	Distributor cam	1	Bosch Ft 1 v 4	Grease felt sparingly
12	Gearbox	1	EP oil SAE 80 (3 US pints=1.4 litre)	Check every 6,000 miles (10,000 km), change every 12,000 miles (20,000 km)
13	Latch, rear side window	2	Vaseline	Grease
14	Front wheel bearings	2	SAAB Special Chassis grease	Repack at overhaul
15	Rear wheel bearings	2	SAAB Special Chassis grease	Repack at overhaul
16	Drive shaft, outer joint, L & R	2	SAAB Special Chassis grease	Repack at overhaul
17	Drive shaft inner joint, L & R	2	SAAB Special Chassis grease	Repack at overhaul
	Rear shock absorber, (station wagon only)	2	Shock absorber oil	Check every 12,000 miles (20,000 km)
	Battery	1	Distilled water	Refill
	Radiator	1	Coolant	Check
	Tires	5		Check

* The brake fluid should be changed every 36,000 miles (60,000), or at intervals not exceeding 3 years.

Location of engine serial number—two-stroke to 1965

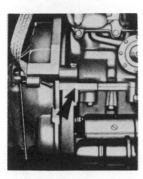

Location of engine serial number—two-stroke from 1966

Location of engine serial number—four-stroke V4

oil (pre-diluted by the manufacturer) is recommended during the winter. This is especially true of the GT-850 and Sonett models. Having a separate oil system, they have an oil pump sensitive to oil viscosity (which rises with decrease in temperature), and is sometimes subject to oil-feeding problems if thick oil is used. During summer months, any good grade two-stroke oil of at least 30–40 weight (SAE) meeting HD— ML, MM and MS requirements may be used. With models other than the GT-850, mixing the oil with an equal quantity of gasoline during cold weather, before filling, aids lubrication.

The normal ratio of oil to gasoline is 1:33 (3% by volume) for all models other than the GT-750. The high output and increased load requirements of this engine require that a 1:25 (4% by volume) mixture be used. Self-mixing oil, being diluted and thus thinner, also must be mixed in a 1:25 ratio for all engines except the GT-750. The GT-750 should have self-mixing oil mixed at 5% by volume. *CAUTION: Under no circumstances should multigrade oil be used in any two-stroke SAAB. NOTE: A 1:33 mixture is 1 quart per 8¼ gallons; a 1:25 mixture is 1 quart per 6¼ gallons.*

All lubrication requiring chassis grease should be accomplished using SAAB special grease. If such grease is not available, any good grade commercial chassis grease may be used, although the service interval should be halved. It is recommended that SAAB grease never be mixed with any other brand; therefore, use one or the other, but never alternate. *NOTE: When lubricating ball*

Chassis Number Identification

	Model Year					
Model	1960	1961	1962	1963	1964	1965
GT–750	100,001–112,500	112,501–139,600	139,601–150,000			
95	1–1,700	1,701–3,684	3,685–6,623	6,624–10,800	10,801–N.A.	23,101–28,701
96 (incl. Sport)	100,101–112,500	112,501–139,600	139,601–168,000	168,001–201,400	201,401–N.A.	310,001–349,693

	Model Year				
Model	1966	1967	1968	1969	1970
GT–750					
95	30,001–37,300	42,001–50,197	52,001–62,059	65,001–74,986	80,001–
96 (incl. Sport)	370,001–400,750	420,001–458,526	470,001–507,018	520,001–552,859	560,001–

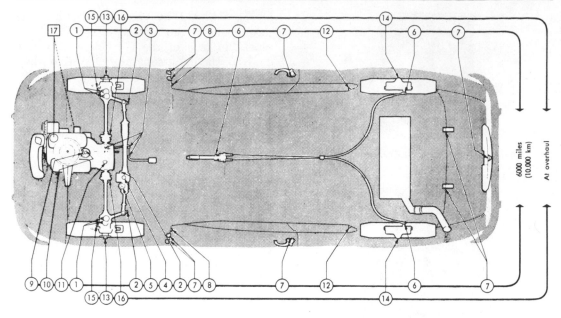

Lubrication table—four-stroke models (V4)

6,000 MILES (10,000 KM) OR TWICE A YEAR

Index	Lubrication points	Number	Lubricant	Instructions
1	Upper and lower ball joints, L and R	4	SAAB Special Chassis grease	Grease gun
2	Steering gear and ball joints	3	SAAB Special Chassis grease	Grease gun. Steering wheel turned fully to the left
3	Accelerator	4	SAE 40 oil	Oil can
4	Hydraulic brake system	1	Brake fluid SAE 70 R 3	Check intervals of max. 3 months*
5	Hydraulic operated clutch	1	Brake fluid SAE 70 R 3	Check intervals of max. 3 months*
6	Handbrake links	3	SAE 40 oil	Oil can
7	Hinges and locks	9	SAE 40 oil	Oil can
8	Door stops	2	Vaseline	Grease
9	Breaker cam	1	Bosch ft 1 v 4	Grease
10	Distributor lubr. felt under rotor	1	Motor oil	Oil
11	Gearbox	1	EP oil SAE 80 (3 imp. pints 1.7 litres)	Check every 6,000 miles (10,000 km), change every 12,000 miles (20,000 km)
12	Latch, rear side window	2	Vaseline	Grease
13	Front wheel bearings	2	SAAB Special Chassis grease	Repack at overhaul
14	Rear wheel bearings	2	SAAB Special Chassis grease	Repack at overhaul
15	Drive shaft, outer joint, L and R	2	SAAB Special Chassis grease	Repack at overhaul
16	Drive shaft inner joint, L and R	2	SAAB Special Chassis grease	Repack at overhaul
17	Engine			Note. Replacement of oil filter. Use original filter only.

* The brake fluid should be changed every 36,000 miles (60,000 km), or at intervals not exceeding 3 years.

joints, jack up car to get good grease distribution.

Four-Stroke Models

Body and running gear maintenance is the same as for the two-stroke models. The engine, however, carries its own oil supply, which must be changed at regular intervals. Engine oil meeting Ford specification ESE-M2C-101-B should be used; viscosity should be selected on the basis of prevailing temperature. In summer months, use either straight SAE 20, 30, 40 grade or a suitable multigrade 10W-30 or 20W-40. During the winter, use either straight SAE 10W or a suitable multigrade 10W-30 or 10W-40. At temperatures constantly below —4°F., use a multigrade 5W-20.

Maintenance Jobs— Two-Stroke Models

AT 1,200 MILES (2,000 KILOMETERS)

1. Change transmission oil (1.4 qts. EP 80); clean magnetic drain plug.
2. Inspect rubber bellows at driveshaft U-joints, ball joints, steering gear.
3. Grease upper and lower ball joints and tie-rod ends.
4. Tighten engine mounting bolts, front and rear.
5. Check exhaust system for leakage; tighten all brackets and clamps.
6. Tighten steering gear to body bolts, two per side.
7. Grease distributor gear.
8. Grease steering box, with wheels turned hard left.
9. Check radiator and hoses for leaks.
10. Check fanbelt tension.
11. Check and adjust spark plugs.
12. Check and adjust distributor points.
13. Check all ignition wiring and spark plug wire connections.
14. Check and adjust ignition timing.
15. Tighten fuel pump mounting bolts.
16. Tighten intake manifold and carburetor mounting bolts.
17. Check fuel lines for leakage.
18. Check battery level and specific gravity.
19. Tighten crankshaft pulley nut.
20. Tighten exhaust manifold bolts.
21. Torque cylinder head bolts with engine cold.

22. Tighten engine side support.
23. Check brake lines and hoses for leakage.
24. Check clutch hydraulic system for leakage.
25. Check hydraulic fluid in brake and clutch reservoirs.
26. Check and adjust clutch pedal free-play.
27. Adjust rear brakes.
28. Adjust parking brake.
29. Tighten rear axle hold-down bolts (four).
30. Tighten body side link, two bolts per side.
31. Check operation of lights, wiper and horn.
32. Check and lubricate door hinges and striker plates.
33. Check tire pressure (spare, too).
34. Check front end alignment.
35. Tighten front suspension mounting bolts (eight per side).
36. Check idle speed.

AT 6,000 MILES (10,000 KILOMETERS) AND EVERY 6,000 MILES (10,000 KILOMETERS) THEREAFTER

1. Check transmission oil level.
2. Check rubber bellows at driveshaft U-joints, steering gear, ball joints and tie-rod ends.
3. Grease upper and lower ball joints and tie-rod ends.
4. Check tire pressure (spare, too).
5. Check front end alignment.
6. Check brake linings/pads for wear.
7. Check radiator and hoses for cracks and leakage.
8. Check fanbelt tension.
9. Clean air filter or replace.
10. Lubricate throttle linkage with light oil.
11. Check battery level; clean terminals with sandpaper and baking soda, grease with Vaseline.
12. Check spark plugs and adjust or replace.
13. Adjust distributor points.
14. Grease distributor cam lubricator (felt), oil distributor bearings.
15. Clean and check all ignition and spark plug wires.
16. Adjust ignition timing.
17. Grease distributor gear.
18. Grease steering gear box, with wheels turned hard left.

19. Check hydraulic fluid in brake and clutch reservoirs.

20. Adjust clutch pedal free-play.

21. Adjust rear brakes.

22. Oil parking brake pivot points.

23. Check operation of lights, horn and wipers.

24. Check headlight adjustment (must be done on special machine).

25. Grease door stops, striker plates, window catches with Vaseline.

26. Oil all door, hood and trunk hinges.

27. Check idle speed.

NOTE: Replace rear resonator of exhaust system at 18,000 miles. Replace entire exhaust system at 42,000 miles. (service item).

At 12,000 Miles (20,000 Kilometers) and at Every 12,000 Miles Thereafter

1. Change transmission oil (1.4 qts. EP 80); clean the magnetic drain plug.

2. Inspect rubber bellows at drive shaft U-joints, ball joints, steering gear and tie-rod ends.

3. Check tie-rod ends and replace if wear is evident.

4. Grease upper and lower ball joints/ king pins and tie-rod ends.

5. Check exhaust system for leakage; tighten all brackets and clamps.

6. Check radiator and hoses for leakage; replace cracked hoses.

7. Check fanbelt tension and adjust if necessary.

8. Replace air filter.

9. Clean carburetor float chambers, mesh filters and needle passages.

10. Clean fuel pump filter.

11. Check fuel lines and hoses for leakage.

12. Lubricate the throttle linkage with light oil.

13. Check battery level, clean terminals with sandpaper and baking soda and apply Vaseline to terminals.

14. Check spark plugs and replace if necessary. (Plugs normally last 6,000 miles.)

15. Adjust or replace distributor points.

16. Grease distributor lubrication felt; oil distributor bearings.

17. Clean and inspect all ignition wiring and spark plug wires.

18. Adjust ignition timing.

19. Inspect brake linings/pads.

20. Adjust rear brakes.

21. Check brake hoses and lines for leak-

age; check that master and wheel cylinders are tightened properly. Hoses are normally changed at around 36,000 miles, as are all rubber parts in hydraulic system.

22. Adjust parking brake lever.

23. Lubricate all parking brake pivot points.

24. Check Station Wagon rear shock absorber oil.

25. Check all rubber shock absorber bushings for wear.

26. Check condition of undercoating. The dealer is best equipped to handle any problems in this area.

27. Check clutch hydraulic system for leakage.

28. Adjust clutch pedal free-play.

29. Check hydraulic fluid in brake and clutch reservoirs.

30. Lubricate distributor gear.

31. Grease steering gear box, with wheels turned hard left.

32. Check headlight, wiper and horn operation.

33. Check headlight adjustment (must be done on special machine).

34. Lubricate door locks, striker plates and hinges.

35. Grease door stops, striker plates and window catches with Vaseline.

36. Lubricate trunk, hood and pedal friction points.

37. Check that front seat rails are tightened properly; grease with Vaseline.

38. Check tire pressure (spare, too).

39. Check front end alignment.

40. Check idle speed.

Maintenance Jobs— Four-Stroke (V4) Models

At 1,200 Miles (2,000 Kilometers)

1. Tighten engine mounting bolts, front and rear.

2. Tighten body side link, two bolts on each side.

3. Tighten and adjust door striker plates.

4. Check operation of headlights, wipers and horn, plus all other lights.

5. Check radiator and hoses for leakage.

6. Check clutch pedal free-play.

7. Check engine for oil leaks.

8. Tighten exhaust manifold bolts.

9. Torque cylinder head bolts.

10. Tighten engine side support.

11. Tighten steering gear box to body bolts.

12. Tighten front suspension bolts, eight per side.

13. Tighten intake manifold and carburetor bolts.

14. Check fanbelt tension.

15. Check fuel lines for leakage.

16. Check brake hoses and lines for leakage.

17. Check battery level and specific gravity.

18. Check hydraulic fluid level in brake and clutch reservoirs.

19. Check clutch hydraulic system for leakage.

20. Remove and clean air filter; lubricate choke shaft.

21. Check distributor points.

22. Check valve clearance and adjust if necessary.

23. Check ignition timing and adjust if necessary.

24. Check rubber bellows at driveshaft U-joints, tie-rod ends, steering gear and ball joints.

25. Grease upper and lower ball joints and tie-rod ends.

26. Grease steering gear box with wheels turned hard left.

27. Check the exhaust system for leakage and tighten all brackets and clamps.

28. Tighten rear axle hold-down bolts (four).

29. Adjust rear brakes.

30. Change transmission oil (1.9 qts. EP 80); clean magnetic drain plug.

31. Change engine oil (3.5 qts. incl. filter).

32. Check tire pressure (spare, too).

33. Check front end alignment.

34. Check and adjust carburetor (mixture and idle).

At 6,000 Miles (10,000 Kilometers) and at Every 6,000 Miles (10,000 Kilometers) Thereafter

1. Check operation of headlights, wipers and horn, plus all other lights.

2. Grease door stops, window catches and striker plates with Vaseline.

3. Oil door and trunk hinges.

4. Remove and clean air filter; lubricate choke shaft.

5. Tighten intake manifold bolts.

6. Disassemble and clean PCV valve.

7. Clean and adjust spark plugs. (Plugs

normally last 9,000 miles.)

8. Adjust valve clearance.

9. Check engine compression.

10. Check and adjust ignition timing.

11. Check distributor points and lubricate felt.

12. Check radiator and hoses for leakage.

13. Adjust clutch pedal free-play.

14. Change engine oil (3.5 qts. incl. filter); change oil filter.

15. Check transmission oil level.

16. Clean fuel filter.

17. Check hydraulic fluid level in brake and clutch reservoirs.

18. Check battery level; clean terminals with sandpaper and baking soda, then grease with Vaseline.

19. Check fanbelt tension.

20. Check tire pressure (spare, too).

21. Check headlight adjustment (must be done on special machine).

22. Check brake lining/pad thickness.

23. Adjust rear brakes.

24. Lubricate parking brake pivot points.

25. Check front end alignment.

26. Check rubber bellows at driveshaft U-joints, tie-rod ends, steering gear and ball joints.

27. Grease upper and lower ball joints and tie-rod ends.

28. Grease steering gear box, with wheels turned hard left.

29. Lubricate throttle linkage with light oil.

30. Check carburetor and adjust as needed.

At 12,000 Miles (20,000 Kilometers) and at Every 12,000 Miles (20,000 Kilometers) Thereafter

1. Check operation of headlights, wipers and horn, plus all other lights.

2. Tighten door striker plates and door hinges.

3. Grease door stops and window catches; oil hood hinges, lock and both pedals.

4. Check seat rails, tighten if necessary, lubricate with Vaseline.

5. Change engine oil (3.5 qts. incl. filter); change oil filter.

6. Change transmission oil (EP 80); clean magnetic drain plug.

7. Replace or clean air filter; lubricate choke shaft.

8. Remove and clean, or replace, vacuum servo air filter.

9. Disassemble and clean PCV valve.

10. Clean carburetor float chamber, mesh filters and jet passages.

11. Clean fuel filter.

12. Clean and adjust, or replace, spark plugs.

13. Check valve clearance and adjust, if necessary.

14. Check engine compression.

15. Adjust distributor points, replace if necessary.

16. Check ignition timing and adjust, if necessary.

17. Check radiator and hoses for leakage; replace cracked hoses.

18. Check fanbelt tension.

19. Check hydraulic fluid level in brake and clutch reservoirs.

20. Adjust clutch pedal free-play.

21. Check clutch hydraulic system for leakage.

22. Check fuel lines and hoses for leakage.

23. Check battery level; clean terminals with sandpaper and baking soda, grease with Vaseline.

24. Check tire pressure (spare, too).

25. Check headlight adjustment (must be done on special machine).

26. Check tie-rod ends for wear and replace if necessary.

27. Check brake lining/pad thickness.

28. Adjust rear brakes.

29. Lubricate parking brake pivot points.

30. Check brake lines and hoses, check that master and wheel cylinders are properly tightened. Rubber components in the hydraulic system should be replaced at 36,000 miles and all fluid changed.

31. Check shock absorber rubber bushings.

32. Check exhaust system for leakage; tighten all clamps and brackets.

33. Check body undercoating. The dealer is best equipped to handle problems in this area.

34. Check the rubber bellows at driveshaft U-joints, tie-rod ends, ball joints and steering gear.

35. Grease tie-rod ends and upper and lower ball joints.

36. Grease steering gear box with wheels turned hard left.

37. Lubricate the throttle linkage with light oil.

38. Check oil level in Station Wagon rear shock absorbers.

39. Check front end alignment.

40. Check carburetor adjustment.

Troubleshooting the Two-Stroke

The localization of faults in a car is often the most difficult part of any repair job, and no written instruction on the subject can replace familiarity with the car and knowledge of its construction. For this reason, serious repairs should be left to the dealer if at all possible, as he has both the tools and experience necessary for a good job.

SOURCE OF TROUBLE	REMEDY

ENGINE

STARTING DIFFICULT—COLD ENGINE

SOURCE OF TROUBLE	REMEDY
Dirty spark plugs, or crossfiring in ignition system due to moisture on plug insulators, ignition cables, coil and/or distributor cap.	Clean or replace spark plugs and wipe ignition cables, plug terminals, ignition coil and distributor cap.
No fuel at the carburetor.	Check that the pump is feeding fuel by pulling off hose at carburetor and running with starter motor. If no fuel is supplied, check pump filter, pipes and hoses for leaks and clogging. If fuel supply still fails after a new test, cranking with starter motor for about 12–15 seconds, the pump itself is probably defective. Remove the pump for examination, and repair if necessary.
Jets and ducts in the cold-starting device plugged up.	Blow ducts and jets clean with air.
No primary current to coil and distributor. No secondary current.	Check all cable connections, especially at ignition switch, to confirm that current is supplied to ignition system when starter motor is on. Cable might be broken at the ignition switch.

STARTING DIFFICULT—WARM ENGINE

SOURCE OF TROUBLE	REMEDY
Float riding too high in carburetor.	Adjust float level.
No primary current to coil and distributor. No secondary current.	Check and correct as per last step in cold engine, preceding.

PINGING

SOURCE OF TROUBLE	REMEDY
Ignition timing too far advanced.	Adjust ignition timing.
Wrong jets in carburetor. (Mixture too lean.)	Fit jets of correct size.
Automatic ignition advance in distributor sticks at earliest timing.	Test distributor on a distributor machine, if available. Clean and lubricate all parts. Replace any worn parts.
Spark plugs too hot.	Check that spark plugs of correct type and heat range are installed.
Heavy deposits of carbon in combustion chambers due to excessive city driving.	Decarbonize cylinder head.

IGNITION BY INCANDESCENCE

SOURCE OF TROUBLE	REMEDY
Incandescence under light loads at high rpm. Ignition timing retarded, or wrong spark plugs installed.	Check ignition timing and that correct type of plugs are installed.
Incorrect combination of jets in carburetor. Fuel mixture too lean.	Install jets of the correct size.

EXCESSIVE FUEL CONSUMPTION

It should be kept in mind that apparently excessive fuel consumption may result from extraneous causes, such as roof rack, winter tires, city driving, etc. To check fuel consumption, use smaller tank in the engine compartment in front of the fuel pump so that the same pump pressure is obtained. *A test based merely on consumption between two fill-ups cannot be regarded as completely reliable.*

SOURCE OF TROUBLE	REMEDY
Incorrect carburetor adjustment. Float riding too high, wrong type of jets fitted, or incorrect mixture adjustment.	Check carburetor settings and adjust as necessary.
Choke incorrectly adjusted.	Check that control wire returns properly.
Clogged air cleaner.	Blow out or replace air cleaner to remove dirt.
Dragging brakes.	Check brake adjustment and free rolling of wheels. *NOTE: Make sure that handbrake cable returns properly.*
Leaky fuel system.	Check for leaks and repair if necessary.

LACK OF ENGINE PERFORMANCE

Engine not firing on all cylinders.	Inspect spark plugs and check connections at plug terminals and distributor cap. Test radio interference suppressor, if installed.
Plugged or restricted exhaust system. Muffled exhaust noise.	Check entire exhaust system, paying particular attention to rear muffler.
Incorrect carburetor adjustment.	Check carburetor jet sizes, float level and mixture adjustment.
Ice in the emulsion jet. Induction preheat tube removed from air cleaner.	Connect preheat tube to air cleaner. Preheater must always be connected. From 1966—put the preheat valve in the "Winter" position.
Poor compression. Sticking or damaged piston rings.	Test compression. Disassemble engine, decarbonize piston rings and install new ones if necessary.

ENGINE NOISE

It is helpful to remove the fanbelt before trying to isolate engine noises. If the engine runs too long without the belt, however, overheating will result. To determine whether noise is in transmission or engine, depress clutch pedal—continuing noise is in engine.

Grinding noise from engine.	If the noise sounds different when clutch pedal is depressed (and when axial load applied to the crankshaft), defective main bearings may be suspected. Disassemble crankshaft and inspect the main bearings. *NOTE: The front main bearing is exchangeable.*
Knocking, related to engine rpm and more pronounced when engine speed goes down from high to low.	Piston scoring due to overheating or other cause. Pistons can be roughly checked by removing intake and exhaust manifolds, and possibly cylinder head. If scoring is found, disassemble engine, change the worn pistons and recondition scored cylinder bores by honing or reboring. Excessive piston clearance may cause similar knocking after considerable mileage. In most cases, elimination of this noise involves replacing pistons, and reclassification may be necessary if specified clearances are not maintained with the new pistons.
Rustling noise when engine is idling. If noise is thought to originate from distributor or distributor gear, touch distributor housing for confirmation.	Grease breaker cam assembly in distributor. Refill distributor gear grease cup. If noise disappears temporarily but reappears after driving a few miles, check the distributor gear and replace if necessary.
Irregular ticking. Broken piston ring or ring retainer.	Largely the same checks and measures as under "B," above.
Rattle occurring in all gears at roughly the same rpm.	Retighten nut for vibration damper with torque of 36 ft. lbs.
Nut on crankshaft for vibration damper not properly tightened. A similar noise can be caused by front muffler baffles.	If noise persists, try a new front muffler.

SOURCE OF TROUBLE	REMEDY

OVERHEATING

Fanbelt slipping.	Adjust belt tension.
Faulty thermostat.	Inspect thermostat and check its opening temperature. Try a new thermostat in the car.
Ignition timing retarded.	Check ignition timing and adjust if necessary.
Incorrect carburetor adjustment (mixture too lean).	Check jets and carburetor adjustments.
Cooling water hoses dissolved by oil and grease.	Inspect hoses and replace if necessary.
Blocked cooling system.	Flush cooling system.

NOTE: On early SAAB models, remove the two circular plates in the right and left front wheel wells during hot weather to avoid overheating. Take care to reinstall these plates when weather turns cool again.

ENGINE MISSES ON ACCELERATION, FAILS TO REV UP PROPERLY

Defective or dirty plugs.	Clean and test spark plugs, installing new ones if necessary.
Crossfiring in spark plug wires. Moisture in distributor cap.	Inspect and wipe wires and distributor cap; replace if necessary.
Defective ignition coil.	Test coil and replace if necessary.
Incorrectly gapped and/or burnt contact points.	Examine breaker points and replace if necessary. Adjust to correct gap, 0.012–0.016″.
Restricted exhaust system.	Check exhaust system, paying particular attention to rear muffler.
Water in fuel.	Look for water in fuel pump filter (at lowest point) and in float chamber.
Irregular fuel supply.	Examine jets, float level, etc. and check fuel pump pressure. Check that no air leakage occurs at gasket between induction manifold and engine block or at carburetor.

FUEL SYSTEM

FUEL PUMP WORKS IMPROPERLY

Leakage at connections and filter housing.	Inspect connection at fittings for fuel hoses; check gaskets in filter housing.
Impurities in fuel.	Check that filter and fuel lines between tank and carburetor are not blocked.
Condensate in fuel, causing frozen fuel lines, pump or tank (winter).	Check fuel pump filter and fuel lines for ice. Add alcohol to fuel.
Leaky pump diaphragm and valves.	If necessary, drain tank and fill up with fresh fuel. Inspect pump diaphragm and valves, replacing if necessary. If diaphragm is defective, there is often considerable fouling of No. 2 cylinder spark plug.
Leakage between engine block and fuel pump.	Check gasket and shim. If necessary, smooth the pump contact surface.

FAULTY FUEL GAUGE

Fuel gauge registers too low or too high.	Remove tank sender unit and adjust by carefully bending float arm.
Fuel gauge works intermittently or not at all.	Install a new gauge or tank sender unit in order to localize the fault. Faulty part can be replaced or repaired by SAAB dealer.

SOURCE OF TROUBLE   REMEDY

EXHAUST SYSTEM

Loss of Performance

Loss of performance due to restricted exhaust system. | Rear muffler is one most often blocked. Another thing to check is that the tailpipe is not bent closed.

LOW COOLANT TEMPERATURE

Difficulty in maintaining sufficiently high coolant temperature (winter weather). | Check thermostat opening temperature, possibly by testing a new thermostat installed in the car. Inspect the air valve in water outlet pipe on cylinder head. To screen airflow, close radiator blind or block grill with cardboard.

ELECTRICAL SYSTEM

Battery Run Down

Fanbelt slipping. | Adjust belt tension.

Battery cells dry. | Check electrolyte level in cells and top up as necessary.

Faulty battery. | Check that specific gravity is same in all cells after charging.

Generator or relay not giving sufficient current. | Carry out charging test. Check cable connections.

Short circuit in starter switch. | Disassemble switch and inspect contacts.

Defective Lights

Bulbs constantly burn out; charging voltage too high. (Poor cable connections, leading to crystalization of bulb filaments.) | Check charging settings of relay. Inspect all cable connections.

Weak headlights. | Check bulbs, connections, reflectors, panel switch and dimmer switch.

Stop lights or flashers, front and rear, not working. | Check light ground leads to fenders. Check bulbs and flasher relays.

For faults in ignition system, see Engine Troubleshooting.

CLUTCH

Clutch Slips

No clearance between release bearing and clutch. | Adjust release bearing clearance. The clearance should be 0.16″ measured at the slave cylinder.

Shaft for clutch release fork piston in master or slave cylinder, or clutch pedal, sticking. | Check and lubricate these parts to counteract sticking.

Oil on clutch lining. | Remove inspection cover plate. Check for leakage past clutch shaft seal. If leakage exists, remove engine from car and disassamble clutch for cleaning and possible replacement of lining. Install new shaft seal.

Worn clutch linings. | Install new clutch linings. Check flywheel, pressure plate and clutch-spring tension.

Clutch pressure plate springs defective (too weak). | Check pressure plate springs.

Defective or incorrectly adjusted pressure plate. | Inspect pressure plate and check adjustment.

Incomplete Disengagement

No clearance between release bearing and clutch. | Adjust release bearing clearance. The clearance should be 0.16″ measured at the slave cylinder.

Pressure plate (release) levers incorrectly adjusted. | Engine must be removed for checking and adjustment of pressure plate levers.

SOURCE OF TROUBLE	REMEDY
Warped disc or linings too thick (after refacing).	Check disc for runout. Ensure that correct lining is installed.
Disc hub binding on disc center.	Remove inspection cover plate. Lubricate sparsely with a few drops of graphite oil. For perfect results, remove engine and lubricate shaft and hub with graphite grease.
Clutch shaft (pilot) bushing at rear end of crankshaft damaged.	Remove engine. Trim bushing, or replace if necessary. Lubricate with graphite grease.
Defective tension pin holding clutch fork to release shaft, allowing movement with fork and shaft.	Disassemble transmission and install new tension pin, fork and shaft as required.

CLUTCH GRABS

Oil on clutch lining.	Same as under *clutch slips, "C."*
Release shaft, clutch operating mechanism or clutch pedal sticking, releasing jerkily.	Same as under *clutch slips, "B."*
Faulty or incorrectly adjusted pressure plate.	Same as under *clutch slips, "F."*

RELEASE BEARING

The release (throwout) bearing, a grease-packed ball bearing, always must be removed when the transmission case is being cleaned. Water, cleaning fluid or other extraneous matter will damage the bearing.

Grating noise when clutch pedal is depressed.	Remove engine and replace bearing, treating it as an integral unit.

BRAKES

Poor braking is usually due to incorrect brake adjustment, air in the brake system, or worn brake linings. Always use genuine SAAB linings as replacements. If linings of a newer type are installed on older cars, they always must be installed on *both* front or rear wheels, as applicable.

UNEVEN BRAKING

Car swerves to one side when brakes are applied. Grease on brake linings.	Remove brake drums and inspect linings. Install new linings and wheel bearing seal, if necessary.
Brake drums unevenly worn on opposite sides.	Machine drums in pairs or replace worn or scored drum.
Car swerves to one side with brake pedal too low. One circuit is inoperative due to leakage.	Inspect brake lines, brake hoses and brake pistons for leaks and repair if necessary.

BRAKES DRAG

Dragging brakes may be caused by excessively adjusted brake shoes or by jammed brake pistons.	Remove brake drum for inspection, and possible adjustment. Check piston return.
Return hole (compensating port) in master cylinder not uncovered when brake is released, due to incorrectly adjusted pushrod or swollen gaskets.	Check that clearance exists between pushrod and pedal. (Correct clearance is 0.024–0.047″, or 0.12–0.24″ at pedal tip.) If gaskets in master cylinder are in poor condition, replace them.
Incorrect or low quality brake fluid in hydraulic system.	Check condition of brake fluid. If bad, flush system thoroughly with methylated spirits and install new rubber gaskets throughout.
Brake hoses clogged, preventing return of fluid after braking.	Check that brakes release immediately when pedal is released.
Poor handbrake cable return or sticky brake cylinders.	Check, clean and lubricate.

BRAKE WARNING LIGHT GLOWS

The light glows due to long pedal travel; braking effect is good.	Adjust the rear wheel brake shoes.
The light glows due to long pedal travel; braking effect is poor or uneven.	Carefully examine system and repair leaks in brake lines, hoses or cylinders.

SOURCE OF TROUBLE   REMEDY

FRONT ASSEMBLY AND STEERING GEAR

Grease Leaking at Front Wheel Hub

Bearing grease on brake drum with damaged brake linings. Grease also may be visible on outside of brake drum or on rim through inspection hole in drum.

Remove wheel, brake drum and seal retainer. Install new seal and brake linings. (Check brake drum sealing surface against seal.)

Play in Wheel Bearings

This is easily determined with car jacked up to relieve wheels from load. Noise, especially when cornering abnormal tire wear and poor roadholding may be caused by play in wheel bearings. Permissible play 0.08″ measured at edge of wheel rim.

Install new wheel bearing and the seal between wheel bearing and universal joint. When changing bearings, pack the new one with ball bearing grease of good quality. Check rubber boot over outer universal joint.

Play in Driveshaft Universal Joints

Play in driveshaft universal joints occurs very seldom. If it occurs, it may be accompanied by knocking in conjunction with shaft rpm when car is freewheeling at low speeds. Same noise may also occur as the result of wear of ball and ball seat on inner or intermediate driveshafts.

Slight play in universal joints and driveshafts has no adverse effect, and, consequently, no direct action is called for. Inspection and possible renewal of rubber boots and grease in universal joints is recommended. Noise can be eleminated *only* by replacement of damaged parts.

Stiff Steering

Steering gear adjustment too tight.

Insufficient lubrication of, or use of wrong lubricant for, steering gear and/or ball joints.

Refill steering gear and ball joint grease cups. While lubricating, turn steering wheel to full lock in both directions.

Steering column bushings binding.

Relieve tension by adjusting steering column bracket bolts.

Abnormal Kickback in Steering Wheel

Poorly lubricated outer driveshaft universal joints.

Disassemble joint for lubrication. Replace damaged or worn parts.

Saab 95 and 96 (1965). Intermediate driveshaft rusted onto splines in yoke for inner universal joint.

Lubricate with oil can (hole on yoke). It may be necessary to disassemble the driveshaft on these models. Always lubricate sparsely.

Saab 95 and 96, Saab Sport and Monte Carlo 850, all from 1966.

Poorly lubricated inner driveshaft universal joints.

Disassemble joint for lubrication. Replace damaged or worn parts.

Tires Unevenly Worn

Uneven tire wear usually is due to lack of balance in the wheels—either inherent in wheels and tires or resulting from mud or tar on the inside of the rims.

Rotate wheels regularly, left front to left rear and right front to right rear. Check wheel balance at regular intervals and adjust if necessary.

Worn tread centers or edges are the result of excessive or insufficient tire pressure, respectively.

Adjust tire inflation to recommended pressures, with due allowance for load carried.

Scraped-off, feathered or cross wear is caused by incorrect wheel alignment.

Check toe-in, caster, camber, kingpin inclination and turning angles.

Worn wheel bearings or tie-rod ends; possibly bent rims.

Check wheel bearings and steering assembly. Check rims for runout.

Wheel Shimmy

Unbalanced wheels.

Clean rims and rebalance wheels if necessary.

Poorly lubricated driveshaft universal joints. Intermediate driveshaft rusted onto splines in yoke for inner universal joint. (Applicable to Saab 95 and 96 model 1965.)

See under previous heading.

SOURCE OF TROUBLE	REMEDY

CAR SWERVES TO ONE SIDE

Tire pressure too low in one front tire.	Check and adjust tire pressure.
Wrong camber adjustment.	Readjust camber. If driver is nearly always alone in car, compensation can be made by adjusting camber to ½° left side and 1° right side.
Rims bent or tires out-of-round.	Check rims and tires.
Poorly lubricated driveshaft universal joints and splines for intermediate driveshaft in yoke for inner universal joint. (Applicable to Saab 95 and 96 model 1965.)	See under previous heading.

Troubleshooting the Four-Stroke V4

ENGINE

STARTING DIFFICULT, COLD ENGINE

Faulty spark plugs. Gaps too wide.	Clean, adjust and test or replace.
Faulty distributor.	Check, adjust.
Poorly charged battery	Check condition of battery. Recharge if the specific gravity of the electrolyte has dropped to 1.23 or lower.
Faulty condenser.	Replace
Weak ignition coil.	Test and replace if necessary.
Faulty interference suppressors on spark plugs.	Replace
No fuel in the carburetor.	Check that the pump is feeding fuel by pulling off hose at carburetor and cranking with starter motor. If no fuel is supplied, check pump filter, pipes and hoses for leaks and clogging. If fuel supply still fails after a new test, cranking with starter motor for about 12–15 seconds, the pump itself is probably defective. Remove the pump for examination and repair if necessary.
Clogged jets and passages.	Blow out jets and passages with air.
No primary current to coil and distributor. No secondary current.	Check cable connections, especially the starter switch, to confirm that current is supplied to ignition system with starter motor on. The cable may be broken at the ignition switch.
Choke plate fails to close.	Remove air cleaner. Check that choke spindle rotates easily. If spindle binds clean its bearing surfaces with gasoline or trichcloroethylene.
Faulty carburetor gaskets.	Replace
Incorrect fast idle adjustment.	Check adjustment. See section headed *fast-idle adjustment.*
Oil too thick or dirty.	Change oil.
Poor compression caused by worn cylinders, pistons or piston rings. Piston rings stuck in ring grooves; burnt valves.	Check compression in all cylinders.
Leaking cylinder head gasket.	Replace gasket, mill heads if necessary.

STARTING DIFFICULT, WARM ENGINE

Incorrect float level. Damaged float or leaking needle valve.	Check and adjust if necessary. Replace any faulty parts.
No primary current to coil and distributor. No secondary current.	Check, correct as previously described.
Dirt in jets or passages.	Blow out jets and passages with air.
Flooded carburetor.	Check needle valve and float; clean or replace.

SOURCE OF TROUBLE	REMEDY

Engine Does Not Idle

Incorrect float level; leaking needle valve.	Check, adjust if necessary.
Idle fuel jet clogged with dirt.	Clean
Improperly adjusted idle screw and/or air regulating screw.	Check, adjust if necessary.
Faulty gasket between intake manifold and carburetor.	Replace gasket.
Leakage at vacuum connection.	Check, repair.

Pinging

Ignition timing too far advanced.	Adjust ignition timing.
Wrong jets in carburetor. (Mixture too lean.)	Install jets of correct size.
Automatic ignition advance in distributor sticks in advanced position.	Test distributor on test stand, if available. Clean and lubricate all parts; replace any worn part.
Heavy deposits of carbon in compression chambers due to excessive city driving or too cold plugs.	Decarbonize cylinder heads.
Too low octane rating of fuel.	Change to premium fuel the next time tank is filled.

Ignition by Incandescence

Wrong spark plugs.	Make certain that spark plugs of the correct type are installed.
Heavy deposits of carbon in compression chambers.	Decarbonize cylinder head.
Engine idles too fast.	Adjust idle speed.

Excessive Fuel Consumption

It should be kept in mind that apparently excessive fuel consumption may result from extraneous causes, such as roof rack, snow tires, predominately city driving, etc. A small tank installed in the engine compartment may be used to check fuel consumption. Connect the small tank ahead of the fuel tank so that the same pump pressure is obtained. *A test based merely on consumption between two fill-ups cannot be regarded as reliable.*

Damaged fuel tank.	Check, repair if necessary.
Damaged fuel line.	Check, replace if necessary.
Leaking nipples or fittings.	Tighten or replace.
Ignition timing improperly adjusted.	Check, adjust.
Faulty distributor.	Test, adjust.
Faulty ignition coil.	Test, replace if necessary.
Faulty condenser.	Replace.
Carburetor improperly adjusted. Float level too high, wrong type of jets installed, or air regulating screw improperly adjusted.	Check carburetor settings and adjust if necessary.
Automatic choke improperly adjusted.	Check, adjust.
Clogged air cleaner.	Blow out air cleaner; replace if necessary.
Dragging brakes.	Check brake adjustment and free rolling of wheels. *NOTE: Make sure that handbrake cable returns properly.*

Lack of Power

Engine not firing on all cylinders.	Check spark plugs and connections at plug terminals and distributor cap. Check radio interference suppressors, if installed. Set air preheat device to winter position.

SOURCE OF TROUBLE	REMEDY
Carburetor adjusted improperly.	Check carburetor jet sizes, float level and mixture adjustment.
Ice in carburetor.	Set air preheat device to winter position.
Unsatisfactory or contaminated fuel.	Drain and clean tank.
Leaking valves in fuel pump.	Replace.
Fuel pump filter clogged with dirt.	Remove and clean.
Air cleaner clogged.	Remove and clean.
Dirt in jets.	Clean.
Poor compression caused by worn cylinders, pistons or piston rings.	Check compression in all cylinders.
Burnt valves.	Decarbonize and grind valves.

OVERHEATING

Insufficient coolant.	Replenish coolant as required.
Fanbelt slipping.	Adjust belt tension.
Damaged pump impeller.	Replace.
Faulty thermostat.	Test, replace if necessary.
Clogged radiator.	Clean.
Hoses and passages clogged by dirt and sludge.	Clean.
Clogged water distribution pipe.	Remove, clean.
Ignition timing retarded.	Check, adjust if necessary.
Air/fuel mixture too lean.	Clean, adjust carburetor.

ENGINE MISSES

Unsatisfactory or contaminated fuel.	Drain, remove and clean tank.
Partially clogged fuel line.	Check, flush clean.
Faulty fuel pump.	Check, repair if necessary.
Poor contact at ignition coil connection.	Check, test and repair.
Open contacts at primary circuit connections.	Check, correct.
Primary circuit open or shorted.	Check, correct.
Faulty spark plug wires.	Clean connections. Replace wires if insulation is damaged.
Burnt breaker contact points.	Replace.
Incorrectly gapped breaker contact points.	Check, adjust.

EXCESSIVE OIL CONSUMPTION

Oil consumption can be affected by high-speed driving, abrupt acceleration, or too high oil level. When filling the crankcase, it is not strictly necessary for the oil to come up to the upper mark, so long as the level never falls below the lower mark.

Leakage at oil pan gasket.	Tighten the bolts. Replace gasket if broken.
Faulty gasket between fuel pump and cylinder block.	Replace gasket.
Damaged gasket in transmission cover.	Replace gasket.
Damaged crankshaft seal.	Replace seal.
Leakage at valve cover.	Check that cover is correctly installed; replace gasket if necessary.

SOURCE OF TROUBLE	REMEDY
Faulty seal at oil filter.	Check, replace oil filter cartridge if necessary.
Worn cylinders, pistons or piston rings.	Check compression.
Piston rings broken or stuck in grooves.	Replace piston rings.
Damaged valve stem seals.	Replace seals.
Worn valve guides.	Ream valve guides; install oversize stem valves.

Low Oil Pressure

Faulty oil pressure gauge.	Test, replace if necessary.
Damaged wiring to oil pressure gauge.	Replace wiring.
Relief valve stuck in open position.	Remove valve and replace.
Relief valve spring broken or too weak.	Replace.
Worn relief valve plunger.	Replace.
Oil pump strainer clogged with dirt.	Clean.
Worn pump rotor.	Replace.
Damaged or worn main and/or connecting rod bearings.	Replace. Regrind crankshaft if it is damaged or worn.
Faulty overflow valve in oil filter.	Replace oil filter cartridge.

Engine Jerks and Spits on Acceleration

Faulty spark plugs.	Test, replace if necessary.
Crossfiring in spark plug wires. Moisture in distributor cap.	Check and wipe spark plug wires and distributor cap; replace if necessary.
Faulty ignition coil.	Test, replace if necessary.
Accelerator pump inlet valve leaks.	Blow out with air.
Accelerator pump outlet valve leaks.	Blow out with air.
Accelerator jet clogged with dirt.	Clean jet.
Water in fuel.	Look for water in fuel pump filter (at lowest point) and in float chamber.
Irregular fuel supply.	Check jets, float level, fuel pump pressure, etc. Check that no air leaks exist at gasket between intake manifold and cylinder block or at carburetor.

Fuel Pump Operates Improperly or Not at All

Leakage at connections and pump housing cover.	Check fuel hose connections at fittings and cover gaskets.
Impurities in fuel.	Check that pump filter and fuel lines between tank and carburetor are not clogged.
Condensed water in fuel causes fuel system to freeze up in winter.	Check for icing in fuel pump filter and fuel lines. Drain tank and refill with fresh fuel if necessary.
Leaking pump diaphragm and valves.	Check pump diaphragm and valves, and replace if necessary. Check pump pressure.

Carburetor Floods or Leaks Fuel

Dirt in needle valve.	Clean valve and seat.
Worn valve or seat.	Replace.
Incorrect float level.	Check float level.
Excessive fuel pump pressure.	Check pressure.
Leakage at fuel pipe connections.	Replace faulty connections.
Damaged float.	Replace.

SOURCE OF TROUBLE	REMEDY

Uneven Idling

Volume control screw adjusted improperly.	Adjust.
Dirt in idling jet.	Remove, clean.
Idle passage clogged.	Remove carburetor and clean passage.
Air leaks at carburetor or intake manifold gaskets.	Tighten screws or replace gaskets.

Faulty Fuel Gauge

Fuel gauge registers too low or too high.	Remove tank sender unit and adjust by carefully bending float arm.
Fuel gauge works intermittently or not at all.	Install a new gauge or tank sender unit in order to localize the fault. Faulty part can be replaced or sent to local SAAB dealer for repair.

COOLING SYSTEM

Low Coolant Temperature

Difficulty in maintaining sufficiently high coolant temperature in winter.	Check thermostat opening temperature. (One method is to install a new thermostat for comparison. It is recommended that airflow be blocked at the grill.

ELECTRICAL SYSTEM

Battery Runs Down

Fanbelt slipping.	Adjust belt tension.
Battery cells dry.	Check electrolyte level in battery.
Faulty battery.	Check that specific gravity is same in all cells after charging.
Alternator or relay giving insufficient current.	Make charging test; check cable connections.
Short circuit in starter switch.	Disassemble and inspect switch.

BRAKES

Brake Warning Light Glows

The light glows because of too long pedal travel; braking effect is good.	Adjust the rear wheel brake shoes.
The light glows because of too long pedal travel; braking effect is poor or uneven.	Investigate and repair hydraulic leaks on brake lines, hoses or cylinders.

Chapter 2

Two-Stroke Engine and Clutch

Part I—Engine

The SAAB two-stroke engine is a three-cylinder, in line, water-cooled unit employing crankcase scavenging, piston-controlled port timing and cylinder scavenging on the Schnürle principle. Lubrication is accomplished by mixing motor oil with the fuel supply, except in GT-850 models.

SAAB 95 and 96 models use an identical 850 cc. engine, while the GT-750 uses a 750 cc. unit, similar to that used in the older 93 model. The engine used in the Sonett II is basically the same as that used in the Monte Carlo 850, with the exception of a different water outlet which has a connection for a thermostatically operated switch and for a hose to an expansion tank. The oiling system of the Sonett engine has an oil tank with no glass gauge, and a capacity of 3 quarts. In addition, this engine has two fuel pumps (Bendix) and a three-carburetor system employing Solex 40 DHW carburetors.

The cylinder block and lower crankcase half are made of cast nickel alloy steel and are machined to match. Matching numbers are stamped on each side of the joint at the right rear of the engine.

The cylinder head is made of light alloy (aluminum) and the crankshaft is built up by pressing separate sections together. The crankshaft has six webs and seven crankpins, permitting the use of single ball bearings and double or single bearings as main and connecting rod bearings. A torsional vibration damper is utilized.

Seals of the piston-ring type separate the three crankcase compartments and the flywheel end of the engine. At the front of the engine, the crankcase is sealed by rubber gaskets on the covers of the distributor gear housing. With the two-stroke design, it is extremely important that the crankcase be sealed.

The connecting rods are made of drop forged and hardened steel, the wristpin being carried in a caged needle bearing and the big end designed so that its internally ground surface forms the outer race of the connecting rod bearing.

Connecting rods in later model engines (850 cc., and 750 cc. from chassis No. 118.980) are piston guided, while in earlier 850 cc. enginess and 750 cc. engines up to chassis No. 118.979 they are crank guided.

The standard 850 cc. engine uses Ringstreifin pistons, while the 750 cc. engine uses aluminum units. All engines utilize chrome-steel piston rings.

The GT-850 engine is lubricated in a somewhat different manner than the engines used in the 93, 95 and 96 models. Instead of adding oil to the fuel, a supply reservoir is filled every 900–1,200 miles. Steel pipes

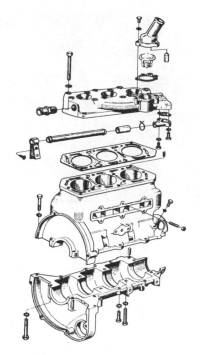

ENGINE BODY WITH CYLINDER HEAD

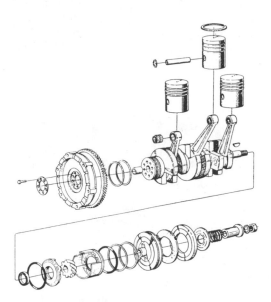

CRANKSHAFT WITH PISTONS

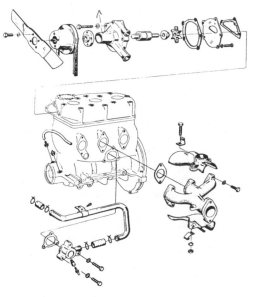

WATER PUMP AND CONNECTING PARTS, LEFT

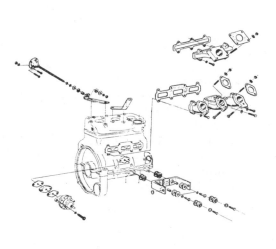

CONNECTING PARTS, RIGHT

Internal engine components—two-stroke

within the engine convey the oil to the three cylinders and the four main bearings under pressure from a separate oil pump. The distributor drive pinion is driven off the front of the crankshaft and is fitted with a slip clutch which operates if the oil pump jams or if the oil is too viscous.

The GT crankshaft is slightly different from the crankshaft used in other models. More material on the crank webs results in a higher crankcase compression pressure (volume is reduced) and, thus, higher power output.

IMPORTANT: The methods described

here are derived from factory-recommended procedures, which require special tools. Substitutes for these tools are mentioned and other, equally suitable, procedures are possible so long as a certain amount of care is exercised. In any case, the proper tool usually can be purchased through the SAAB dealer network.

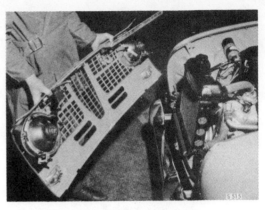

Removing grill panel

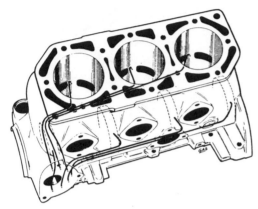

Engine block cutaway, showing oil passages— SAAB Sport and Monte Carlo 850

Engine Removal

1. Disconnect battery ground cable.

2. Remove the hood. Open the hood wide enough to remove the securing pins, if any, on the pivot pins. Take hold of the hinge bracket and bend it slightly inwards to release the pin on one side. The hood now may be easily lifted off. On the Sonett, simply open the hood and remove the two pivot bolts, then, with the help of an assistant, lift off the hood.

3. Drain the cooling system.

4. Disconnect the headlight and turn signal wires. On the Sonett, this must be done before removing hood.

5. Disconnect the radiator blind cord and hood lock mechanism.

6. Remove the four screws for the front panel and the two radiator supports from the body plate. Remove the clamping straps from the radiator. (*NOTE: Not necessary on Sonett.*)

7. Carefully lift off the front panel.

8. Disconnect the upper and lower radiator hoses from the engine.

9. Remove the two lower radiator bolts, then remove the radiator.

10. Disconnect the distributor primary wire, the ignition coil wire and generator wires. Remove the vent hose (if utilized) from the distributor cap.

11. Remove the air cleaner and preheat pipe.

12. Disconnect the fuel line from the pump.

13. Disconnect the cold starting (choke) control and throttle linkage from the carburetor.

14. Disconnect the two heater hoses and the temperature gauge sender from the engine.

15. Disconnect the engine side brace.

16. On the SAAB Sport and Sonett cars, disconnect the oil pressure monitor line and the hose from the oil pump. Bend the hose upward and fasten it so as to prevent losing oil from the tank. Cover all connections to keep dirt from entering the oil system.

17. Remove the two muffler flange bolts and loosen the exhaust pipe clamp.

18. Loosen the muffler retaining nut and tie the muffler out of the way to avoid damaging the pipe.

19. Remove the six front engine mount bolts from beneath the engine compartment floor.

20. Lift engine slightly and block up the transmission case with a 3½″ wood block.

21. Remove the two starter bolts and lay the starter on the floor of engine compartment with the cables still connected.

22. Loosen and remove the bolts that hold the engine to the transmission case, then pull the engine out carefully so as not to damage the clutch shaft.

Engine Installation

1. Lower engine into the car. Check the clutch shaft splines—if undamaged, coat them with grease.

2. Bolt the engine to the transmission case and reconnect the engine ground cable.

3. Install the starter.

4. Remove the wood block from under the transmission case, then lower the unit.

5. Refasten front engine mounts and the side brace.

6. Reconnect the muffler by fastening it to the exhaust manifold and muffler bracket. Don't tighten the bracket nut.

7. Tighten the flange bolts, the bracket nut and the exhaust pipe clamp—in that order.

8. On SAAB Sport and Sonett cars, reconnect the hose to the oil pump and the cable to the oil monitor on the pump. Turn the pump shaft about 100 times by hand.

9. Reconnect heater hoses and temperature gauge sender unit.

10. Reconnect throttle and cold starting device controls.

11. Install air cleaner and preheat pipe, then connect fuel hose.

· 12. Connect the distributor and generator wires. Replace the distributor vent hose.

13. Connect the radiator hoses.

14. Replace the front panel, along with the clamping strap and two radiator braces.

15. Install the radiator blind cord and the hood light mechanism.

16. Connect the headlight and turn signal wires.

17. Refill the radiator.

18. Replace the hood.

19. Connect the battery ground cable.

20. Check the clutch pedal free-play and adjust if necessary.

21. Adjust ignition timing and test engine.

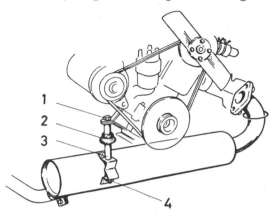

Front muffler
1. Bolt
2. Rubber seal
3. Spacer
4. Nut and washer

Basic ignition timing when installing distributor

Engine Disassembly

1. Clean the engine, using Gunk and kerosene.

2. Remove the fanbelt and generator.

3. Remove the intake manifold, complete with carburetor.

4. Remove fuel pump.

5. Remove exhaust manifold.

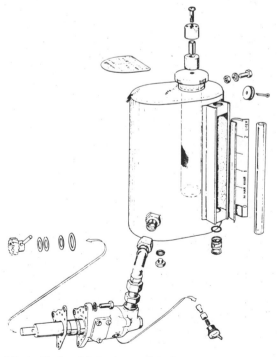

Monte Carlo oil injection tank and pump

6. Take off radiator inlet hoses.

7. Loosen cylinder head bolts and remove head; remove head gasket.

8. If the water pump and thermostat are to be removed, take off fan and pulley, then detach water pump from the cylinder head. Disconnect the upper inlet pipe and remove the thermostat and valve.

9. Loosen the distributor clamp bolt and the distributor.

10. On SAAB Sport cars, loosen the oil pump bolts and remove the pump.

11. Turn the engine right side up, making sure the surface is clean and flat.

12. Loosen the crankshaft pulley nut and remove the vibration damper and the pulley. (Use puller 784055 if available.)

Removing outer cover using pulley No. 784054

18. Take off the outer cover of the distributor housing and put it aside, along with the retaining ring and shims.

19. On SAAB 95 and 96, remove the distributor pinion with a puller (784051), then remove the inner cover together with O-ring.

On SAAB Sport, remove the distributor pinion together with the fiber washer. Remove and put aside the two slip clutch pins and springs.

20. Remove the piston retaining rings and drive out the piston pins using a brass drift or Tool 784061.

Removing front pulley using tool No. 784055

13. Insert spacers (784209 or 784065) under clutch levers and remove the retaining screws and clutch.

14. Release the lockwasher and loosen the flywheel bolts, then remove flywheel.

15. Remove the engine mounts from the lower crankcase half.

16. Remove the bolts and lift off the crankcase lower half.

17. Lift out the crankshaft, along with pistons. Take great care so as not to bend the connecting rods or damage the pistons. Removal is simplified by inserting a clutch centering tool (784064) into the flywheel end and screwing tool (784057), onto the stub at the other end of crankshaft.

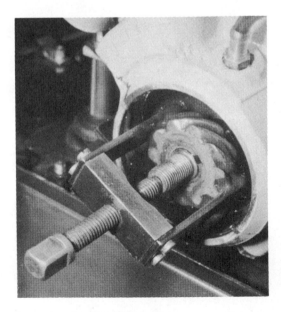

Removing distributor drive pinion

Engine Assembly

Inspect and clean all engine parts. Replace defective parts and all gaskets. A new cylinder head gasket *always* must be used regardless of the condition of the old one.

1. Install piston rings using piston ring pliers.
2. Install pistons onto connecting rods, using a dummy shaft and driver (784061) to locate needle bearing. Install piston pin with the driver and install retaining rings. Always install the pistons with the arrow pointing forward.
3. On the SAAB Sport, make certain the sealing ring is fitted at the ignition end of the crankshaft. If it has been removed, make sure the sealing rings are located with the openings 180° apart.
4. Put the Woodruff key in the end of the crankshaft. Oil the pistons and cylinder bores before assembly and use care not to damage pistons or rings. On SAAB 95 and 96 engines, make sure that the sealing rings are located vertically and that gaps are 180° apart.
5. Insert tool No. 784057 into the front end of the crankshaft and put the centering tool into the crankshaft bushing. Locate the piston ring gaps to coincide with the locking pins in the pistons and lower the crankshaft, with pistons, into the engine block. The center piston should be lowered first.
6. In SAAB Sport engines, place the two slip clutch springs and pins in the ignition end of the crankshaft, then refit the distributor pinion so that the pointed pin enters the notch on the pinion. Install the distributor pinion fiber washer. Oil all parts before continuing assembly.
7. Install the lower crankcase half, tightening the large bolts first. Begin in the middle and tighten alternately toward each end. Tighten the 5/16″ bolts to 18 ft. lbs. and the 3/8″ bolts to 29 ft. lbs. No sealing compound or gasket may be used between the lower half and the block; the surfaces must be clean and lightly oiled.
8. On SAAB 95 and 96 engines, install the inner cover of the distributor gear housing along with O-ring and shaft seals. Use tool No. 784056 (or homemade sleeve) to avoid damaging the shaft seals. Locate the cover with the cutaway opening opposite the hole for the distributor; install the distributor pinion with the chamfered side inwards.

On SAAB Sport engines, check that the ignition distributor pinion is located with the pointed pin in the groove, then insert the fiber washer.

9. Install the outer cover, with O-ring and shaft seal, (using tool No. 784057, or tool No. 784127 for the SAAB Sport engine) onto the crankshaft stub and press the cover in place by screwing in the tool.
10. Insert shims outside of the cover and install the retaining ring, making sure it is firmly seated in its groove. Loosen the tool about 1/2 turn and make sure the shims are tight against the retaining ring. If not, remove the ring and insert more shims.

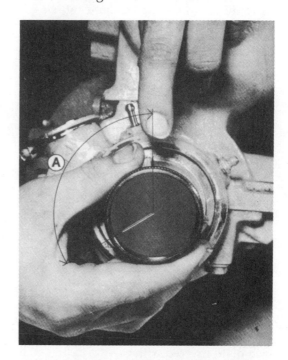

Shimming the outer cover. A=¼-⅛ turn

11. Install the flywheel, using a new retaining ring. Tighten the bolts to 22 ft. lbs. and secure them. (Special bolts are used for the flywheel.)
12. Insert the clutch plate and install the clutch, making sure the three spacers are properly positioned. Center the clutch plate with arbor No. 784069, or an old transmission main shaft while tightening the bolts, then remove arbor and spacers. Some flywheels and clutches are paint marked to indicate proper balance. These parts are to be installed with the marks 180° apart.
13. Install the pulley and vibration damper, using a new retaining ring under the nut. Torque the nut to 36 ft. lbs.

14. On SAAB Sport engines, install the oil pump and its gasket.

15. Install the engine mounts.

16. Install the lower water inlet neck and pipe; coat both sides of the gasket with Permatex.

17. With the surfaces dry and clean, place the cylinder head gasket on the block, making certain the broad part of the folded-on lining is against the cylinder head. Never use Permatex or oil on cylinder head gasket.

18. Install the cylinder head and tighten the bolts, in sequence, as described in the next part of this chapter.

19. Reconnect the water pump, pulley and fan, then hook up the hose for the engine inlet pipe.

20. Install the thermostat, the valve and the upper outlet pipe; reconnect the heater pipe.

21. Install the intake manifold and carburetor.

22. On the SAAB Sport, pour 1.7 fluid ozs. of motor oil into the distributor gear housing through the hole for the distributor.

23. Install the distributor.

24. Install the generator and fanbelt, then adjust the belt tension.

25. Install the exhaust manifold and gaskets.

26. On SAAB 95 and 96 models, fill the distributor housing with chassis grease.

Cylinder Head

The engine must be cool before the head is removed so as not to distort the casting.

Check the head surface with a straight-edge and correct any irregularities with a face plate covered with valve grinding compound. Don't indiscriminately mill the head to increase compression because the piston to head clearance can be decreased to the point where contact is made. Clean the spark plug threads with a round wire brush or with a M 18 V 1.5 mm. thread chaser. Carbon deposits in the lower parts of the thread can cause damage when a new plug is installed. Such damage, if it occurs, can be repaired using Heli-Coil inserts.

The head gasket is black composition material with rolled metal O-rings around the cylinders. When installing, the head surface must be clean and dry and the gasket carefully centered with the broad side of the folded metal O-rings facing the head.

Before installing the cylinder head bolts,

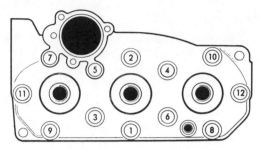

Cylinder head bolt tightening sequence—850 cc. engines

clean the threads with a wire brush and lightly coat the threads with oil or graphite grease. Tightening is done in steps—on 850 cc. engines, first tighten to 22 ft. lbs., then further tighten 90° (1/4 turn). This is equal to 36 ft. lbs. torque and is a better method than simply tightening to 36 ft. lbs. On 750 cc. engines, there are eight bolts instead of twelve. There are two types of bolts used as well—marked "80" and "100." The bolts marked "100" are tightened to 58 ft. lbs., the bolts marked "80" to 47 ft. lbs.

Start the engine, after assembling all other components, and allow it to warm up. Shut off the engine and allow it to cool to at least 86°F. Tighten all bolts again (without first loosening them) an additional 20° in the case of 850 cc. engines; to the prescribed torque for 750 cc. engines. After 1,200 miles, retighten an *additional* 20° or check prescribed torque (with engine cold).

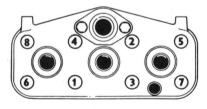

Cylinder head bolt tightening sequence—750 cc. engines

Cylinder Block

The cylinder block and crankcase are machined to match and it is impossible to replace one without replacing the other. The crankcase number is stamped on both sides of the common joint at the right rear of the engine. The engine number is stamped as illustrated in Chapter 1. The bore class is stamped on the left-hand side of the block.

DISASSEMBLY AND ASSEMBLY

Follow the procedures at the beginning of this chapter, with the following hints: when crankcase is fitted to the block, the surface must be perfectly clean. No form of gasket, sealing compound or similar material may be used. The surfaces should be lightly coated with oil. There are two bolt sizes, having different tightening torques. Tighten the large bolts first, beginning in the center and tightening alternately outwards in each direction. Make sure to tighten the rear bolts on the flywheel side.

HONING CYLINDERS

When pistons are replaced due to wear or damage it is often necessary to hone the cylinder bores in order to remove ridges and scoring, as well as to match the clearance of the piston class to be used.

BORING CYLINDERS

If reboring is necessary, select an oversize that will correct any damage to the bores. The ports always must be chamfered as indicated in the illustration, otherwise broken piston rings could result. This job can be done with a scraper or a rotary grinder. Make sure that all dust and chips are removed after this operation and that the port shape is not radically changed (which could result in unbalanced gas flow).

CHECKING OIL PASSAGES—SAAB SPORT AND MONTE CARLO 850

The block casting includes seven steel pipes which direct oil from the oil pump to the main bearings and the three cylinders. Check for blockage by passing a nylon thread about 0.04″ thick (fishing line) through the oil passage. If the oil passage is blocked, it can be cleaned with a piece of music wire 0.02″ thick. It is extremely important that oil passages be checked after reboring.

Pistons and Piston Pin Bearings

PISTONS—95 AND 96

The engine in the SAAB 95 and 96 is fitted with Ringstreifen pistons. This type of piston is distinguished by a steel ring which is cast-in below the bottom piston groove. All piston rings are of hard-chrome steel and are of the same thickness.

PISTONS—SAAB SPORT, MONTE CARLO 850, AND GT-750

The pistons in the SAAB Sport and Monte Carlo are made of aluminum and have very thick skirts. The three piston rings are made of steel and are molybdenum coated all around their periphery. The bottom ring is thinner than the other two and serves as an oil scraper. (The oil scraper is beveled at the top and has a sharp bottom edge.)

CONNECTING ROD GUIDANCE

The late-model connecting rods are piston-guided, meaning that they are guided axially at the piston pin bearing and have a large clearance at the big end connecting rod bearing.

When fitting piston, pin and needle bearing to the connecting rod, it is recommended that a guide pin (No. 784061) be used. When installing the piston pin, hold the piston firmly with the hand to avoid distorting the connecting rod. Always install the piston pin retaining rings.

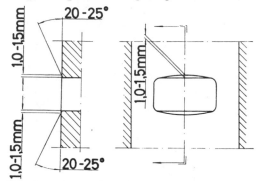

Chamfering ports after reboring cylinders

PISTON PIN BEARING

The piston pin bearing is a needle bearing. To ensure an accurate fit, a series of nine bearings is available.

MARKING OF NEEDLE BEARINGS

The basic diameter of the needles is 0.07847″ and the marking indicates the deviation from this value in thousandths of a millimeter. The bearing marked —9 has the smallest needles, while the biggest needles are installed in the bearing marked +7. Bearings marked with a plus sign are a kind of oversized bearing and normally are used on replacement crankshafts. When reconditioning piston pin bearings, both piston pin and needle bearings should be replaced.

Before reassembling the piston, the piston pin must be matched with a needle bearing to give the correct fit in the connecting rod. There should be practically no play, although it should not be necessary to force the piston pin into the needle bearing when the latter is fitted in the connecting rod.

Light thumb pressure is the maximum permissible pressure when fitting needle bearings. The piston pin should rotate easily between two fingers and should be free of play.

Pistons and Cylinder Classes

The markings on the cylinder block indicate the cylinder class of each bore. This

Piston and block marking codes

makes it possible to choose the proper piston. The choice of piston class is made from the following table.

Standard Classes	Oversize Classes Cyl. Bore, Piston Mark
A	O.D. 0.5 A
AB	O.D. 0.5 B
B	O.D. 1.0 A
C	O.B. 1.0 B

As shown, there are four standard classes of pistons and cylinders, and two oversizes,

0.5 and 1.0 mm. (.020″ nom. and .040″ nom.) with two classes each. Piston and cylinder class normally must agree. However, when the engine is properly broken in, or worn, pistons of a larger class can be fitted into the SAAB 95 and 96 engines. Remember that the difference between classes B and C is far greater than between other classes and that no deviations are permitted.

Measuring Cylinder Bores

If the cylinder bore is damaged by piston scoring, or if excessive wear is measured, the block must be rebored.

Normally, the bores are worn most at the upper part, although they also wear out-of-round.

It is necessary to measure each bore at several points—both across and lengthwise. To determine the true amount of wear, the micrometer must be set at the lower tolerance limit of the cylinder class concerned. Check taper by measuring at two points, 0.39″ and 1.97″ from the upper edge.

Measuring Pistons

Measure the piston diameter with a micrometer 0.8″ (0.6″ for the SAAB Sport and GT-750) from the bottom of the skirt and at right angles to the pin. Measure out-of-roundness by measuring parallel with, and at right angles to, the piston pin.

Checking Piston Clearance

Should the proper equipment for measuring bores and pistons be unavailable, pistons can be fittted with the aid of a feeler gauge, 1/2″ wide and about 8″ long, and a spring scale graduated to 1,000 grams (2.2 lbs.).

Clean the bore and lightly coat with oil. Place, for example, a .002″ feeler gauge along the bore, compression side, and insert the piston into the bore (minus the rings). Measure the clearance at right angles to the pin. Now, pull the feeler gauge from the bore with the spring scale and note the amount of pull; it should be 600–1,000 grams (1 lb. 5 oz.—2 lbs. 3 oz.). If the pull is less, try pistons one class larger; if more, try pistons one class smaller. Continue until the correct fit is obtained. The amount of pull should be checked at different piston depths.

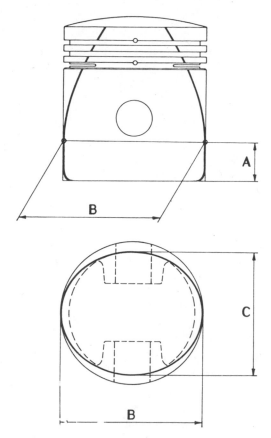

Measuring piston taper and out-of-roundness. A=distance from piston skirt bottom is 0.8" for 95/96, 0.6" for Sport and Monte Carlo. B= diameter at right angles to piston pin. C= diameter parallel to piston pin.

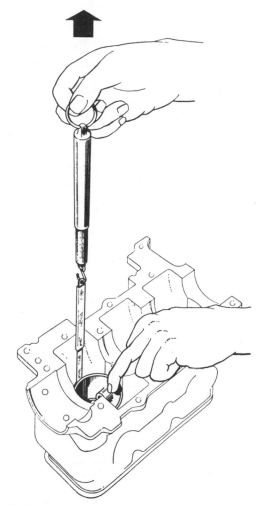

Checking piston clearance with feeler gauge and scale.

Part II—Clutch

General

The clutch in the two-stroke models is a single dry-plate type manufactured by Fichtel and Sachs or Borg and Beck.

The pressure plate assembly consists of a steel cover and cast pressure plate with six coil springs providing pressure. The unit is secured to the flywheel with six bolts.

A ball-type throwout bearing with a graphite or teflon coating is held in the clutch fork by two clip-type springs.

Clutch Removal

1. Remove engine, as previously described.

2. Loosen the six bolts that hold pressure plate to flywheel, placing spacers (tool No. 784209) as shown in the illustration.

Clutch Installation

1. Insert clutch disc and replace pressure plate assembly using spacers, as shown in illustration, to assure proper location of pressure plate in flywheel. Balanced clutch and flywheel combinations are color marked and should be assembled by locating the color marks as close to 180° apart as possible. Parts may be assembled in any position, or the same as they were before removal.

2. Center the clutch disc with arbor tool No. 78064 or a clutch shaft from an old transmission.

3. Tighten the six pressure plate bolts slowly and evenly and remove the spacers.

Clutch Adjustment—Cable Type

The clutch pedal free-play is adjusted by means of an adjusting screw on the side of

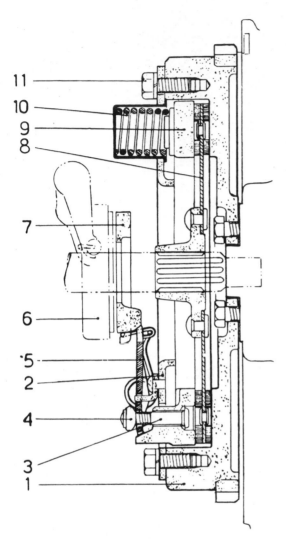

11
10
9
8
7
6
5
2
4
3
1

Two-stroke clutch assembly

1. Flywheel	6. Release bearing
2. Clutch cover	7. Release plate
3. Stud	8. Clutch disc
4. Adjusting nut	9. Pressure plate
5. Clutch lever	10. Spring
	11. Screw

the clutch housing opposite the slave cylinder. The free-play is increased by turning the screw to the left. Check the clearance by pressing the slave cylinder connection towards the clutch arm—movement of 0.16″ (A), indicates the correct clutch clearance.

Clutch Adjustment—Sonett Mechanical Linkage

The adjustment screw on the clutch cable is accessible from the left side of the engine compartment. Screwing in increases pedal play and vice-versa. Adjust for a pedal play

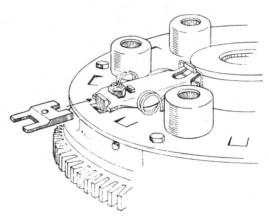

Fitting spacers when removing or installing pressure plate assembly

of 3/4–1″—clutch wear may cause the clearance to decrease to 3/8″ or so before clutch replacement is necessary.

Removal and Installation of Throwout Bearing

1. Remove engine.
2. Turn clutch lever forward, along with the two spring clips that hold the bearing in the clutch fork. The graphite ring must not be worn flush with its retainer. If worn, replace ring or bearing assembly.
3. Reinstall in reverse sequence, making certain spring clips are properly located.

Clutch Master Cylinder

DISASSEMBLY

To examine or renew parts, disconnect pushrod from pedal and remove from dash panel. Carefully move back the dust cap. Use longnose pliers to remove lock-ring. After removing pushrod, the entire piston assembly can be removed. The piston assembly can be disassembled by lifting the retainer spring leaf over the tongued end of the piston. Carefully remove the piston seal and the end seal. Push down on the piston return spring, allowing the valve spindle to slide through the key-shaped hole in the retainer so that the spring lets go. Remove the valve spacer carefully so as not to damage the elastic washer under the valve head. Remove the seal from the valve head.

If the cylinder bore is smooth, not scored or distorted, new seals may be installed safely.

Four-Stroke (V4) Engine and Clutch

Part I—Engine

Description

This engine is a four-cylinder, four-stroke, water-cooled overhead valve unit with the cylinders arranged in a 60° vee. The carburetor is a single downdraft type having an automatic choke. The cylinder heads have separate intake ports and common exhaust ports for each bank of cylinders; the cylinder block is one-piece cast iron.

The cylinder heads are identical, with partially machined combustion chambers and 14 mm. threads for the spark plugs. The valve guides and valve seats are machined directly in the heads. The cast iron crankshaft has three identical main bearings with hardened and ground journals and drilled oil passages.

The camshaft, case hardened and phosphated, is gear driven from the crankshaft at a 2:1 ratio through a fiber gear. The tappets, actuated directly by the camshaft, are carried in the cylinder block and move the valves, pushrods and rockers.

The connecting rods are shrunk onto the piston pins and are not detachable from the pistons; therefore, only a piston and connecting rod assembly is available as a spare part. The pistons are made of aluminum, having two compression rings and one oil

control ring. The upper ring is chrome-plated and plain, while the lower compression ring is of an oil scraping design. The oil control ring is tripartite. The lubrication system is force feed type, pressure being generated by a rotor-type pump driven by the camshaft. The pump is mounted inside the oil pan under the crankshaft. The pump

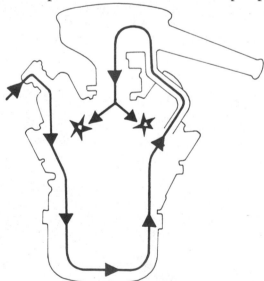

Semi-enclosed crankcase ventilation

forces the oil past a relief valve incorporated in the pump, through the full-flow oil filter and the oil passages to the various lubrication points.

33

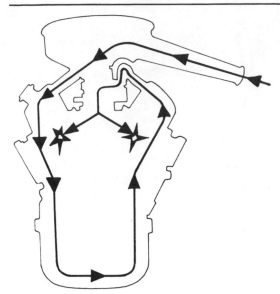

Fully enclosed crankcase ventilation

The engine in the Sonett V4 is identical to those used in the 95 and 96 models with the exception of heavier valve springs.

Engine Removal

If work is to be done on the engine only, the entire power unit should be removed and the engine separated from the transmission. Removal of the engine alone is not recommended.

1. Disconnect battery ground cable.

2. To remove hood first open it wide enough to remove the locking springs for the hood hinges. Now, bend the hood brace slightly inward to release the pin on one side. On Sonett V4, remove the two pivot bolts, then, with the help of an assistant, lift off the hood.

3. Drain engine oil and cooling water.

4. Disconnect headlight and turn signal wires. (*NOTE: This must be done before removing hood on Sonett.*)

5. Loosen the four screws that hold the grill panel and remove the two radiator supports. Detach the clamping straps from the radiator, then remove the hood lock and control wire.

6. Remove the grill panel, using care so as not to damage paint.

7. Disconnect the upper and lower radiator hoses.

8. Loosen the lower radiator retaining bolts and remove radiator.

9. Disconnect all hoses and cables from the engine. Note the proper location of wires to the alternator (tag them).

10. Remove the air cleaner.

11. Disconnect the throttle control, engine side support and air preheat casing.

12. Remove the flange nuts for the exhaust pipes at the cylinder heads. Remove the lower exhaust pipe clamps at the engine mounting pads.

13. Remove the rubber cushions for the middle exhaust pipe (under the floor).

14. Remove the spacers at the cylinder heads and lower the muffler as far as possible.

15. Remove the two front engine mounts (from above).

16. Disconnect freewheel control.

17. Remove the rear retaining bolt for the clutch cylinder and wire unit out of the way. Collect any shims used between the cylinder and transmission.

18. Remove the gearshift joint from the transmission, after removing the tapered pin.

19. Disconnect the speedometer cable.

20. Lift floor mat and remove the rubber plug so the center bolt of the rear engine bracket becomes accessible. Remove the bolt, using a 9/16″ socket and extension.

21. Jack up car and place jack stands under the front edges of the sills so that the front wheels clear the floor.

22. Remove the large clamps from around the rubber boots on the universal joints.

23. Attach a lifting device (GC 6000) to the engine.

24. Connect the lifting device to a suitable lifting hook, carefully lift the engine about 2″ and pull the transmission stub out of the rear engine bracket.

Removing engine with factory lifting brackets

25. Disconnect the inner universal joints, first on the right side, then on the left. Do this with the T-shaped pieces of the drive-shafts located vertically and with the engine pushed as far as possible in the opposite direction. (Fit protective cover 731762 in the rubber boots and 783846 on the inner drivers, if available.)

26. Lift the engine-transmission unit out of the engine compartment. Make sure the distributor vacuum chamber does not hit the cross brace.

Engine Installation

1. Make sure that the inner universal joints are filled with the proper grease.

2. Lower the engine-transmission unit into the engine compartment, using the lifting device.

3. Lower just far enough so that the engine brackets are about 0.2″ from the engine mounts.

4. Place the T-pieces of the inner shafts into the inner universal joints. Do this with the T-pieces located vertically and with the power unit pushed over as far as possible in the opposite direction. First assemble the left side, then the right.

5. Attach the engine side support; tighten after engine is in place.

6. Lower the engine into position and tighten the front engine mounts.

7. Lower the car onto its wheels.

8. Place new clamps on the inner universal joints.

9. Tighten the bolts for the rear engine bracket. Make sure the limit washer on the rear of the engine bracket is in position. If the washer is missing, the fan could hit the radiator.

10. Reinstall the rubber plug and replace floor mat.

11. Reconnect speedometer cable and freewheel control.

12. Install the gearshift rod joint.

13. Install the clutch cylinder, along with any shims; adjust the clutch.

14. Connect the exhaust pipes to the cylinder heads, using new gaskets.

15. Reinstall the clamps and the exhaust pipes.

16. Reconnect the throttle control.

17. Reconnect all hoses and cables to the engine. Do not confuse the leads to the alternator, as wrong wiring could ruin the unit. (Connect the black leads to D—.)

18. Install air cleaner.

19. Install radiator and hoses.

20. Install the front grill panel, radiator clamping straps, radiator braces and hood lock.

21. Reconnect the headlight and turn signal wires.

22. Fill and bleed the cooling system.

23. Check the oil level in the transmission.

24. Fill the engine with oil.

25. Reconnect the battery ground cable.

26. Start engine, check oil pressure and coolant temperature.

Separating Engine-Transmission Unit

DISASSEMBLY

1. Remove the flywheel housing cover plate from beneath the clutch housing.

2. Remove the bolts that connect the engine and transmission.

3. Remove the starter.

4. Separate the engine and transmission.

ASSEMBLY

1. Reinstall transmission. Make certain the guide sleeves line up correctly in the clutch housing.

2. Tighten the clutch housing bolts evenly to the proper torque.

3. Install the housing cover plate for the flywheel.

Engine Service

DISASSEMBLY

1. Ideally, the engine should be attached to the proper SAAB engine stand (using fixture GC 6010). If one is not available, place engine upright on a sturdy wooden bench or roller stand.

2. Remove the distributor cap and wires.

3. Remove the distributor vacuum line and fuel inlet line by applying pressure with a screwdriver behind the washers at the flexible connections.

4. Remove the carburetor.

5. Remove the distributor clamping bolt, clamp and distributor.

6. Remove the fuel pump, pushrod and gasket. Mark the end of the pushrod which normally rests against the camshaft.

7. Remove the spark plugs.

8. Loosen the water supply tube clamps and slide them away from the connections. Remove the tube.

Removing fuel pump (3), gasket (2), and push-rod (1)

9. Remove the oil pressure gauge sender.
10. Remove the valve covers. Release the rocker arm assembly by loosening the two bolts alternately, then removing the oil return plates.
11. Remove the pushrods, keeping them in the correct order.
12. Remove the thermostat housing, thermostat and gasket.
13. Remove the intake manifold retaining bolts and nuts. It may be necessary to tap the underside of either end with a fiber mallet in order to break the seals. *Do not pry with a screwdriver or similar tool.*
14. Remove the side bracket.
15. Remove the cylinder head bolts. Lift off the heads and inspect the cylinder head gaskets for signs of leakage.

Removing rocker arm assembly
1. Rocker shaft and arms
2. Oil return plate

16. Remove the tappets, using a bar magnet or bent wire; keep them in the correct order.
17. Remove the oil pan and gaskets.
18. Remove the balance shaft pulley.
19. Remove the transmission cover bolts.
20. Tap the rear of the water pump with a fiber mallet to loosen the transmission cover from the intermediate plate.
21. Disconnect the water pump from the transmission cover.

Removing water pump

22. Take the oil seal for the balance shaft out of the transmission cover (using slide-hammer or tool GC 6059).
23. Remove the oil filter.
24. Remove the oil pump and its drive-shaft.
25. Remove the bolt and washer for the camshaft drive gear. Take out the camshaft gear by hand.
26. Pull off the balance shaft gear.
27. Remove the two intermediate plate retaining bolts, then remove the plate and gasket.

Engine block, as seen from the front
1. Intermediate plate   2. Retaining bolts

28. Remove the camshaft thrust plate, the key and the spacer, then carefully pull the camshaft out of the bearings (toward the front).

29. Carefully remove any ridges or carbon deposits from the upper end of the cylinder bores, using a scraper or milling cutter, without touching the piston ring travel area of the bores.

30. Mark all connecting rods and caps, so that they can be reinstalled in their original positions. Remove the bolts and caps and push the pistons, with connecting rods, out of the bores using the handle end of a hammer. When removing connecting rods and pistons, the connecting rod and cap must be marked as indicated in the illustration.

Connecting rod marking

31. Remove the bearing inserts from the connecting rods and caps, then mark the caps and rods so that they can be installed in their original positions.

32. Remove the crankshaft retaining bolt and remove the gear with tool GC 6306 or suitable gear puller.

33. Remove the flywheel. Before removing the crankshaft flange and flywheel, they must be marked with relation to one another.

34. Using a soft mallet, drive the balance shaft rearwards until the Welch plug is out. Carefully remove the balance shaft from the rear of the block.

35. Remove the bolts from the main bearing caps. Remove the main bearing caps, together with bearing inserts.

36. Lift the crankshaft carefully out of the block.

37. Remove the rear oil seal from the rear of the crank.

38. Remove the main bearing inserts from the caps and block and keep them in the proper order.

Assembly

1. Place all bearings in position, after coating them lightly with oil.

2. Place the crankshaft carefully in the bearing seats.

3. Install the bearing caps and inserts. Apply a thin coat of sealing compound to the rear part of the contact surface of the rear main bearing cap. The arrows on the center and front main bearings must point to the front.

4. Tighten the front and rear bearing caps to 72 ft. lbs. Finger-tighten the bolts for the center bearing cap. Do not confuse the cylinder head bolts and the main bearing cap bolts—they are the same diameter, but the bolts for main bearing caps are 0.4″ longer. After engine No. 74900, the bolts are an additional 0.4″ longer and there is less danger of confusion.

5. Push the crankshaft forward and pry the center bearing cap to the rear. Tighten the cap bolts to a torque of 72 ft. lbs, while holding the crankshaft forward. This is necessary so that both halves of the bearing insert are equally capable of bearing axial loads.

6. Lubricate the inner diameter of the new crankshaft seal with engine oil and push the seal onto tool GC 6701-B (if available); in any case, drive seal into the main bearing until it bottoms. Fit piston rings, as described below, then go on to Step 7.

Fitting of Piston Rings

New or Rebored Cylinder

Push the piston rings one by one into the bore, using a piston turned upside down so that the ring takes the proper position. Measure the piston ring gap with a feeler gauge. The correct figures are found in the Appendix. If the gap is too small, the ring ends must be trimmed with a fine file.

Worn Cylinder

When installing piston rings into a worn bore, the ring gap must be measured with the ring in the lower piston reverse position, as the bore is the smallest at this point.

7. Install new connecting rod bolts. This should be done each time the crankshaft has been removed.

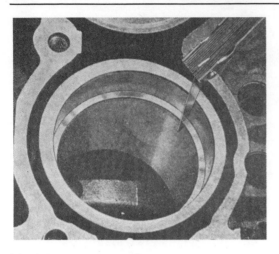

Measuring piston ring and gap

Installing balance shaft cover plate

8. Coat the pistons, rings and cylinder bores with engine oil. Position the piston rings in the following manner:

The oil control ring center spring gap 180° from the mark on the top of the piston; the oil segments with the gaps staggered 1″ on either side of the center spring gap; the lower compression ring gap 150° from one side of the center spring gap, and the upper compression ring gap 150° from the other side of the center spring gap. Installation as above is essential for optimum seating and low oil consumption.

9. Install the piston, together with the connecting rod, using tool 786228 or other suitable ring compressor, by carefully driving the piston down with the handle of a hammer. Be certain the mark on the top of the piston faces forward.

10. If new bearings are installed, check the oil clearance. The procedure is described later in this chaper.

11. Install the bearing inserts (dry) into the connecting rods, then coat them with oil. Put on the bearing caps and tighten the nuts to the proper torque.

12. Coat the balance shaft journals and bearings with engine oil and install the balance shaft from the rear end of the block.

13. Apply a thin coat of sealing compound to the new balance shaft Welch plug, then drive it into the block until it bottoms. Install with the flat side out.

14. Coat the two wedge-shaped seals with sealing compound and press them into the rear main bearing cap with a blunt screwdriver. The domed side of the seal must be turned to face the main bearing cap.

15. Install the flywheel, using new bolts.

16. Locate the key in the crankshaft. Fasten the gear to the shaft using a bolt and washer; tighten to 36 ft. lbs. Do not tap the gear because this could damage the bearings.

17. Coat the camshaft bearings with engine oil and install the camshaft.

18. Install the spacer, with the countersunk side toward the camshaft; insert the key.

19. Put the thrust plate over the front of the camshaft so that it covers the main oil gallery hole. The spacer is a little thicker than the camshaft thrust plate. (The difference in measurement corresponds to the axial play in the camshaft.) To indicate the size group, the spacers have red or blue markings. When installing new parts, choose a spacer giving the correct axial play. (A red spacer gives a small clearance and a blue one a larger clearance.)

20. Apply a thin coat of sealing compound to the mounting surface of the intermediate plate on the front of the block; put the gasket on the block and install the plate loosely with the two retaining bolts. Temporarily install the two lower bolts as guide dowels, then tighten the two retaining bolts. Make sure the lower edge of the plate is in line with the level of the pan, then remove the guide bolts.

21. Turn the crankshaft until the mark on the crankshaft gear faces the camshaft.

22. Press the camshaft gear onto the camshaft so that the mark matches the mark on the crankshaft gear. Secure the camshaft gear with a retaining bolt and washer.

23. Install the balance shaft gear so that the mark matches the mark on the crankshaft gear.

24. Install a new balance shaft seal in the transmission cover (using tool GC 7600-B).

Transmission gear timing marks properly aligned

25. Apply a thin coat of sealing compound to the gasket mounting surfaces of the intermediate plate and transmission cover. Put the transmission cover gasket against the intermediate plate, then center the transmission cover (with the special pilot tool GC 6059 if possible) and fasten it with the nine bolts. To facilitate the installation of the water pump, fasten it to the transmission cover *before* installation.

26. Lubricate the inside of the balance shaft seal with engine oil. Line up the pulley keyway with the balance shaft key and install the pulley; fasten using bolt and flat washer.

27. Insert the oil pump driveshaft into the block (pointed end first). The stop plate on the shaft must be positioned 5.02″ from the blunt end.

28. Install the oil pump and gasket. Tighten the pump bolts first, then the suction line bolt.

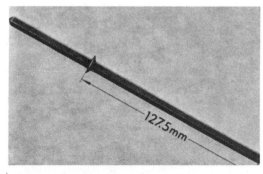

Oil pump drive shaft, with stop ring

29. Insert the rubber seal into the groove in the rear main bearing cap.

30. Apply a coat of sealing compound to the two corner joints where the transmission cover, the intermediate plate and the edges of the oil pan meet. Position the oil pan gasket on the block and insert the two tabs on the cork gasket under the recesses in the rear bearing cap rubber seal.

31. Install and secure the oil pan. Position the two bolts with the rubber washers at the rear balance shaft bearing; see arrows in illustration.

Installing oil pan

32. Lubricate the tappets and their bores with engine oil and install the tappets in their original positions.

33. Install cylinder head gaskets. The gaskets are marked "Front" and "Top."

34. Install the complete cylinder heads, insert the bolts and tighten all bolts in the sequence indicated to the correct torque,

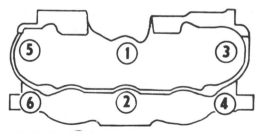

Cylinder head bolt tightening sequence—V4

tightening in three stages: first to 40 ft. lbs., then to 50 ft. lbs. and finally to 68 ft. lbs.

35. Install the side stay bracket.

36. Dip the pushrod ends in engine oil and install the pushrods into their original tappets.

37. Lubricate the ends of the rocker arms with engine oil, then install the oil return plates and rocker arm assembly. Fasten the

rocker arm assembly by alternately tightening the two bolts.

38. Apply sealing compound to the intake manifold gasket surfaces on the cylinder heads. Install the intake manifold gasket and make sure that the protruding part of the righthand cylinder head gasket enters the notch in the intake manifold gasket.

39. Install the intake manifold. Tighten

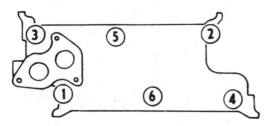

Intake manifold tightening sequence—V4

the bolts and nuts in two stages, to the correct torque:

Stage 1: Bolts—2.9–58 ft. lbs.
           Nuts—2.2–36 ft. lbs.
Stage 2: Bolts—16–21 ft. lbs.
           Nuts—11–13 ft. lbs.

40. Install the thermostat, the gasket and thermostat housing cover.

41. Adjust the valve clearance as described later in this Chapter.

42. Install a new oil filter. Tighten by hand until the oiled rubber seal makes contact with the cylinder block, then tighten it another 1/2 turn.

43. Install the pump pushrod, gasket and fuel pump. Install the pushrod with the same end on the cam as before.

44. Apply sealing compound to the threads of the oil pressure gauge sender and install.

45. Install the water distribution pipe.

46. Install the clutch, after aligning the disc with tool No. 784064 or other suitable pilot shaft.

47. Install the carburetor and gasket.

48. Connect the fuel lines to the carburetor and fuel pump. Make certain the washers on connections are positioned properly.

49. Install spark plugs.

50. Install fanbelt pulley and fan.

51. Install alternator and bracket; adjust fanbelt (0.2–0.3″ deflection under thumb pressure).

52. Insert new gasket into valve cover

grooves. Press the clamp ends of the gasket into the notches in the cover. Install and tighten the bolts equally to the proper torque. Cover with oil cap goes on righthand bank. (Before replacing the covers, the lubrication of the rocker shaft should be checked with the engine running.)

53. Install the distributor.

54. Connect the vacuum line to the distributor.

55. Install the distributor cap and spark plug wires.

56. Install the dipstick.

57. Install the air filter.

Adjusting Valve Clearance

Rotate the engine by hand, while cold, until the mark on the pulley lines up with the dead center mark on the transmission cover. With both valve covers removed, rotate the engine very slightly back and forth; the rocker arms on the first (No. 1) or fourth (No. 4) cylinder will move slightly in opposite directions. If the No. 1 cylinder rockers move, rotate the engine, in the normal direction, one more full revolution and check again; No. 4 cylinder rockers should now move.

With the engine in this position, check the valve clearance for No. 1 cylinder by inserting feeler gauges between the valve stems and the rocker arms. Turn locknuts to adjust clearance. Now, rotate the engine one-half turn (180°) in the normal (clockwise seen from front) direction of rotation until the No. 2 cylinder rockers move, then adjust the No. 3 cylinder valve clearance. Continue in the same manner, i.e., when the rocker arms of No. 1 cylinder move, the No. 4 cylinder valves are adjusted; when the rocker arms of No. 3 cylinder move, the No. 2 cylinder valves are adjusted. Intake valves are adjusted to 0.014″ cold; exhaust valves to 0.016″ cold.

Rocker Arm Disassembly and Assembly

Drive the roll pins out of the shaft, using a drift. Remove the spring washers and rocker shaft brackets. During assembly, the oil holes in the rocker arms must be turned down against the cylinder head. This position is marked by a ground area at the end of the rocker shaft; see arrow in illustration.

Drive a roll pin into the shaft, then install the various parts as indicated in the illustration. The rocker shaft bracket with the oil outlet must be positioned at the rear on the right-hand side of the engine and at the front on the left-hand side of the engine.

Selecting Main and Rod Bearing Inserts

Standard bearing inserts are of two thicknesses. One is marked with a red dot and one with a blue dot; they also have different part numbers. Blue inserts are slightly thicker than red ones; red inserts increase, blue inserts decrease, the clearance.

First, attempt to obtain the correct clearance by using red inserts, regardless of the color with which the engine block, the bearing caps, the crankshaft and connecting rods are marked. Should the clearance be too great with two red inserts, install a red and a blue one, or two blue ones, to obtain a lesser clearance. Should the clearance be too great with two blue inserts, the crankshaft journals must be machined to the next possible undersize and inserts of the corresponding sub-class installed. *CAUTION: Never, under any circumstances, grind the bearing caps or place shims under the bearing inserts to reduce clearances.*

MEASURING BEARING OIL CLEARANCE

Clearance is measured using Plastigage. Plastigage is supplied in three thicknesses, type PG-1 (green) must be used, since this type permits measurement of 0.00098–0.00299″ clearances.

1. Support the engine with the cylinder head down to prevent crankshaft weight from affecting the measurement.

2. Make certain the parts to be measured are free of oil and dirt. Install a dry bearing insert into the bearing cap and put a strip

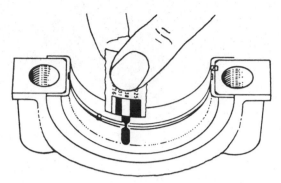

Measuring crushed Plastigage to determine oil clearance

tighten the bearing cap bolts to the prescribed torque. Do not rotate the crankshaft when measuring. When measuring connecting rod clearance, make sure the rod is not moved.

4. Remove the bearing cap. The Plastigage strip will be found pressed in the bearing cap or on crankshaft journal.

5. Using the scale printed on the Plastigage packing, measure the Plastigage at its widest point; do not touch it with the fingers.

Conicity (axial taper) of a crankshaft journal exists if one end of the flat pressed Plastigage strip is wider than the other.

After taking the above measurement, another measurement must be taken after turning the crankshaft through 90°. The difference between the two measurements indicates the ovality (egg-shape) of the journal.

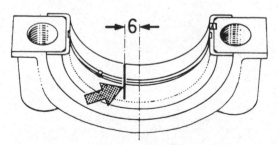

Proper location of Plastigage in bearing cap

of Plastigage into the insert, about 0.236″ off center.

3. Make sure the crankshaft is set about 30° after bottom dead center. With the crankshaft in this position, install the bearing cap with insert and Plastigage and

Part II—Clutch

General

The clutch consists of a single dry plate disc, pressure plate assembly and release bearing.

The clutch plate consists of a resilient steel disc attached to a splined hub which slides on the clutch shaft. The clutch linings are riveted to both faces of the disc.

The pressure plate assembly, which consists of the clutch cover and a cast pressure plate kept under pressure by coil springs, is attached to the flywheel by means of bolts. The coil springs are kept in place by guides on the pressure plate and the clutch cover. Three clutch release levers are carried on struts, riveted to the clutch cover.

Clutch and flywheel assembly

1. Clutch housing and pressure plate
2. Clutch disc
3. Flywheel

The pressure plate assembly is held together by three clutch levers, which are secured by lugs on the struts. A spring-loaded steel disc, against which the release bearing is pressed during disengagement, rests on the inner ends of the clutch levers.

The release bearing consts of a ball bearing held in a bearing housing, which is retained in the clutch fork by springs. A graphite ring or teflon coating on the ball bearing presses against the release plate during disengagement. When replacing the release bearing it must be noted if the bearing has teflon coating. If so, the release plate must be surface ground and *not* teflon coated.

The clutch is hydraulically actuated, and service to this part of the system, including bleeding operations, is the same as for the similar two-stroke unit—see Chapter 2.

Clutch Removal

1. Remove the engine from the car.
2. Loosen evenly and remove the six bolts that hold the pressure plate assembly to the flywheel.
3. Remove the pressure plate assembly, then the clutch disc.

Clutch Installation

1. Place the clutch disc and pressure plate assembly against the flywheel; loosely insert the six retaining bolts.
2. Center the clutch disc with arbor tool No. 784064 or another suitable pilot shaft which fits into the pilot bearing in the crankshaft end.
3. Tighten the six retaining bolts evenly all around.
4. Install the engine.

Clutch Pedal Free-Play Adjustment

The clearance between the release bearing and release plate is gradually decreased by wear of the clutch linings.

Adjust the clutch pedal free-play by turning the screw on the clutch housing.

The free movement is increased by loosening the screw (turning to the left).

The clearance is checked by moving the slave cylinder connection to the clutch arm. A movement of 0.16″ here indicates the correct clutch clearance.

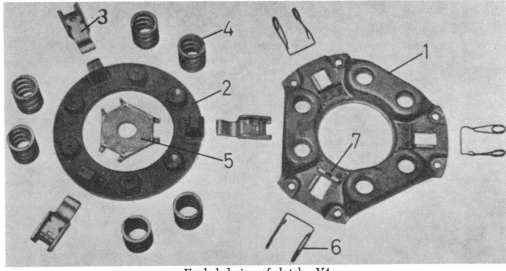

Exploded view of clutch—V4

1. Clutch cover
2. Pressure plate
3. Clutch reiease lever
4. Spring
5. Release plate
6. Retaining spring
7. Strut

Two-stroke models have used many carburetor types, depending on year, the more common of which are the Solex 40 AI, Solex 40 BI, and Zenith 34 VNN. SAAB Sport, Sonett two-stroke, and Monte Carlo models have always had a triple carburetor set-up, using three Solex 34 W units mounted on a common throttle body, three separate Solex 34 BIC units, or three sidedraft Solex 40 DHW units (Sonett II). A triple carburetor set-up was also available on some 95 and 96 models from 1966, although few were imported. The GT-750 was equipped with a Zenith 34 VNN carburetor originally, although a dual-downdraft Solex 44 PII carburetor was available for competition tuning.

SAAB 95, 96, and Sonett models having the V4 engine were equipped with either a Solex 28-32 PDSIT-7 or 32 PDSIT-4 carburetor up to and including 1968, a Ford C8GH-9510-H smog carburetor in 1969, and a Ford 70TW-9510-AA carburetor in 1970.

Both electric and diaphragm-type fuel pumps have been used on the various SAAB models. Of the electric pumps, the SU is the more common, although Monte Carlo models from chassis No. 168,001 are equipped with Bendix pumps, as are Sonett two-stroke models having the 40 DHW carburetors. The GT-750 model with the dual Solex 44 PII carburetor and special (2.01″) exhaust system required two SU pumps connected in tandem (see Chapter 8).

Solex 40 AI and 40 BI Carburetor

These carburetors have a "cold starting device," which supplies a richer than normal fuel mixture during starting. The fuel-air ratio is determined by starting air jet (8) and fuel jet (9). The device is turned on by means of a control on the dashboard. When the cold start device is used, the throttle should be fully closed.

The high speed system includes main jet (4), emulsion jet (1), and emulsion tube (2). The correct combination of these parts gives the right carburetor compensation.

Idle speed is regulated by means of air jet (2), fuel jet (3) and the volume control screw (5). A richer mixture is obtained by unscrewing the volume control screw.

This design permits access to all the jets, except the idle air jet, without disassembly.

Disassembly and Assembly

1. Remove air cleaner.
2. Disconnect fuel line from pump.
3. Disconnect cold start control.
4. Remove rubber boot from plate on the throttle spindle.
5. Remove the carburetor.
6. Clean the carburetor externally.
7. Remove the float chamber cover.

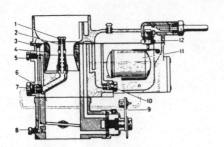

SOLEX 40 BI CARBURETOR SECTIONED

1. Emusion tube jet
2. Emulsion tube
3. Idling air jet
4. Choke tube
5. Idling fuel jet
6. Main jet
7. Jet carrier
8. Adjusting screw, idling mixture
9. Starter air jet
10. Starter fuel jet
11. Float
12. Needle valve

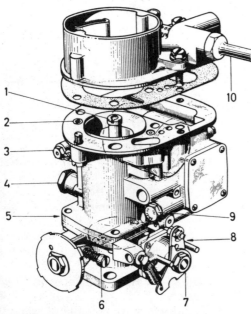

Solex 40 BI carburetor

1. Emulsion tube jet
2. Idling air jet
3. Idling fuel jet
4. Main jet carrier
5. Adjusting screw, idling mixture
6. Adjusting screw, idling speed
7. Cold-starting device
8. Starter air jet
9. Starter fuel jet
10. Union and filter

8. Check the needle valve and gasket.

9. Check the float lever and spindle.

10. Check the float for leaks.

11. Check the main jet, the idle jet and the emulsion jet.

12. Check the slide of the cold starting device for surface wear. Check the starting air jet and starting fuel jet, as well as the return motion.

13. Check the throttle spindle for wear.

14. Reassemble and install carburetor, after cleaning all parts.

15. Reconnect fuel line and controls and start engine.

16. Check float level, if necessary.

17. Install air cleaner; when engine is warm, adjust idle speed.

Idle Speed Adjustment

1. With engine warm, adjust idle speed to about 600–750 rpm with the slow speed adjustment screw.

2. Screw in mixture screw until bottomed, then unscrew 1½–2 turns.

3. Readjust the slow speed adjustment screw until 600–750 rpm is obtained, then recheck the volume control screws as before. Repeat until proper idle speed is obtained.

Float Level Adjustment

1. Allow engine to idle.

2. Switch off engine without touching the throttle.

3. Remove air cleaner.

4. Detach fuel line from carburetor. This must be done in order to prevent additional fuel from entering the float chamber.

5. Remove the float chamber cover.

6. Measure the float level with a caliper depth gauge. The distance from the top of float chamber to the fuel should be 0.8″ ± 0.04″. If the engine is hard to start when warm, the float level may be lowered to 0.87″.

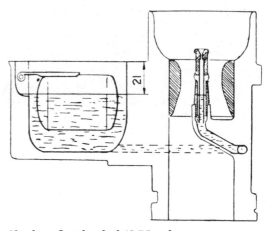

Checking float level of 40 BI carburetor

7. Raise the float level by filing the fiber washer under the needle valve; lower it by adding an extra washer.

Carburetor Cleaning

1. Remove air cleaner.
2. Detach fuel line.
3. Clean filter in the banjo fitting.
4. Remove float chamber cover.
5. Clean needle valve.
6. Remove screw which acts as the float level spindle; lift out float.
7. Remove main jet (4).
8. Remove idle jet (3).
9. Remove starting jet (9).
10. Blow out the float chamber passages and jets.
11. Reassemble in reverse order, making certain the float chamber gasket is perfect.

Zenith 34 VNN Carburetor

The main difference between the Zenith and the Solex is the type of cold start device used—the Zenith has a butterfly valve type choke.

Pulling the choke control closes the spring-loaded butterfly valve. At the same time, linkage opens the throttle to allow the engine to idle. It is *not* necessary to depress the accelerator when starting the engine with the choke.

Disassembly and Assembly

1. Remove air cleaner.
2. Disconnect fuel line.
3. Disconnect choke control.
4. Remove rubber boot from throttle spindle plate.
5. Remove carburetor from intake manifold.
6. Clean the carburetor externally.
7. Remove the four bolts that hold the float chamber and remove chamber. Before lowering the float chamber, pull it out sideways a small distance in order to free the emulsion orifice.
8. Check the condition of the needle valve and its gasket.
9. Examine the float lever and spindle.
10. Check the float for leaks.
11. Loosen the two screws that hold the emulsion block; remove block from the float chamber.
12. Remove all jets.
13. Remove the choke and spindle.
14. Loosen stop screw (10) and remove the choke tube.

15. Check all the gaskets and blow out all passages.
16. Reassemble carburetor and adjust fast idle link.
17. Reinstall carburetor. Allow engine to warm up and adjust idle speed.

Fast Idle Link Adjustment

1. Loosen the stop screw (1) and open the throttle butterfly .043″ by inserting a No. 57 drill or a wire .043″ in diameter between the throttle butterfly and the carburetor body.
2. Close the choke butterfly completely, then check that the lever (2) of the throttle control rests against the projection on the throttle control. Tighten stop screw (1).

Fast Idle Speed Adjustment

1. Adjust the volume control screw (6) to give the highest idle speed, after first seating it.
2. Readjust the slow speed adjustment screw (3) until the proper idle speed is obtained, 600–750 rpm, then recheck the position of the volume control screw (6) to give highest idle speed. Repeat procedure until correct idle speed is obtained.

Float Level Adjustment

The float level is determined by the thickness of the washer under the needle valve. The correct float level is obtained by using a washer with a thickness of 0.12″ (0.08″ for 1965 and earlier models). To check the level, the float chamber must be removed as follows:

1. Allow engine to idle, then switch off without touching throttle.
2. Remove fuel line from carburetor to prevent flooding from pump.
3. Remove air cleaner.
4. Loosen the float chamber screws and lift the chamber out. Use care not to spill any of the fuel in the chamber.
5. Measure the distance from the upper edge of the float chamber to the fuel while holding the chamber in a level position. When the float is in place, the distance should be 1.0″ (0.89″ for 1965 and earlier models) (1.18″ without the float).
6. To lower the float level, install additional gasket under the float valve. To raise the level, file down the existing gasket.
7. After adjustment, recheck level.

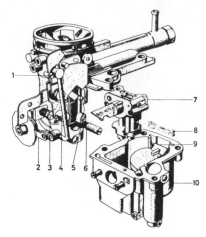

Zenith 34 VNN carburetor

1. Stop screw, throttle/choke link
2. Throttle-control lever
3. Adjusting screw, idling
4. Choke-control holder
5. Vacuum connection for distributor
6. Air-regulating screw, idling mixture
7. Emulsion block
8. Float carrier
9. Float
10. Float chamber

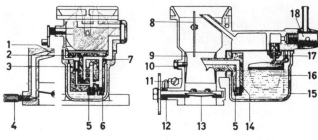

Zenith 34 VNN carburetor

1. Idling duct
2. Idling air jet
3. Idling fuel jet
4. Air-regulating screw, idling mixture
5. Main jet
6. Compensating jet
7. Main air jet
8. Choke butterfly
9. Choke ring
10. Stop screw, choke ring
11. Adjusting screw, idling
12. Throttle-control lever
13. Throttle flap
14. Emulsion block
15. Float chamber
16. Float
17. Needle valve
18. Fuel filter

Triple Carburetors— Monte Carlo up to 1965

This system consists of three Solex 34 BIC carburetors mounted on a common intake manifold with separate cast-in induction passages. A thin balance channel connects the main passages. The air idle system volume screw is located on the intake manifold; this controls the amount of air fed to the individual carburetor idle systems through cast-in channels in the manifold. The carburetors have individual volume control screws that are locked and preset at the factory.

With this system, only the center carburetor contains a cold starting device. The throttle spindle between the three carburetors is equipped with an adjusting screw for synchronization purposes, while the slow idle speed is set by turning the throttle screw on each carburetor.

Disassembly and Assembly

1. Remove the intake manifold and carburetors from engine.

2. Remove fuel lines and carburetors from manifold.

3. Clean carburetors externally, using gasoline or thinner.

4. Remove float chamber cover from one carburetor. It is a good idea to place the other carburetors aside so that parts confusion is eliminated.

5. Inspect needle valve for scoring and gasket for cracks.

6. Inspect the float for leakage; clean float chamber.

7. Inspect main jet, pilot jet, correction jet and emulsion tube for damage.

Carburetors and intake manifold—three carb system to 1965

1. Channel to cylinder
2. Balance channel
3. Air-idle distribution channel
4. Air volume screw
5. Air hose to volume screw
6. Mixture screw (must not be moved)

8. Inspect cold starting device slide for excessive surface wear, then inspect fuel jet, air jet and lever free movement.

9. Check the throttle spindle for excessive wear.

10. Clean all parts in thinner and reassemble unit, then proceed to other carburetors and disassemble as above.

11. Install all reassembled carburetors onto manifold.

12. Install throttle linkage, companion screws and springs. The front carburetor gets the weakest spring, the second carburetor the next weakest and the control shaft the strongest.

13. Install carburetors and manifold, then connect fuel lines, generator bracket, throttle linkage and cold starting device linkage.

14. Install air cleaner and start engine. It may be necessary to adjust float level at this time.

Float Level Adjustment

1. Allow the engine to idle for a few minutes.

2. Turn off ignition without touching accelerator pedal.

3. Disconnect fuel line at the fuel pump (outlet).

4. Remove float chamber cover and air cleaner, if it was installed.

5. Measure the fuel level using a vernier depth gauge or steel ruler; the clearance between the float chamber top and the fuel surface should be $0.78 \pm .04''$. Because of the installed inclination of the carburetor, take the measurement near the choke tube wall. Float level is changed by changing the thickness of the washer under the needle valve; a thicker washer lowers the float level, a thinner washer raises it.

Idle Speed Adjustment and Synchronization

1. Start the engine and allow it to warm up; turn off engine.

2. Remove the air cleaner, then unscrew the companion screws, (4) and (5), about 0.080''.

3. Turn the volume control screw on the

Adjusting volume control screw—three carb system to 1965

manifold until it gently bottoms, then back it out 1½ turns.

4. Start the engine and adjust the idle speed to 600–750 rpm, using the throttle screws.

5. This step requires use of a "Synchro-Test" or "Uni-Syn" device. Place the device

Adjusting throttle screw using Uni-Syn device

on one of the carburetors and adjust the valve to bring the float to the middle of the sight tube.

6. Move the device to the next carburetor and adjust the carburetor throttle screw to bring the float to the same mark as on first carburetor. A grease pencil is handy for marking position of float on sight tube.

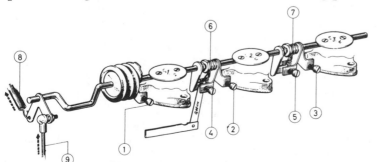

1., 2., 3. Throttle screws for cylinders
4., 5. Companion screws
6. Stiff spring
7. Weak spring
8. Return spring
9. Throttle control

Throttle linkage—three carb system to 1965 (front cylinder is No. 3)

7. Move device to next carburetor and repeat. Continue moving device around until an idle speed of 600–750 rpm is attained with the float at the same level on all carburetors. The volume screw on the manifold can be adjusted ± 1/2 turn from its original 1 1/2 turn position to obtain smoother idle. NOTE: *If a synchronization device is not available, a short length of rubber hose can be used to determine airflow through the carburetors. Place one end of the hose at the carburetor throat and the other end near your ear. The sound level is a fair indication of flow so long as the hose is located at the same place for each carburetor.*

8. Turn in the companion screws to give 0.002″ clearance, as illustrated.

9. Install the air cleaner, preheat tube and manifold hose.

Triple Carburetors—Sport, Monte Carlo and 95/96 from 1965

This induction system consists of three downdraft Solex 34 W units mounted on a common throttle body, each cylinder having a separate induction passage.

A balance passage is cast into the intake manifold. The carburetors have jets for four systems which include high speed, low speed, idling and cold starting systems.

The high speed system consists of the choke tube (K), the main jet (Gg), with its calibrated holder (Y) mark "A," the emulsion jet (a) and the emulsion tube (s), which combine to insure the correct fuel-air mixture for the high speed range.

The low speed system includes fuel jet (g), the air jet (u), which is not removable, and three passages drilled in the carburetor body immediately over the throttle butterfly.

The idling system consists of the fuel jet (gN) and an idling jet, which is not removable, and the air regulating screw (W) for the fuel-air mixture. Prior to 1966, the screw is located on the induction tube; since 1966, the air regulating screw is found on the float chamber.

Fuel and air first pass through separate jets, after which the two components are mixed and pass through the adjustable air regulating screw out into the induction pipe. From 1966 on, only the center carburetor has an idling system or a cold starting system. Through a special passage, this connects to the intake manifold. The cold start system consists of fuel jet (Gs), the air jet (Ga) and a slide valve for regulating the volume of the fuel-air mixture. The slide valve has two positions—one-half open and fully open. The fully open position is spring-loaded for automatic return to the one-half open position.

Disassembly and Assembly

1. Remove air cleaner.
2. Disconnect fuel line.
3. Remove rubber boot from throttle spindle plate.
4. Remove cold start control and fuel lines.
5. Remove carburetor and intake manifold as a unit.
6. Remove throttle body assembly, with carburetors, from intake manifold.
7. Clean carburetors externally and detach from throttle body.
8. Remove the cover of the float chamber and examine the retaining spring between needle valve and float arm, as well as the needle valve and its gasket.
9. Check the float lever and bearing and make sure the float does not leak.
10. Clean the bleed filter in the float chamber cover.
11. Check the main jet, low speed jet, idling jet, emulsion jet and emulsion tube.
12. Examine the cold starting device slide for wear on face. Check fuel and air jets and lever return.
13. Check the throttle spindle for wear.
14. After thorough cleaning, reassemble carburetors. Take care when assembling the lid of float chamber. The bearing pin for the float must enter both grooves in the float chamber, otherwise the pin will become bent or jammed. Also, make certain the needle valve retaining spring is connected to the float.
15. Complete assembly of carburetors and manifold to the engine. Allow engine to warm up before adjusting idle.

Float Level Adjustment

1. Remove air cleaner.
2. Allow engine to idle about 30 seconds, then stop engine without touching throttle.
3. Disconnect the fuel line at carburetor

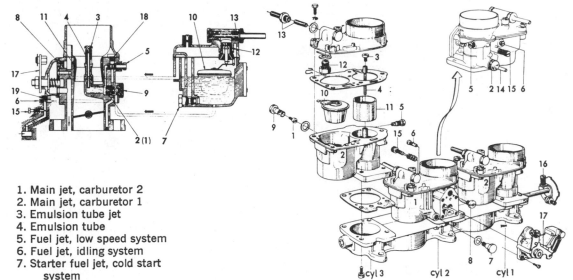

1. Main jet, carburetor 2
2. Main jet, carburetor 1
3. Emulsion tube jet
4. Emulsion tube
5. Fuel jet, low speed system
6. Fuel jet, idling system
7. Starter fuel jet, cold start
   system
8. Starter air jet, cold start
   system
9. Carrier main jet
10. Float
11. Choke tube K 28
12. Needle valve

Solex 34 W carburetor

13. Connection with filter
14. Vacuum connection
15. Air-regulating screw, idling
    mixture

16. Adjusting screw, idling
17. Cold start control
18. Air-jet, low speed system 80
19. Air jet, idling system 80

and remove the float chamber cover and float.

4. Measure the lever with a vernier depth gauge. The distance between the dividing plane of the float chamber cover and the

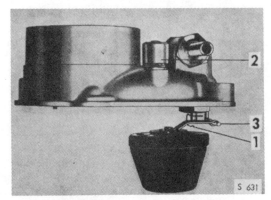

Float chamber cover

1. Spring for needle
   valve
2. Bleed filter
3. Float bearing

surface of the fuel should be $0.96 \pm 0.04''$ for the 1965 SAAB Sport, $1.04 \pm 0.04''$ for the SAAB 95 and 96 and the Monte Carlo from 1966. The measurement must be made at the carburetor neck because the carburetors are inclined at an angle.

5. If adjustment is necessary, file down or remove the washer under the needle valve and recheck the level.

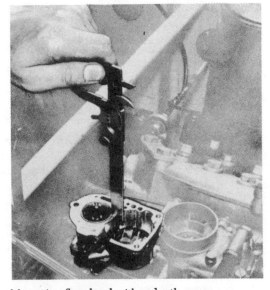

Measuring float level with a depth gauge

Idle Speed Adjustment

1. Allow engine to idle until warm.
2. Adjust idle speed to make engine run as slowly as possible (400–500 rpm).
3. Screw in the volume control screw 1/4 turn and wait until the engine speed stabilizes. Repeat until the engine stops.
4. Unscrew the volume screw 1/4 turn and restart engine.
5. Slowly give more fuel, and check that

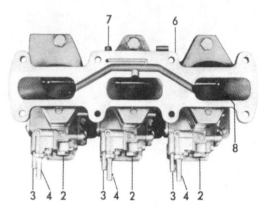

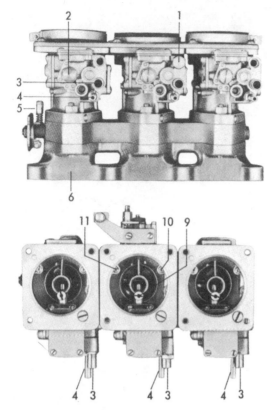

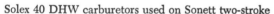

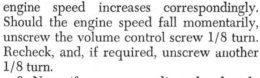

1. Idle fuel jet
2. Retainer, main jet
3. Outlet pipe, fuel
4. Inlet pipe, fuel
5. Low-speed adjustment screw
6. Suction pipe
7. Volume-control screw
8. Throttle valve
9. Emulsion jet
10. Bypass air jet
11. Idle air jet

Solex 40 DHW carburetors used on Sonett two-stroke

engine speed increases correspondingly. Should the engine speed fall momentarily, unscrew the volume control screw 1/8 turn. Recheck, and, if required, unscrew another 1/8 turn.

6. Now, if necessary, adjust the throttle screw until a suitable idle speed is obtained in the 600–750 rpm range. On cars equipped with AC alternator, switch on headlights and check idle speed.

Triple Carburetors—SAAB Sonett Two-Stroke

This system uses three sidedraft Solex 40 DHW carburetors mounted on a common throttle body. Through the throttle body runs a common shaft, to which the three throttle butterflies are attached. A tube is cast into the manifold to provide balance between the carburetors, and a common float chamber (mounted on the engine compartment floor) serves all three carburetors. This system uses two electric

fuel pumps, one of which pumps fuel from the gas tank to the float chamber, the other of which pumps fuel from the chamber to the carburetors. Excess fuel is diverted back to the float chamber to be recirculated.

These carburetors have four fuel systems —high-speed, low-speed, idle, and cold-starting. The high-speed system consists of the choke tube, main jet, emulsion jet, and emulsion tube. The low-speed system consists of the fuel jet, air jet, and three channels drilled into the throttle body close to the butterfly of each carburetor. The idle system consists of the fuel jet, the air jet, and the mixture regulating screw on the throttle body. Only the center carburetor has this idle system. Idle speed is adjusted by turning the air regulating screw and the setscrew on the throttle shaft. The cold-starting system consists of the fuel jet and a sliding valve to regulate the quantity of fuel-air mixture supplied to the engine. This sliding valve has two positions—one-half open and fully open. In the wide open position, a spring tends to make the valve return automatically to the one-half open position. For this reason, the accelerator must not be moved when starting the car, otherwise the cold-starting device will not operate.

Removal, Disassembly, Assembly, Installation

1. Remove the air cleaner, then disconnect the fuel line from the secondary pump at the T and plug the hose.

2. Remove the rubber cover from the throttle shaft, then remove cold-starting control cable, fuel lines, and alternator bracket.

3. Remove the intake manifold and carburetors as a unit.

4. Cover the intakes on the engine to prevent entry of dirt.

5. Remove throttle body assembly, with carburetors, from intake manifold.

6. Clean the carburetors with solvent, then remove them from the throttle body.

7. Check all jets for wear or clogging, then check the cold-starting slide for wear.

8. Check the throttle shaft for wear, then clean all parts, replace any defective parts, and reassemble carburetors.

9. Reassemble throttle body to manifold and install by reversing removal procedure. NOTE: *Always use new gaskets to prevent air leaks.*

Float Level

The float level is determined by carburetor design and cannot be adjusted. The common float chamber, while adjustable, usually does not need adjustment. The float level in this chamber can vary over a wide range without any adverse effects, and only should be disassembled if it overflows or is empty.

Idle Speed Adjustment

1. Start the engine and allow it to warm up to operating temperature.

2. Adjust the idle speed to about 600–750 rpm, using the low-speed screw.

3. Adjust the volume screw to give the highest idle speed possible, then readjust the low-speed screw to obtain 600–750 rpm again.

4. If the car stumbles or hesitates when the accelerator is floored at about 40 mph, it may be necessary to loosen the volume screw an additional 1/4–1/2 turn, then readjust the low-speed screw to obtain 600–750 rpm.

Adjusting the idle speed with the air regulating screw—Solex 40 DHW

Adjusting the idle speed with the throttle shaft setscrew

Fuel Pump and Filter— Two-Stroke

Diaphragm Pump

The diaphragm-type fuel pump is mounted on the engine crankcase. The pressure variations in the crankcase actuate the diaphragm, causing the pump to feed fuel to the carburetor.

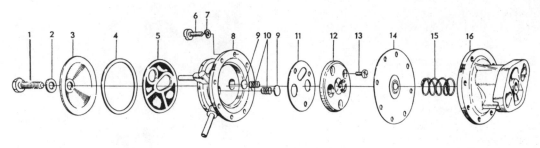

Fuel pump

1. Screw	5. Filter	9. Valve	13. Screw
2. Washer	6. Screw	10. Valve spring	14. Diaphragm
3. Cover	7. Washer	11. Gasket	15. Diaphragm spring
4. Gasket	8. Upper pump housing	12. Valve plate	16. Lower pump housing

CLEANING THE FILTER

Loosen the screw on top of the pump and remove the cover with its gasket. Clean the filter. This should be done every 12,000 miles. When reassembling, make sure filter and gasket are undamaged.

DISASSEMBLY

1. Remove fuel pump from engine.
2. Mark relative positions of pump halves.
3. Loosen bolts that hold the pump halves together and separate.
4. If valves are to be changed, loosen the three bolts that hold the valve plate and remove gasket, valve discs, and valve springs.
5. Loosen the screw that holds the cover on top of the filter. Remove filter, together with gasket.
6. Check sealing surfaces of pump and correct, if necessary, using a face plate with fine valve grinding compound. Replace the diaphragm and valves.

ASSEMBLY

1. Mount the valve springs, with the small diameter turned towards the guide pin.
2. Put on the valve discs, refit the gasket and valve plate and secure the bolts by use of a centerpunch.
3. Refit the pump spring and diaphragm. Locate the diaphragm with the rivet head toward the lower part of the housing.
4. Put the pump halves together in the previously marked position and tighten the bolts.
5. Fasten the pump to engine block with a gasket on either side of thick fiber spacer that fits between block and pump.

Alternate Fuel Pump

In 1966, an alternate fuel pump was introduced with a different valve system—see illustrations for major differences.

Fuel Pump Testing

1. Disconnect the fuel hose at the carburetor and connect hose to a fuel pressure test gauge (0–10 psi).
2. Remove the ignition coil high-tension wire.
3. Run the starter without touching the throttle.
4. The pressure should be 2.8–3.5 psi; it must not fall appreciably when starter is turned off. If the pressure drops rapidly, there is probably leakage in gaskets, valves or diaphragm.

SU Electric Pump

The SU electric fuel pump is made up of three main parts—the pump body, containing valves and fuel filter, the magnet and diaphragm assembly and the contact breaker assembly. SU pumps can be of either 6-volt or 12-volt design. To determine the voltage designation, remove the bakelite cover and check the leads—green coil leads indicate a 6-volt unit; red, black or brown coil leads a 12-volt unit.

DISASSEMBLY

1. Remove pump from wheel housing.
2. Wash pump with kerosene or gasoline.
3. Referring to the illustration, remove the six bolts which hold the magnet housing to the pump body.
4. Separate pump into major component groups, then unscrew diaphragm assembly

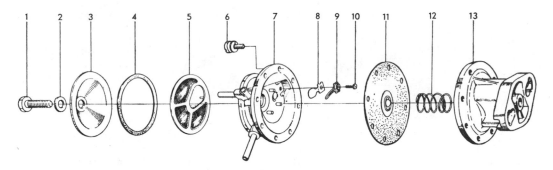

Alternate fuel pump

1. Hexagon screw
2. Gasket
3. Casing
4. Gasket
5. Filter
6. Screw
7. Upper pump
    housing
8. Inlet valve
9. Stop for inlet valve
10. Stop screw
11. Diaphragm
12. Diaphragm spring
13. Lower pump
    housing

(3) from trunnion in contact breaker and release bronze pushrod.

5. Remove diaphragm, retrieving the 11 guide rollers (19).

6. Remove volute spring (4).

7. Turn pump over and remove retaining nut (22) and the bakelite cover (9).

8. Loosen the two bolts (23) that hold pedestal (8) to magnet housing (5). Leaving one bolt in place, completely remove the other (with ground lead).

9. Remove hinge pin (20) from bakelite molding.

10. The "throwover" unit (6) now can be removed sideways.

11. Remove bolt (24), spring blade (7) and coil terminal.

NOTE: *Unless pedestal or magnet assemblies are to be replaced, further disassembly is unnecessary.*

12. Remove nut (28).

13. Remove the other screw that holds pedestal (23).

14. Slip a thin screwdriver blade between the terminal tag and the bakelite pedestal, or use a knife to loosen lead washer (27).

15. Remove terminal, screw (26) and spring washer (25).

16. Remove outlet fitting (10) from pump body.

17. Remove fiber washer (15).

18. Remove valve cage (11). Turn pump upside down and shake out washer (14) and valve disc (12).

19. Remove filter plug (17), filter (16) and fiber washer (15).

ASSEMBLY

1. Clean all parts and blow dry with compressed air.

2. Insert square-head terminal screw into bakelite pedestal.

3. Install coil terminal tag onto screw, after installing spring washer.

4. Install lead washer.

5. Install terminal nut, concave side down, and tighten to compress lead.

6. Loosely install pedestal to magnet housing using screw (23) and spring washer.

7. Assemble "throwover" unit and insert it between pedestal and magnet housing. Adjust outer rocker to eliminate side-play, then connect ground lead.

8. Install the other screw (23)—do not tighten. Fit ground terminal tag and spring washer.

9. Install rocker hinge pin, making sure the center of rocker spring points towards contact points. Hinge pin is special hardened steel—no substitutes are possible.

10. Tighten pedestal screws (23) evenly. Do not overtighten or pedestal will crack.

11. Install volute spring onto diaphragm pushrod, with large diameter end facing away from diaphragm. Fit impact washer.

12. Slide pushrod through magnet core and turn rocker trunnion so that pushrod can be screwed in a few turns.

13. Install 11 guide rollers in position around armature, inside diaphragm.

14. Hold magnet assembly firmly in left hand in a horizontal position. Screw in diaphragm pushrod, pushing in and out on

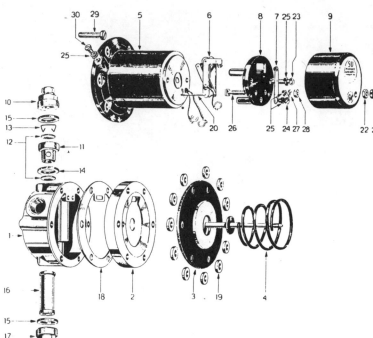

1. Pump body
2. Spacer
3. Diaphragm
4. Volute spring
5. Magnet housing
6. Throwover mechanism
7. Spring blade
8. Bakelite pedestal
9. Bakelite cover
10. Outlet union
11. Valve cage
12. Valve disc
13. Spring clip
14. Fiber washer, thin
15. Filter washer, thick
16. Filter
17. Filter plug
18. Gasket
19. Armature guide roller
20. Rocker hinge pin
21. Terminal nut
22. Cover nut
23. Pedestal screw
24. Screw for blade
25. Spring washer
26. Terminal screw
27. Lead washer
28. Nut
29. Assembly screw
30. Ground terminal

SU electric fuel pump

diaphragm while doing so. The breaker mechanism will at first flop over hard. Continue adjustment and stop screwing in pushrod when the mechanism flops over lightly. The pedestal contact blade should be moved out of the way during this adjustment.

15. Unscrew the diaphragm and armature 2/3 turn (four holes), then install one screw to hold the adjustment.

16. Secure the pedestal contact blade, with coil terminal tag and spring washer.

17. Check and, if necessary, adjust the spring blade so that when contacts are separated the blade rests on the ledge formed in the bakelite pedestal.

18. Check that contact points coincide when circuit is closed. If not, adjust spring blade.

19. Tension on the spring blade should be such that the outer rocker can make a full sweep to deflect blade. Contact points should close when rocker is in middle of travel. To check this, place a finger against spring blade and hold it against the ledge. There should be, in this position, a clearance of 0.030″ between the magnet housing and the white rocker roller. There should also be a 0.030″ clearance between the rocker and the bakelite pedestal.

20. Seat the suction valve disc in the pump body, with the smooth face against the seat. Install delivery valve disc in the same manner.

21. Install thin fiber washer into pump body below valve cage.

22. Install valve cage and disc; secure with spring clip (facing outwards).

23. Install thick fiber washer above valve cage.

24. Install fuel outlet fitting.

25. Install filter and fiber washer onto filter plug; install plug into pump body.

26. Place a new gasket between pump body and spacer.

27. Install spacer with concave side facing magnet housing and all holes lined up properly.

28. With pump body, spacer and magnet housing assembled, the diaphragm must be flat. This can be achieved by placing a wedge between the white rollers of the outer rocker and pressing under tips of inner rocker until pushrod trunnion is lifted as far as it will go. The six assembly bolts now can be installed. NOTE: *The drain hole must match the filter plug.*

29. Tighten six bolts.

30. Remove wedge.

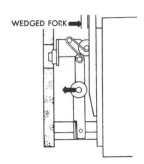

Wedged fork being used to stretch pump diaphragm—SU electric pump

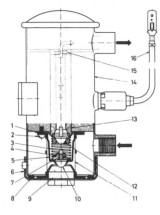

Bendix fuel pump used up to chassis No. 201,400

1. Gasket	10. Valve
2. Screw	11. Filter
3. Plunger spring	12. Valve
4. Spring retainer	13. Plunger
5. Valve housing	14. Pump housing
6. Bayonet cap	15. Damping spring
7. Valve spring	16. Electrical
8. Gasket	connection
9. Magnetic body	

31. Lubricate rocker hinge with a few drops of light oil.

32. Test pump by hooking it up to a battery.

33. If pump operates, install bakelite cover and install pump into car.

Bendix Electric Pump

The Bendix fuel pump consists of a solenoid section, a breaker unit, a pump plunger, valves and a fuel filter. The Bendix gives higher pressure than the double-action SU and it always must be mounted with the bayonet cap downwards.

CLEANING FILTER

1. Remove the bayonet cap from the lower end of the pump.

2. Remove filter and clean it in thinner; blow dry with compressed air.

3. Remove all particles from the magnetic plug.

4. Reassemble pump filter.

DISASSEMBLY (UP TO CHASSIS No. 201.400)

1. Remove bayonet cap, gasket and filter.

2. Loosen the three bolts which hold the valve housing. Remove the housing.

3. Remove the inlet valve, retainer and spring from valve housing.

4. Remove piston and spring from pump housing.

DISASSEMBLY (FROM CHASSIS No. 201.401)

1. Remove bayonet cap, gaskets, filter and magnetic plug.

2. Unhook lock wire, remove washer, O-ring and inlet valve from the barrel.

3. Remove spring, piston and delivery valve.

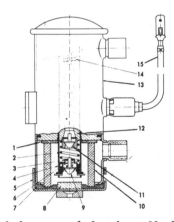

Bendix fuel pump used after chassis No. 201,401

1. Gasket	9. Valve
2. Plunger spring	10. Filter
3. Spring retainer	11. Valve
4. Valve housing	12. Plunger
5. Bayonet cap	13. Pump housing
6. Valve spring	14. Damping spring
7. Gasket	15. Electrical
8. Magnetic body	connection

ASSEMBLY (UP TO CHASSIS No. 201.400)

1. Wash all parts in thinner and blow dry with compressed air. Examine all parts for wear and replace as required.

2. Coat the plunger assembly with light oil, install the plunger spring and push plunger into the barrel.

3. Install the inlet valve, with spring and washer, into the valve housing.

4. Install the valve housing, with gasket and screws, into the pump housing; tighten the screws.

5. Install the filter and the bayonet cap, with gasket.

Assembly (from Chassis No. 201.401)

1. Wash all parts in thinner and blow dry with compressed air. Examine all parts for wear and replace as required.

2. Coat the plunger assembly with light oil, install the plunger spring and push plunger into the barrel.

3. Install inlet valve, spring and retainer into the valve housing.

4. Install O-ring, washer and lock wire.

5. Install filter into valve housing, then install bayonet cap with gasket and plug.

Solex Carburetor—V4 Models

The carburetor is a Solex downdraft type. Up to engine No. 16,100 (chassis No. 434,-173 for the SAAB 96 and Monte Carlo, and No. 46,137 for the SAAB 95) the designa-tion is 28–32 PDSIT-7. From engine No. 16,101 (chassis No. 434,174 for the SAAB 96 and Monte Carlo, and No. 46,138 for the SAAB 95) the designation is 32 PDSIT-4. The fuel supply is regulated by fixed jets mounted in the carburetor body. The body contains not only fuel drillings but also air drillings, and a certain amount of air is mixed with the fuel at an early stage in the emulsion tube.

The carburetor features an automatic choke device with fast idle povisions, an accelerator pump and a pressure-controlled booster system known as an Econostat.

Carburetor with Automatic Choke (Prior to 1969)

Removal

1. Drain some of the cooling water.

2. Remove air filter.

3. Disconnect the lines from the auto-matic choke.

4. Disconnect the throttle control linkage and the vacuum line.

5. Disconnect the fuel line.

6. Remove the carburetor.

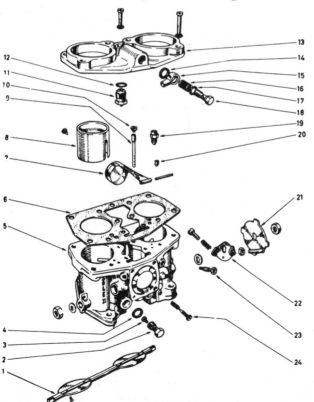

1. Trottle spindle
2. Main jet carrier
3. Main jet
4. Fiber gasket
5. Carburetor body
6. Gasket
7. Float and spindle
8. Choke tube
9. Emulsion tube
10. Emulsion jet
11. Needle valve
12. Spacer washer
13. Cover
14. Fiber gasket
15. Banjo union
16. Filter
17. Fiber gasket
18. Banjo screw
19. Emulsion tube attachment
20. Idle air jet
21. Plate for the throttle control bellows
22. Idle speed adjustment device
23. Idle fuel jet
24. Volume control screw

Solex 44 PII dual-throat carburetor used for competition tuning

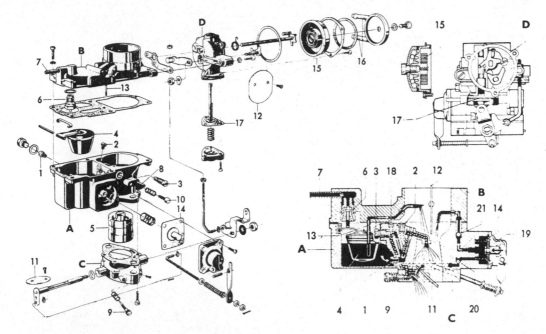

Solex 28-32 PDSIT-7 carburetor

1. Main jet
2. Emulsion jet
3. Idling jet, fuel
4. Float
5. Choke tube
6. Float valve
7. Connection, fuel hose
8. Connection, vacuum hose, distributor
9. Air-regulating screw, idling mixture
10. Adjusting screw, idling
11. Throttle flap
12. Choke flap
13. Ascending pipe, additional system (Econostat)
14. Diaphragm, acceleration pump
15. Bimetal spring for automatic choke
16. Water connections
17. Diaphragm for vacuum control of automatic
    choke
18. Idling air jet (drilling)
19. Acceleration pump
20. Inlet valve, acceleration pump
21. Outlet valve, acceleration pump
A. Float chamber
B. Float chamber cover
C. Throttle body assembly
D. Housing, automatic choke

7. For 32 PDSIT-4, first disconnect the hose from the valve cover, then remove the intermediate flange.

INSTALLATION

On 32 PDSIT-4, first install the intermediate flange, with new gaskets.

1. Using a new gasket, install the carburetor and tighten bolts evenly.
2. Reconnect the fuel and vacuum lines.
3. Connect the throttle control.
4. Reinstall water hoses.
5. Refill the cooling system.
6. Install air filter.

DISASSEMBLY

1. Remove the retainer from the control rod between the automatic choke and the throttle butterfly, then detach the link from the throttle butterfly arm.

2. Unscrew and lift off the float chamber cover; remove the gasket.
3. Unscrew the needle valve.
4. Take out the float and float chamber.
5. Remove the plug from the float chamber and remove the main jet.
6. Pull off the accelerator pump jet (over the accelerator pump).
7. Unscrew the idle and emulsion tube jets.
8. Unscrew the accelerator pump cover and check the diaphragm.
9. Unscrew the idle mixture air regulating screw.
10. For carburetor 32 PDSIT-4, remove the intermediate flange valve.

ASSEMBLY

1. Install the spring, diaphragm and cover for the accelerator pump.

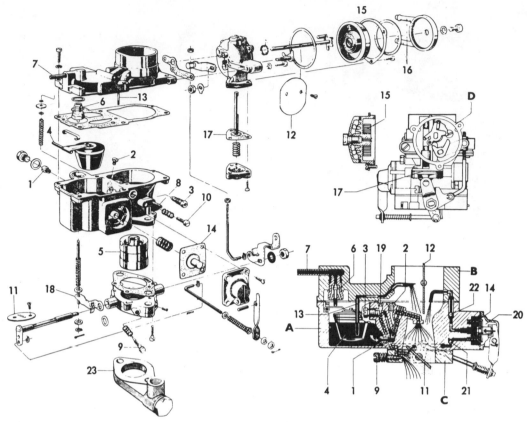

Solex 32 PDSIT-4 carburetor

1. Main jet	11. Throttle flap	18. Retaining device, float
2. Emulsion jet	12. Choke flap	chamber ventilation
3. Idling jet, fuel	13. Ascending pipe, addition	19. Idling air jet (drilling)
4. Float	system (Econostat)	20. Acceleration pump
5. Choke tube	14. Diaphragm, acceleration	21. Inlet valve, acceleration
6. Float valve	pump	pump
7. Connection, fuel hose	15. Bimetal spring, automatic	22. Outlet valve, acceleration
8. Connection, vacuum hose	choke	pump
distributor	16. Water connections	23. Intermediate flange
9. Air-regulating screw, idling	17. Diaphragm for vacuum	A. Float chamber
mixture	control of automatic	B. Float chamber cover
10. Adjusting screw, idling	choke	C. Throttle body assembly
		D. Housing, automatic choke

2. Insert the accelerator pump jet.

3. Screw in the idle and emulsion tube jets.

4. Advance the idling mixture air screw carefully until it bottoms, then back it off one complete turn.

5. Insert the float.

6. Screw the needle valve and gasket into the float chamber cover.

7. Install a new cover gasket.

8. Install float chamber cover.

9. Install the rod between the automatic choke and the throttle butterfly arm; fasten with the retaining ring.

10. Set the butterfly arm in the semi-open position and, at the same time, fully close the choke butterfly with the fingers. Hold the butterfly arm firmly and make sure the throttle butterfly is ajar. The clearance between the butterfly and flange must be 0.032″. This can be checked with a No. 67 drill bit or wire of the same diameter. To adjust the clearance, loosen the nuts on the linkage rod for the fast idle system, then adjust the rod so that the butterfly takes the correct position. Retighten the rod and lock in the correct position. NOTE: *For carbu-retor 32 PDSIT-4, install the intermediate flange valve.*

FLOAT LEVEL ADJUSTMENT

The level in the float chamber should be measured while the engine is idling and should be $0.59 \pm 0.04''$. The level is controlled by the thickness of the float valve sealing washer. If the level is too high, a thicker washer must be fitted; a thinner washer must be fitted to raise the level. The float level is measured from the top of the float chamber cover to the fuel level. Measuring can be done with a transparent fuel standpipe connected at the location of the jet plug in the float chamber.

IDLE SPEED ADJUSTMENT

The idle speed must be adjusted with the engine at normal operating temperature and the headlights switched on.

1. Turn the slow speed adjustment screw slightly clockwise, so that the engine speed is slightly increased.

2. Slowly turn in the volume control screw until the engine begins to run unevenly, then slowly back off approximately 1/4 turn to achieve the best idle setting. The volume control screw never must be screwed in so hard that it bottoms.

3. Screw the volume control screw slowly in or out until the engine runs at the prescribed idling speed.

AUTOMATIC CHOKE ADJUSTMENT

1. Remove the air filter.

2. Connect an accurate thermometer into the water hose between the thermostat housing cover and a connector for the water hoses to the automatic choke.

3. Start the engine (cold) and note the temperature at which the choke butterfly opens wide. The correct opening temperature is 140–149°F.

4. If the choke opens at a lower or higher temperature, loosen the three clamping screws and turn the bimetal spring housing so that the proper setting is obtained.

FAST IDLE SPEED ADJUSTMENT

1. Remove air cleaner.

2. Warm up engine, switch on headlights.

3. Connect a tachometer to the engine (between distributor-to-coil primary wire and ground).

4. Adjust the engine to correct idle speed (800–900 rpm).

5. Close the choke a little in order to

Removing choke housing bolts

make it contact the ratchet wheel. Hold the choke in this position and keep pressing it toward the ratchet wheel.

6. Open the throttle butterfly slowly so as to allow the choke to move to the next position. Release the throttle cautiously, then the choke. The step which increases the idle speed is now in the first position of the ratchet wheel.

7. The throttle control must not be touched at this stage, as the ratchet wheel would then revert to the neutral position. For safety's sake, the control rod should be pushed up hard with the fingers.

8. With the throttle butterfly in this position, the engine speed should be 1,100–1,300 rpm. Adjust the control rod. (To increase the speed, lengthen the rod; to reduce the speed, shorten the rod.) After the ad-

Bending throttle valve stop

justment, check that the control rod does not jam the throttle control lever.

9. Now check the speed of the third step (2,700–2,900 rpm).

10. Recheck idle speed.

Carburetor with Automatic Choke (Autolite)

REMOVAL

1. Remove the air cleaner.
2. Remove the water hoses from automatic choke.
3. Remove the throttle control.
4. Detach fuel and vacuum hoses.
5. Remove the carburetor.

INSTALLATION

1. Install new gaskets under the intermediate flange and carburetor. Turn the face

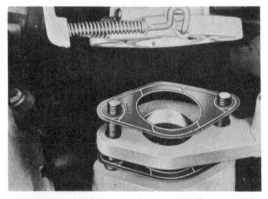

Special gasket, showing correct installation

marked "oben" up. A special gasket is required for this carburetor and must not be confused with the gasket for the Solex carburetor.

2. Reinstall the fuel and vacuum hoses, throttle control, water hoses and air cleaner.

DISASSEMBLY

1. Remove the three bolts and detach the thermostatic spring housing.
2. Unscrew the step cam from the throttle body.
3. Unscrew the bolts that hold the float

Accelerator pump fuel channel ball and weight

chamber cover and lift off the cover. Remove the spring on the float chamber cover; remove the gasket. By holding the float chamber upside down, remove the ball and weight from the accelerator fuel channel.

4. Unscrew the bolts in the accelerator pump cover, then remove cover, diaphragm and spring.

5. Remove accelerator pump rod from the lever of the throttle valve shaft; remove the lever.

6. Remove idle mixture control screw and idle speed adjusting screw; remove the springs.

7. Remove the throttle valve.

8. Remove, using a small file, any burrs from the threaded bores in the throttle valve shaft, then remove the shaft.

9. Remove the float. Unscrew the float needle valve.

10. Unscrew the main jet.

11. Unscrew the automatic choke housing from the carburetor.

12. Pull the pins of the air cleaner mounting yoke and remove.

13. Remove the choke plate.

14. Remove, using a small file, any burrs from the threaded bores in the choke plate shaft, then remove the shaft.

ASSEMBLY

Clean the carburetor. Blow out all channels, passages and jets; renew gaskets and defective parts.

1. Mount the throttle valve shaft in the throttle body. Fit the accelerator pump lever to the throttle valve shaft, turning the side marked "O" up.

2. Install the throttle valve so that the side with two punched marks faces downward when the throttle is held closed. Prior to tightening the bolts, see that the valve centers in the closed position. Check that the throttle shaft moves freely.

3. Install the mixture control and idle adjusting screws and springs.

4. Install the accelerator pump rod between the levers of the accelerator pump and throttle valve.

5. Install the accelerator pump diaphragm and spring. The small end of the spring must face the diaphragm. Replace the cover.

6. Install the choke plate shaft and choke plate. Before tightening, make sure that the choke plate centers in the closed position. Check that the shaft moves freely.

7. Install the air cleaner mounting yoke and drive in the pins.

8. Install the automatic choke housing, with its gasket, and connect the accelerator pump rod to the choke plate shaft.

9. Screw in the main jet.

10. Screw in the needle valve and install the float.

11. Insert ball and weight into the accelerator pump channel.

12. Install the float chamber valve spring into the carburetor cover. Install, then insert the float chamber valve pushrod into, the cover. Tighten the cover.

13. Screw on the step cam.

14. Install the thermostatic spring housing.

FLOAT LEVEL ADJUSTMENT

1. When checking the measurement "A," which must be 1.08″, hold the float chamber cover vertically without pressing on the spring-loaded ball of the float valve. When adjusting, bend the stop gently at the arrow.

2. The lower end position of the float is

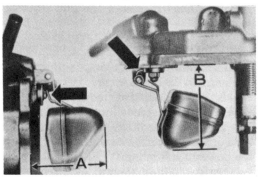

Checking float measurement (see text)

checked by measuring at "B"; (1.34″). When adjusting, bend the stop gently at the arrow.

ACCELERATOR PUMP ADJUSTMENT

1. Loosen the idle adjusting screw until the throttle is fully closed.

2. Using a small screwdriver, depress the accelerating pump diaphragm until it stops.

3. The measurement "A" between the piston and lever must be 0.09–0.10″.

4. If the measurement "A" is not within tolerance, adjust by bending or straightening the yoke of the accelerator pump rod.

AUTOMATIC CHOKE ADJUSTMENT

Normally the automatic choke setting should not need to be altered in any way.

Checking measurement "A"

The setting mark on the thermostatic spring housing is normally in line with the center mark on the automatic choke housing, with the free end of the thermostatic spring fitted into the center slit of the thermostatic spring lever.

VACUUM OPERATION

1. Remove the thermostatic spring housing.

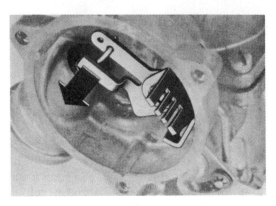

Vacuum piston and position

2. Depress the vacuum piston fully. Move the choke plate toward closed position until the tongue of the thermostatic spring lever contacts the vacuum piston lever. In this position, the opening of the choke plate should be 0.17–0.19″; a No. 12–17 drill may be used as a gauge.

3. Install the thermostatic spring housing; make sure the spring takes the proper position.

4. Check the position of the step cam by inserting a drill gauge; see Step 2. In this position, the mark on the third catch of the step cam must be exactly in front of the stop dog of the throttle valve lever; adjust by bending the link rod.

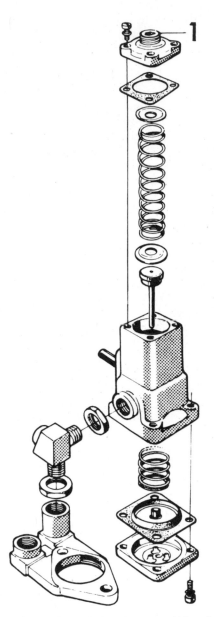

Deceleration valve—1970 USA cars. (1)=adjusting screw

Fuel Pump—V4

Removal

Remove the fuel line from the pump. Remove the nuts and lockwashers, then remove the pump, pushrod and the old gasket. Always use a new gasket and mark the end of the pushrod which rests against the camshaft for easy assembly.

Disassembly

1. Remove the cover, gasket and strainer.
2. Mark the upper and lower part of the pump so that they can be installed in the same relative position.
3. Loosen and remove the screws, then separate the upper and lower parts of the pump. The upper part containing the valves can be disassembled no further.
4. Place the lower part of the pump, with the diaphragm, on a flat surface. Press down the spiral spring lockwasher with a 10 mm. open end wrench and remove the lock-ring from its groove in the diaphragm rod. Remove the spring lockwasher and the spring; replace the lock-ring on the diaphragm rod.
5. A small seal is supplied to seal between the diaphragm rod and the lower part of the pump. This is not replaceable. Because the lips on the shaft seal face the ring groove for the lock-ring, the shaft seal would be completely ruined if the diaphragm rod was withdrawn from the lower part of the pump towards the diaphragm. Because of this, always proceed as follows:
   a. Hold the lower part of the pump in the hand, press the diaphragm lightly inward and remove the lock-ring again. Release the diaphragm only far enough to allow the pins which hold the diaphragm to the diaphragm rod to be removed by pressing with a sharp pin punch.
   b. Pull the diaphragm rod away from the lower part of the pump (towards the drive side). Remove the diaphragm and the compression spring.

Assembly

1. Apply a little grease to the diaphragm rod and connect it, with the pin, to the new diaphragm. Install the spring.
2. Push the lower part of the pump,

air then passes from the bleed hole in the atmospheric side into the intake manifold. This massive air leak results in an overly lean mixture with attendant backfiring, stalling, and rough idle. If both carburetor adjustment and ignition timing are correct, and the above symptoms still exist, check the decel valve by covering the bleed hole with a finger. A defective diaphragm can be replaced—disassembly is obvious from the illustration.

against spring pressure, onto the diaphragm rod until the diaphragm makes contact.

3. Place the lower part of the pump, with the diaphragm, on a flat surface. Install the compression spring with the lockwasher. Hold the lockwasher with a 10 mm. wrench, press it down on the pushrod and insert the lock-ring.

4. Align the upper part of the pump according to the marked flanges. Press the pushrod in far enough that the diaphragm is not under tension. In this position, insert the screws and fasten the two halves together.

5. Install a new strainer and gasket; screw on the cover.

Chapter 5
Transmission and Differential

Part I—Three-Speed

Removal

1. Remove engine.
2. Disconnect freewheel control.
3. Remove rear clutch cylinder bracket and wire cylinder out of way.
4. Remove gearshift shaft joint from the transmission. If both ends of the conical pin are threaded, transfer the nut and use it to remove the pin. A conical pin threaded on only one end is removed by means of tool 784083 or by backing off nut until flush with threads, then tapping gently with hammer.
5. Disconnect speedometer cable from transmission.
6. Peel back or remove front floor mat, then remove rubber plugs to provide access to rear engine mount center bolt.

On older models, a section of the pedal housing must be removed. Remove the center bolt, using a 9/16″ socket wrench.

7. If the tapered engine mount will not move, tap it off with a punch.
8. Remove the steering arm from the upper ball joint on the right steering knuckle housing, then pull the middle driveshaft from the inner joint. On the SAAB Sport, 1966 up, model 95 and 96, and the Monte Carlo 850, the steering knuckle need not be loosened.

9. As the transmission is lifted, move it slightly to the right so that the left drive-shaft comes out of the joint. On the SAAB Sport, Monte Carlo 850, and SAAB 95 and 96 from 1966, use care not to remove the inner drivers (which contain needle bearings).

Three-Speed Transmission Disassembly

The methods described here are derived from factory-recommended procedures, which require special tools. Substitutes for these tools will become obvious as the job progresses. For example, it would be impractical to buy the special transmission jig that the dealer uses, but a large bench vise and suitable arbors and sleeves cut from pipe or other stock can serve the same purpose.

1. Clean outside of transmission and drain all the oil.
2. Remove the inner universal joint with shafts. On the SAAB 96, the joints are connected to the side gears by means of a bolt which passes through the shaft centers.
3. Separate the transmission unit at the joint between the clutch housing and the transmission case. The clutch shaft will have to be turned to a certain position while removing the differential case.
4. Install the transmission case into the fixture, tool No. 784100, as illustrated (if available).
5. Check location of pinion and measure ring gear backlash for correct setting, as

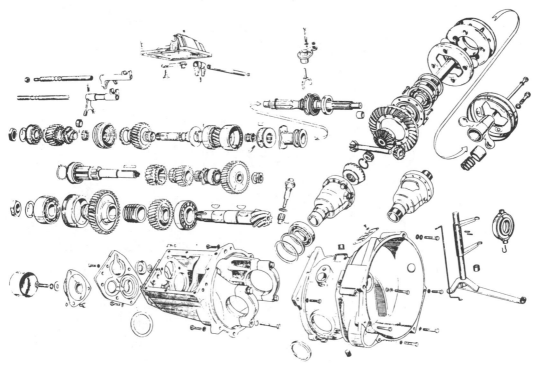

Exploded view of three-speed transmission

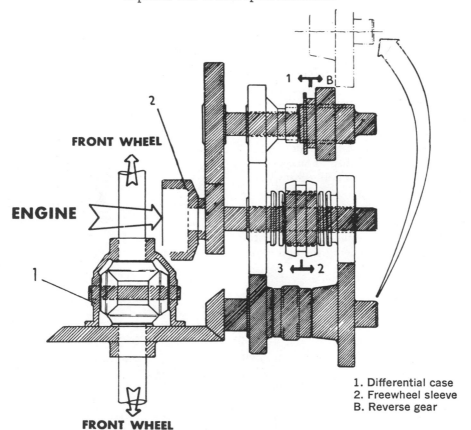

FRONT WHEEL

2

ENGINE

1

1 ← → B

3 ← → 2

FRONT WHEEL

1. Differential case
2. Freewheel sleeve
B. Reverse gear

Power flow in three-speed transmission

1., 3., 4. Spacers and shims
2. Differential case
5. Caps

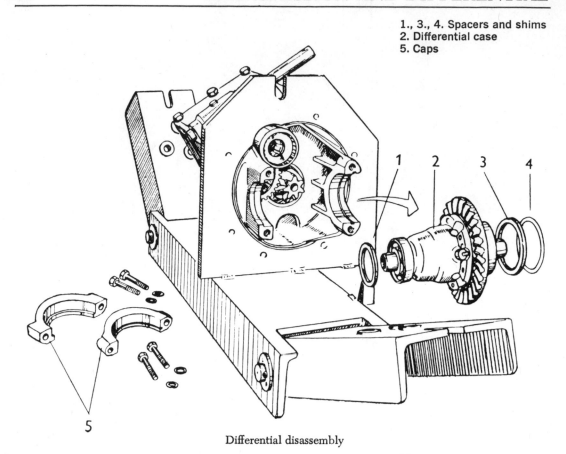

Differential disassembly

described later in this chapter.

6. Remove the two bearing caps and lift out differential. Keep the spacers and shims for each of the two bearings separate and note their positions.

7. Remove freewheel hub, with the six rollers, from its sleeve, using tool No. 784068 and a strong rubber band to prevent the spring-loaded rollers from being thrown out. Next, remove the needle bearing. Make certain none of the rollers are missing.

8. If the pinion shaft or bearings are to be removed, measure the location of the pinion shaft before removing the end cover.

GEARSHIFT FORKS

9. Remove the transmission case cover.

10. Remove the end cover and attached shift fork rail for 2nd and 3rd gears. Take care to prevent the ejection of the poppet ball. Keep the shims and gasket in their respective positions.

11. If only the rear pinion shaft bearing is to be removed, it can be done now. Back off the left-hand thread nut and extract bearing with tool No. 784101 or other suitable puller.

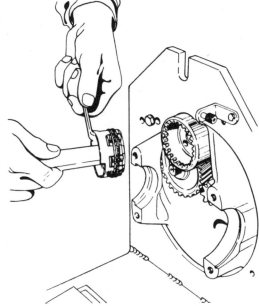

Disassembling freewheel hub using special tool No. 784068

12. Using a screwdriver, push 1st and reverse shift fork rail through the end of the transmission case. Take care to prevent ejection of poppet ball.

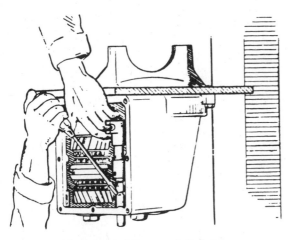

Disassembling 1st and Reverse shift fork

COUNTERSHAFT WITH BEARINGS AND GEARS

13. Shift the synchronizer sleeves to engage two gears at the same time.

14. Back off the nut at front of countershaft. Remove friction wheel and washer. Also back off the end nuts of the primary and pinion shafts if they are to be removed. The pinion shaft nut has left-hand thread.

15. Lift the front end plate of the fixture and make it fast.

16. Locate arbor tool No. 784110, fitted with the shortest point, between the front press screw and the countershaft. Press in shaft until arbor rests hard against the gear. Change the arbor point to the next longest one and press again. Repeat procedure once more with the longest point until the bearing and countershaft are released. Remove tool and drop fixture end plate.

17. Lift the front end of the countershaft, hold the gears with one hand and pull the shaft through the rear bearing hole. Remove the gears. Note the washer between the 1st speed gear and ball bearing; take the two needle bearings from inside 1st gear.

18. Remove retaining ring and drive ball bearing off the shaft.

19. Using an arbor, carefully drive or tap the remaining bearing toward the differential side. Note the retaining ring behind the bearing.

PRIMARY SHAFT WITH BEARINGS AND GEARS

20. Put the rear press screw of the fixture against the primary shaft and locate the arbor tool No. 784104 between screw and shaft.

21. Press shaft out to the front until it is released from the bearings.

22. Extract shaft in forward direction.

23. Hold the synchronizer unit and gears and allow the washer to drop from between the 2nd speed gear and the ball bearing into the case. Lift out gear and synchronizer as a unit.

24. If the twin needle bearings in the 3rd speed gear hub did not come with shaft, remove shaft.

25. Remove the needle bearings from the 2nd speed hub.

26. Disassemble synchronizer.

27. Drive the rear primary shaft bearing out of the case with the press screw in the front end of the fixture, using tool No. 784109 and sleeve No. 784106.

28. Remove the thrust washer and locking pin from shaft.

29. Remove the retaining ring and press ball bearing from the shaft.

PINION SHAFT WITH BEARINGS AND GEARS

30. Attach puller, tool No. 784101, to pinion shaft bearing sleeve and pull sleeve out with bearing. Use the front press screw of the fixture for support against the drive pinion. Collect the spacer and shims from inside the bearing.

31. On transmissions with aluminum casings, use puller No. 784115 instead, as the construction is the same as with the four-speed unit.

32. Remove the speedometer drive gear.

33. Put the rear fixture press screw against the pinion shaft and press out forward. As soon as the unit is free, remove the shaft and lift the gears out of the transmission case.

34. If necessary, drive the roller bearings off the pinion shaft.

Assembly

1. After making certain all parts are completely clean, begin reassembly at the appropriate point.

When fitting new gears, the following are supplied in matched sets.

    3rd speed gear—pinion shaft 3rd gear
    2nd speed gear—pinion shaft 2nd gear
    pinion shaft   —ring gear

For quiet operation, it is essential that gears be replaced in complete sets and installed with matching numbers facing the same side.

Pinion Shaft with Bearings and Gears

2. Press the roller bearing onto the pinion shaft with a sleeve or tool No. 784106 and locate the two Woodruff keys in their grooves. The keys are of different sizes, the thinner one is intended for 2nd gear.

3. Fit the 2nd and 3rd gears into the case, along with the speedometer drive gear. Locate the speedometer drive gear with the beveled side facing the differential. The matching number on the pinion shaft 3rd gear should face the same direction as the number on the 3rd speed gear.

4. Insert the pinion shaft from the front.

5. Locate the 3rd gear in relation to keyway. Make sure the speedometer drive gear is properly engaged, then locate the 2nd gear in relation to the keyway.

6. Locate the front press screw of the fixture against the pinion shaft and press carefully, a fraction of an inch, so that the pinion rides on the shaft. The pinion shaft 2nd gear will now rest against the rear of the case. Make certain that it is at right angles to the pinion shaft.

7. Back off the press screw a few turns, while supporting the gears, and locate the aligning arbor tool No. 784102 in the rear bearing seat. Be sure the shaft end passes into the arbor.

8. Press the arbor in until its flange is flush against the end of the case; leave the press screw in this position.

9. Use the opposite press screw to drive the pinion shaft in from the front until the roller bearing is hard against the 3rd gear.

10. Back off the press screws and remove arbor from the rear bearing seat.

11. Put a spacer 0.14" thick on the end of the shaft. If the pinion shaft or any other parts have not been replaced, use the previously fitted spacer and shims.

12. Refit the twin bearing in its sleeve— the bearing marking should face inwards.

13. Drive in the bearing and sleeve assembly with the press screw and arbor tool No. 784102, using the press screw on the opposite end of fixture for support of the pinion shaft.

14. Fit a new tabbed retaining washer onto the pinion shaft and screw on the left-hand thread nut. Turn the tab of the washer outwards. Don't tighten the nut with a torque wrench until the primary shaft and countershaft have been installed.

15. Replace the speedometer drive.

Primary Shaft with Bearings and Gears

16. Drive the ball bearing onto the primary shaft and install retaining ring. Use tool No. 784107, if available.

17. Install locking pin in shaft and fit the thrust washer behind the ball bearing retainer so that the pin drops into the groove, preventing it from rotating.

18. Reassemble the 3rd speed gear, complete with twin needle bearing, synchronizer unit with rings and 2nd speed gear without its bearings. Pass this assembly into the transmission case and install aligning arbor tool No. 784114 into the end of the case so that it enters the 2nd speed gear hub.

19. Install the primary shaft from the front, turning it gently back and forth so its lands enter the synchronizer hub.

20. Fit arbor tool No. 784104 into the freewheel sleeve. The needle bearing must be removed from the freewheel sleeve to prevent damage.

21. Raise and lock both ends of the fixture and support the arbor in the 2nd speed hub with the rear press screw.

22. Drive in the primary shaft carefully, from the front towards the arbor, using the press screw. Make certain the synchronizer hub slides easily on the shaft.

23. Back off the rear press screw and remove the arbor from the 2nd speed gear hub.

24. Put the needle bearings and steel bushing in the 2nd speed gear and fit the washer onto the shaft. The beveled side of the washer should face outwards.

25. Drive in the primary shaft rear bearing with the rear press screw and tool No. 784109. The press screw and 784104 at the freewheel sleeve will help support the shaft.

26. Back off the press screws and remove the arbors.

27. Install a new tabbed washer, tab facing outwards, and the end nut. Don't tighten with torque wrench until the countershaft is installed.

Countershaft with Bearings and Gears

28. If the countershaft front ball bearing has been removed, drive it into the case from the differential side, until it is tight against the retaining ring. Raise and lock the rear plate of the fixture and drive in the bearing with the press screw and arbor tool No. 784108.

29. Put the countershaft gear on the out-

side of the bearing, holding it with tool No. 784108. Hold with front press screw against the bearing. The machined part of hub must face clutch housing.

30. Assemble the reverse gear and 1st speed gear, with its two needle bearings and washer. Mount these parts as a unit, inserting the countershaft through the rear bearing seat at the same time. If the rear bearing has not been removed from the shaft it can remain in position during reassembly, providing the retaining ring is taken off.

31. Drive in the shaft using the rear press screw and arbor tool No. 784104. Be certain that the shaft passes into the countershaft gear. If the shaft is driven in complete with bearing, tool No. 784109 should be used. This tool also is used to install the ball bearing after installation of the shaft. Make sure to install the ball bearing retaining ring.

32. Shift the synchronizer units to engage two gears at the same time and turn the 3rd speed gear to align the keyways in the countershaft and the countershaft gear. Using an arbor, drive in the key as far as it goes.

33. Install a new retaining ring with tab facing inwards, or mount the friction wheel, with a new friction washer and star washer. Make certain the friction wheel is not located outside the opposing gear and that there is sufficient clearance between the primary shaft ball bearing and the countershaft gear. Tighten the countershaft end nut to 60 ft. lbs. torque, and the primary shaft nut to 35 ft. lbs. Tighten the pinion shaft nut initially to a torque of 90 ft. lbs., then back off and retighten to 45 ft. lbs.

34. Return the synchronizer sleeves to the neutral position.

35. Lock the primary shaft nut. The pinion shaft nut also may be locked unless further adjustments are to be made.

36. Check the end cover shims and adjust if necessary.

GEARSHIFT FORKS

37. Insert the spring and poppet ball into the 1st and reverse gearshift fork. Put the fork in position and install shaft. To simplify this job, use tool No. 784069 to hold the poppet ball in place.

38. Put the 2nd and 3rd gearshift fork in place, with the spring and poppet ball assembled.

39. Check that the rubber washer and the plastic plug are mounted in the end cover and that the oil collector is mounted in the transmission case end.

40. Fit the 2nd and 3rd gearshift fork rail to the end cover. Coat the shims lightly with grease to hold them in place, coat both sides of the gasket with Permatex No. 3 and slide the rail and cover into place. Tighten the end cover bolts to 18 ft. lbs.

41. If necessary, back off the locknut and adjust the 2nd and 3rd gearshift fork so that it is not under axial pressure with 2nd and

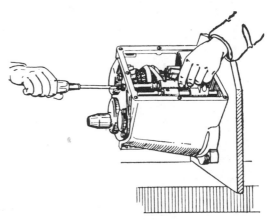

Adjusting 2nd and 3rd shift fork shaft

3rd gears engaged. There must be a definite clearance between the synchronizer sleeve and its respective gear.

DIFFERENTIAL FREEWHEEL

42. Check the drive pinion setting and adjust if necessary. Before measuring the drive pinion setting, be sure to tighten the pinion shaft end nut and end cover bolts to the correct torque.

43. After adjusting drive pinion, check that the shaft nut is locked.

44. Place the differential and ring gear in the bearing seats and adjust the backlash between the drive pinion and ring gear.

45. Install the freewheel hub, complete with rollers in the freewheel sleeve, using tool No. 784068. The hub should engage firmly when turned to the right. It is marked on front face.

46. Put all gears in neutral position; coat sealing surface of transmission cover with Permatex No. 3 and install.

47. Remove transmission from fixture.

48. Coat the sealing surface of clutch housing with Permatex No. 3.

49. Place needle bearing in freewheel sleeve. Check the clutch shaft seal and driveshaft seals and renew if necessary. Install seals so that the dustguard lips face

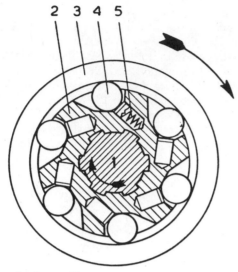

Freewheel assembly

1. Clutch shaft
2. Freewheel hub
3. Freewheel sleeve
4. Roller
5. Coil spring

outwards. Fill the space between the lips with grease.

50. Bolt the clutch housing to the transmission case. Turn the clutch shaft so it clears the differential; drive in the locating pin.

51. Refit the inner universal joints and shafts. Use care not to damage seals.

52. Coat the clutch shaft with graphite grease and fill the transmission with transmission oil.

Part II—Four-Speed

Four-Speed Transmission Disassembly

The methods described here are derived from factory-recommended procedures, which require special tools. Substitutes for these tools will become obvious as the job progresses. For example, it would be impractical to buy the special transmission jig that the dealer uses, but a large bench vise and suitable arbors and sleeves cut from pipe or other stock can serve the same purpose.

1. The removal procedure and the first eight disassembly instructions of the three-speed unit also apply to the four-speed unit.

GEARSHIFT FORKS

2. Remove end cover bolts and drive out

Mounting transmission case in factory disassembly fixture

the 1st, 2nd and 3rd, and 4th gearshift fork shaft (from the front).

3. Remove cover rearwards, keeping the gearshift forks in position. Note the location

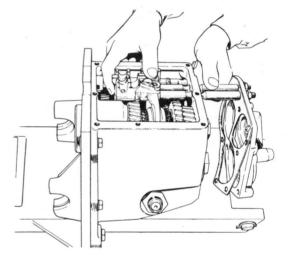

Disassembling end cover and shift fork rails

of shims and collect the shims. Prevent the ejection of the poppet balls in the gearshift forks.

4. If only the rear pinion shaft bearing is to be removed, it can be done now. Engage two gears (3rd and reverse), release the retaining washer and back off the left-hand thread nut on the shaft. The bearing now can be removed with a puller (No. 784115), and a new bearing can be installed and the pinion shaft shimmed.

5. Use a brass driver to release the reverse gearshift fork shaft and withdraw it to the rear. Prevent the ejection of the poppet ball.

6. Lift out the three gearshift forks.

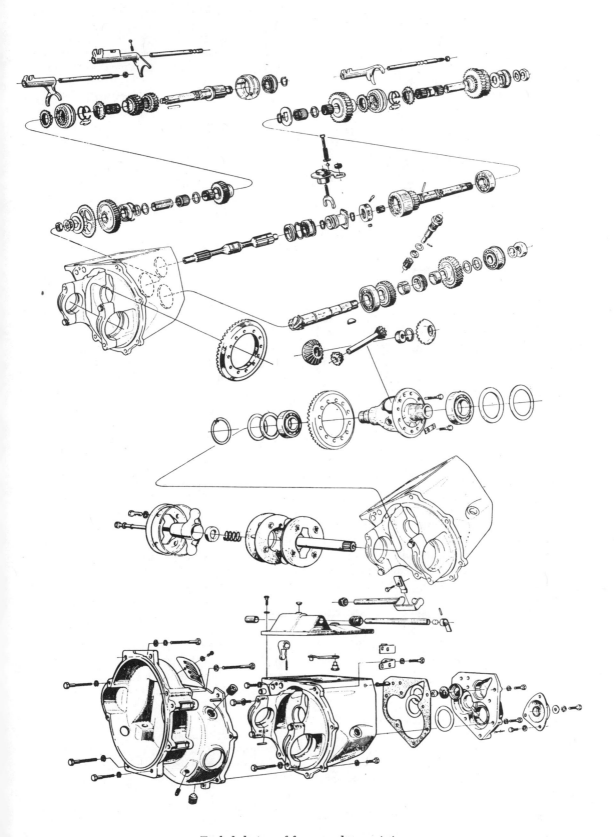

Exploded view of four-speed transmission

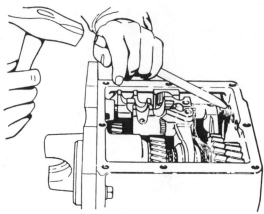

Driving out reverse shift fork rail

Countershaft with Bearings and Gears

7. Engage reverse and 3rd gears at the same time.

8. Loosen nut at the front end of the countershaft. Remove the friction wheel and washer. Loosen nuts of the primary and pinion shaft if these are to be removed; pinion shaft nut has a left-hand thread.

9. Return synchronizer sleeve to the neutral position. Lift up and fasten the front end plate of the fixture.

10. Place arbor tool No. 786058, with shortest point between the front press screw and the countershaft, and press in until the arbor is against the gear. Meanwhile, supporting tool No. 784125 should be located between 1st speed gear and rear of the transmission case. Change the arbor point to the next longer one and again press in the shaft. Repeat procedure with the longest point until the bearing and countershaft are released. Remove tools and drop the fixture end plate.

11. Pull the shaft out rearwards; the countershaft gear will be released. Let the spacer at the front bearing drop while lifting the entire assembly, including the two gears and synchronizer unit, out of the case. Collect the washer and key.

If necessary:

a. Remove the retaining ring from the shaft and drive off the rear ball bearing and bearing seat in order to remove reverse gear.

b. The front countershaft bearing cannot be changed without removing the primary shaft.

Primary Shaft with Bearings and Gears

12. Remove the end nut and retaining

washer. Lift up and fasten the rear plate of the fixture.

13. Place an arbor tool (No. 784104) between the rear press screw and shaft and press in the shaft until it is released from the bearings.

14. Remove the shaft forwards; let the spacer at the rear bearing drop while lifting out gears and synchronizer as a unit.

15. After removal of primary shaft, the front bearing can be removed by tapping it gently toward the differential side.

16. Drive out the rear primary shaft bearing using the front press screw, tool No. 784109 and extension sleeve No. 784106.

If necessary:

a. Remove the thrust washer and locking pin from the shaft.

b. Remove the retaining ring and drive off the front bearing.

Pinion Shaft with Bearings and Gears

17. Remove the speedometer gear drive.

18. Remove the left-hand thread shaft nut and pull out rear pinion shaft bearing with a puller (tool No. 784115), using front press screw to support the shaft. Collect the spacer and shims from inside the bearing.

19. Locate the supporting tool (No. 784121) on the lower side of the shaft between the rear gear and the front end of the case. Make sure the tool is centered on the gear so that the gear does not tip and bind on the shaft.

20. Lift and fasten the rear end plate of fixture, then drive out the shaft forwards, using the press screw, until the roller bearing clears the front of case. Remove the tool and drop end plate of fixture. Lift out the 3rd gear while drawing shaft from case. Retrieve the Woodruff key.

If necessary:

a. Press the front roller bearing and pinion shaft 4th gear from the shaft as follows: Remove the retaining ring from the roller bearing. Place the pinion shaft and supporting tool (No. 784123) in a press and drive out shaft. Make sure the outer bearing race is flush against the gear. The bearing should not be taken apart if it is to be reused; make sure that the rollers do not fall out and install the retaining ring immediately.

b. Press oil collector gently out of the case.

When installing new gears, remember that

the 3rd speed gear and pinion shaft 3rd gear are supplied in matched sets, as are the 4th speed gear and the pinion shaft 4th gear. Quiet operation is assured only if gears are replaced in sets. The pinion shaft and ring gear are also matched sets and must be replaced as sets. Install the gears so that the matching numbers face the same way.

Assembly

PINION SHAFT WITH BEARINGS AND GEARS

1. Locate the front roller bearing, pinion shaft 4th gear, spacers and speedometer drive gear on the pinion shaft. Using a press and tool (No. 784106), drive in the bearing and pinion shaft 4th gear until the inner bearing race is flush with the drive pinion. Check that the matching number faces the same way as on the 4th speed gear.

2. Next, put the pinion shaft into the case from the differential side and place the pinion shaft 3rd gear on the shaft inside the case. Be certain the Woodruff key for the 3rd gear is in the pinion shaft. In some older units, the pinion shaft 4th gear also is held by a key.

3. Turn the shaft to line up the Woodruff key and the keyway in the 3rd gear.

4. Place a guiding arbor tool (No. 784122) in the rear bearing seat so that the pinion shaft passes into it.

5. Secure the arbor with the rear press screw so that the flange is flush with the case.

6. Drive the pinion shaft into place using the front press screw. Be certain the key enters the groove in the 3rd gear.

7. Loosen the rear press screw and remove the arbor from the bearing seat.

8. Place a 0.14″ spacer on the end shaft. If the rear pinion bearing has a split inner ring, the spacer must be placed next to the bearing.

9. Using the press screw and arbor (No. 784122), press the rear ball bearing, with retaining ring, into the case. Use the press screw at the front end of the pinion shaft for support. In the case of a split bearing, first fit the inner ring, then the remaining part, and press in as described above.

10. Loosen the rear press screw and drop both fixture end plates.

11. Install a new tabbed washer onto the pinion shaft, with tab facing out. Install the left-hand thread nut, but don't tighten it with a torque wrench until primary shaft and countershaft are installed.

PRIMARY SHAFT WITH BEARINGS AND GEARS

12. Up to and including transmission No. 276503: refit the front bearing, using tool No. 784107, and place retaining ring, locking pin thrust washer and 4th speed gear needle bearing on the primary shaft. Be certain the locking pin prevents the thrust washer from rotating.

From Transmission No. 276504: fit the oil slinger and front bearing, using tool No. 784107, and place the retaining ring, washer and 4th speed gear needle bearing on the primary shaft.

13. Before pressing in the primary shaft, the countershaft front bearing must be in position. Press in the bearing from the front, using the arbor tool No. 786134, until it is hard against the retaining ring in the bearing seat.

14. Assemble the primary shaft components, the 3rd and 4th speed gears and the synchronizer sleeve and rings, then place the entire assembly into the case while passing the aligning arbor (No. 784114) into the 3rd speed gear through the rear bearing seat. Secure the arbor with the press screw.

15. Slide in the shaft from the front until its splines enter the synchronizer hub.

16. Put arbor tool No. 784104 into the freewheel hub. The needle bearing must be removed from the freewheel sleeve while this is being done.

17. Lift and fasten the front end plate of the fixture and carefully drive in the primary shaft against the arbor in the freewheel sleeve, using the press screw if a fixture is available, until the 3rd speed gear is tight against the rear case. Check that the synchronizer hub does not tip and bind.

18. Remove the aligning arbor from the 3rd speed gear and place the needle bearing spacer sleeve and bushing for this gear onto the shaft inside the gear hub.

19. Place the spacer, with the beveled side facing outwards, and the rear bearing on the primary shaft and drive in the bearing using tool No. 784109. The front press screw and the arbor in the freewheel sleeve will support the shaft.

20. Loosen the press screws and drop the rear fixture end.

21. Place a new tabbed washer, with tab facing outward, and a nut on the shaft. Do not tighten with torque wrench until countershaft is installed.

COUNTERSHAFT WITH BEARINGS AND GEARS

22. Raise and fasten the front plate of fixture and place countershaft gear in position, with the machined part facing the clutch bearing. Use front press screw and tool No. 786134 to hold the countershaft gear and shaft gear.

23. Reassemble the 1st and 2nd speed gears, the 2nd speed complete with needle bearing, spacer and bushing and synchronizer unit with its rings.

24. Place this assembly into the case, passing the countershaft needle bearing, complete with 1st speed gear, through the rear of the case at the same time. If the rear bearing, bearing seat and reverse gear have not been removed, they may remain on the shaft during reassembly. In this case, however, the bearing first must be pressed into the seat and the rear retaining ring removed from the shaft.

25. Put the spacer on the shaft between the 2nd speed gear and the front ball bearing, then slide the shaft through the front bearing and into the countershaft gear.

26. Drive in the countershaft with the press screw and tool No. 784109. Make certain that the shaft splines engage with the synchronizer hub and the shaft passes into the countershaft gear. Use a pin wrench, tool No. 784124, to turn the shaft. Drop both fixture end plates and fasten the rear bearing with the retaining ring (after pressing it in). If countershaft is reinstalled, complete with reverse gear and bearing, use tool No. 784109. This tool also is used if the reverse gear and the seat with the bearing are mounted separately.

27. Engage 2nd and 4th gears at the same time and turn the 3rd speed gear in order to align the keyway in the countershaft gear. Drive in the key using an arbor.

28. Refit the friction wheel, together with new friction and star washers. Tighten countershaft end nut to 60 ft. lbs. Tighten the pinion shaft nut initially to 90 ft. lbs., back off and retighten to 45 ft. lbs. The primary shaft nut must be tightened to 35 ft. lbs. Check that the friction wheel is not located outside the opposing gear and that there is enough clearance between the primary shaft ball bearing and the countershaft gear. Lock the nuts on the main and pinion shafts by bending down the tabs on the washers.

GEARSHIFT FORKS

29. Put the synchronizer sleeve and reverse gear in neutral position and insert gearshift forks. The poppet balls and springs

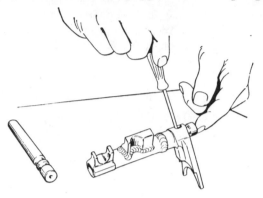

Installing poppet ball into reverse shift fork, using tool No. 784069

must be fitted and secured with tool No. 784069 before forks are placed in case.

30. Install the reverse gearshift shaft through the rear end and retrieve the tool used to hold the poppet ball in position.

31. Make sure the rubber washer and plastic plug are mounted in the end cover and the oil collector is in place in the case end.

32. Check the shims in the end cover.

33. Pass the 1st and 2nd and 3rd and 4th gearshift fork shafts through the rear end, positioning them so that the forks engage their respective shafts.

34. Fit the poppet balls in the forks. This is simplified if the balls are held with two tools (No. 784069) while the cover is pressed in.

35. Retrieve the two tools as they are pressed out of the front ends of the forks,

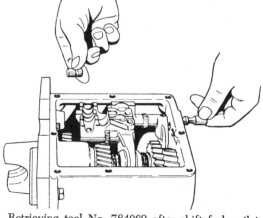

Retrieving tool No. 784069 after shift fork rail is fully seated

then tighten the end cover bolts to 18 ft. lbs. Check that the bolt opposite the reverse gearshift fork is not too long (which would impede fork movement).

36. If necessary, adjust the gearshift fork shafts, so that the forks are not subjected to axial pressure when a gear is engaged. Roughly the same clearance should exist between each synchronizer sleeve and the gear concerned in all gear positions.

DIFFERENTIAL

37. Reinstall differential assembly and spacers and tighten bearing cap bolts to 28 ft. lbs. Be sure the short bolts are installed in the small bearing cap.

38. If the pinion shaft setting has been altered, or parts in the differential were replaced, always check the side clearance of the bevel gear.

39. Reinstall the speedometer drive gear.

40. Coat the top cover with sealing compound and check that the three gearshift

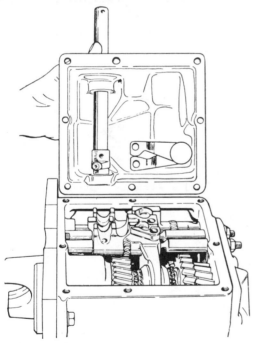

Shift mechanism and catch in transmission case cover

forks and the dogs and catch in the cover are in neutral, then fit the cover. Check the function of the gearshift mechanism.

41. Insert the freewheel hub, using tool No. 784068 in the freewheel sleeve. Be sure an undamaged needle bearing is installed.

42. Check the clutch shaft seal and the driveshaft seals and replace if necessary.

Install the seals so that the dust guard lips face outwards; fill the space between the lips with chassis grease.

43. Coat the sealing surface of the clutch housing with Permatex No. 3 and attach the clutch housing to the transmission case. Turn the clutch shaft so that it clears the differential. Be certain the clutch shaft is not subjected to lateral stress and that the freewheel hub engages the clutch shaft splines.

44. Coat the clutch shaft splines with graphite grease and fill the transmission with oil.

Transmission End Cover

SHIMMING

1. With end cover gasket removed, sealing surfaces clean and all bearings properly installed, place a dial indicator (No. 784237) as shown in illustration; the point of the dial

Measuring rear end cover

indicator to the machined surface of the bearing to be shimmed. The measurement is to be made without shims and with a new end cover gasket.

2. Set the dial indicator to zero.

3. Place the measuring tool in the corresponding bearing in the transmission case; read the dial indicator.

4. Install, into the bearing position in the end cover, a combination of shims that correspond to the measurement, $\pm 0.002''$.

5. Proceed in the same way for all bearings.

6. Coat both sides of gasket and reinstall end cover; torque bolts to 18 ft. lbs.

Shim Selection Chart

Location of Shims or Part	4-Speed Transmission			3-Speed Transmission		
	Spare-Part No.	Thickness (in.)	Thickness (mm)	Spare-Part No.	Thickness (in.)	Thickness (mm)
On primary shaft	708093	0.004	0.10	708093	0.004	0.10
	708101	0.006	0.15	708101	0.006	0.15
	708102	0.012	0.30	708102	0.012	0.30
On countershaft	708094	0.004	0.10	708093	0.004	0.10
	708103	0.006	0.15	708101	0.006	0.15
	708104	0.012	0.30	708102	0.012	0.30
On pinion shaft	708095	0.004	0.10	708095	0.004	0.10
	708105	0.006	0.15	708105	0.006	0.15
	708106	0.012	0.30	708106	0.012	0.30
End cover	708058			710432		
Gasket	716754		(thin)	710430		(thin)

Measuring rear end

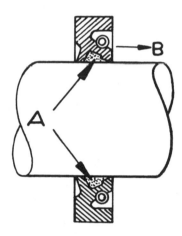

Clutch shaft seal with double seal lips

Clutch Shaft Seal Replacement

1. Remove the release bearing.
2. Pry out the seal (using tool No. 784220)
3. Install new seal—if double type, fill the space between lips with chassis grease, (use tool No. 784220).

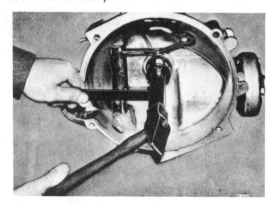

Installing clutch shaft seal

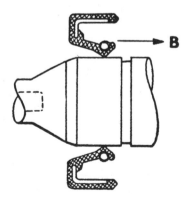

Clutch shaft seal with single seal lips

Clutch Shaft or Bearing Replacement

1. Remove inner universal joints, separate clutch housing from transmission case.

Remove release bearing and clutch shaft seal.

2. Remove retainer ring from the bearing seat inside the seal. Remove the retaining ring which forms the rear stop for the locking sleeve on the shaft.

3. Pull the clutch shaft forwards and retrieve the locking sleeve and freewheel operating fork.

4. Remove the retaining rings from the shaft and drive off the bearing. This bearing's primary function is to locate the shaft in an axial direction.

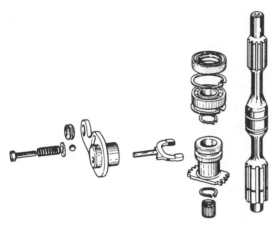

Clutch shaft, bearing, and freewheel mechanism

Clutch Shaft Assembly

1. Place the rear retaining ring in the clutch housing bearing seat.

2. Press bearing onto the shaft and install the two retaining rings.

3. Place the freewheel operating fork and the locking sleeve in position in the clutch housing.

4. The clutch shaft is installed from the front so that it engages the locking sleeve. Fit the rear retaining ring onto the shaft behind the sleeve.

5. Reinstall the front retaining ring into the clutch housing bearing seat and check the function of the freewheel operating mechanism.

6. Install a new seal, then replace release bearing.

Freewheel Disassembly and Assembly

1. Remove the clutch shaft to allow removal of the locking sleeve and operating fork.

2. Back off the operating lever locking screw to provide access to the spring, operating lever and poppet ball. Reassemble in reverse order, after replacing worn parts.

Freewheel Hub

1. When the freewheel unit is disassembled for repair, it is normally necessary to replace only the hub and six rollers.

2. Remove the needle bearing from the freewheel hub.

3. Insert the prongs of tool No. 784068 between the freewheel and sleeve, then insert the other part of the tool into the hub splines. Twist the freewheel so that the rollers are firmly held against the tool prongs, then pull out the hub until the rollers are halfway out of the sleeve. Put a strong rubber band around the rollers and remove completely. If special tool is not available, any tool can be used which can grip the internal splines so that unit may be turned counterclockwise while being drawn out far enough to put on the rubber band.

4. Reassemble the freewheel hub and needle bearing in reverse order and reinstall into transmission. A spring-loaded plunger is under each roller. Always check the plunger for wear, making certain it moves freely in its hole. Check the spring tension. Never reuse old rollers after installing a new freewheel hub. Install hub so that the unit engages firmly when the hub is turned clockwise.

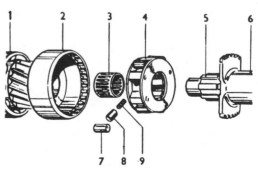

Freewheel mechanism

1. Ball bearing	5. Clutch shaft
2. Freewheel sleeve (primary shaft)	6. Locking device
	7. Roller
3. Needle bearing	8. Plunger
4. Freewheel hub	9. Spring

Chapter 6

Electrical System and Tune-Up

Part I—Two-Stroke Models

The 12-volt negative ground electrical system includes: battery, starter, generator, voltage regulator, ignition distributor, ignition coil, spark plugs, headlights, interior lights, electric clock, windshield wipers, horns, fan motor, stop light switch, cables, wiring, switches and fuses. On the SAAB Sport and Monte Carlo 850, there is also a series resistance for the ignition coil, an electrical temperature sender unit, oil pressure warning relay, electrical windshield washer, and back up light.

Battery

The 12-volt, six-cell battery is rated at 34 Amp./hrs.

For all cars from 1967, the battery is rated at 44 Amp./hrs.

Generator

The generator on the SAAB 95 and 96 (up to and including 1966) and for the 1965 SAAB Sport is connected to a voltage and current regulator of the variode type and supplies a maximum continuous current of 300 Watts. Monte Carlo 850 models from 1966 and Saab 95 and 96 models from 1967 have an alternator. A warning lamp on the instrument panel from 1964, and an ammeter from 1960–63, shows whether or not the generator is charging the battery.

Starter

The starter has a rated output of 0.5 horsepower. The pinion is engaged by means of a solenoid switch (or lever) that is activated by the ignition key.

Ignition System

The engine is equipped with battery ignition, consisting of an ignition coil and distributor. A combined centrifugal and vacuum governor was used on the SAAB 95 and 96 and on the Monte Carlo 850 from 1966. The centrifugal governor regulates the ignition advance in two stages for the SAAB 95 and 96 and in one stage for SAAB Sport and Monte Carlo 850 models. The SAAB Sport of 1965 has a centrifugal governor only.

Lighting

The lights consist of the headlights, turn signals, parking lights, license plate light, and stop lights.

The parking lights are always on with the headlights, regardless of whether the lights are dimmed or not.

The interior panel lights can be dimmed by turning the switch button. From 1968 on the panel lights are regulated by a rheostat to the left of the light switch.

Miscellaneous Electrical Equipment

The interior lighting consists of a dome light operated by a switch on the light itself and by a door switch. After 1967, all cars have a switch on each door.

The turn signals are operated by an automatic return switch located under the steering wheel. Green indicators on the instrument panel indicate when the turn signals are operating.

The windshield wipers are driven by a motor through double links and are controlled by a switch on the instrument panel. This switch is combined with the windshield washer control. The washer is mechanical on the SAAB 95 and 96 and electrical on the SAAB Sport and Monte Carlo 750 and 850.

Oil Warning System—SAAB Sport and Monte Carlo 850

A warning light on the instrument panel glows if the oil pressure fails in the oil pump. The pump is equipped with an oil monitor, operated by oil pressure. It consists of a contact, which opens and closes once for each revolution of the pump. The oil warning relay translates these impulses from the oil monitor to the warning lamp, which is normally not illuminated. If oil pressure fails, the contact on the oil monitor stays closed and the warning light glows.

Battery Service Procedures

The battery is a 12-volt, lead-acid type having six cells. The electrolyte is dilute sulfuric acid having a normal specific gravity of 1.28 at 68°F. with battery fully charged. The battery has a capacity of 34 Amp./hrs. up to and including the 1966 model, which means that it can supply a current of 1.7 Amps. for 20 hours at a temperature of 69°F. From 1967, all cars are equipped with 44 Amp./hr. batteries. The output is 2.2 Amps. for 20 hours. The positive terminal of the battery is connected to the starter and other units, the negative terminal is grounded to the chassis.

REMOVAL AND INSTALLATION

When removing the battery, first disconnect the ground cable to prevent shorting. Engines having an alternator must be stopped before removing cables.

Loosen the wingnuts on the holder and lift out the battery.

Before installing a battery, make sure the entire battery and its terminals are clean. After battery is in place and connected, coat the terminal with Vaseline.

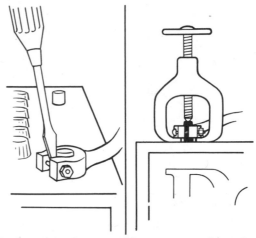

Left—testing battery cable connections by twisting screwdriver in clamp
Right—Removing corroded clamp using a puller

ELECTROLYTE LEVEL

Evaporation and decomposition will cause the electrolyte level to decrease. Top up, using distilled water only, until the level is approximately 0.4″ above the plates. Sulfuric acid may be added *only* to compensate for leakage or to refill the battery if it has been emptied. The specific gravity must be checked whenever sulfuric acid is added.

SPECIFIC GRAVITY OF ELECTROLYTE

The specific gravity of the electrolyte can be checked with a syringe-type hydrometer. The result of the test indicates the charging condition of the battery; see table below.

Charging Condition	*Specific Gravity*
Fully charged	Approx. 1.280
Half charged	Approx. 1.210
Discharged	Approx. 1.120

CELL VOLTAGE

A more accurate test of the state of the battery is made by using a cell tester, a voltmeter combined with a resistance, which is connected in parallel to give a load of 80–100 Amps.

Each cell is tested individually by placing the tips of the cell tester against the cell terminals. The indicated voltage should not fall below 1.6 after 10–15 seconds discharge. A bigger voltage drop indicates a defective or discharged cell.

The normal no-load cell voltage is 2.0 volts; the difference in voltage between any two cells should not exceed 0.2 volt.

CHARGING

The charging rate must be adapted to the capacity of the battery and should not exceed 2.5 Amps.

The battery is considered fully charged when the cell voltage is 2.5–2.7 volts, without load, and each cell has maintained the same voltage for three hours of charging.

Decomposition causes the electrolyte to boil, and release hydrogen gas, and the caps should be unscrewed while the battery is being charged.

Generator Service Procedures

During driving, the generator supplies the current required by the various units and also charges the battery.

The generators used on the SAAB 95 and 96 and Sport models, up to and including 1965, have identical electrical data, but are provided with different retaining lugs for the different models. From 1966, the Monte Carlo 850 is equipped with an alternator; from 1967, all cars use an alternator.

REMOVAL AND INSTALLATION

1. Disconnect the negative battery cable. Engines with an alternator must not be running.

2. Disconnect the generator wires, retaining and adjusting bolts, then remove fan-belt.

NOTE: *On some models, cooling system must be drained and hoses disconnected from water pump.*

3. Lift out the generator.

4. Reinstall in reverse sequence.

5. Adjust the fanbelt tension so that the belt can be pressed down approximately 0.3″ with light finger pressure halfway between the pulleys.

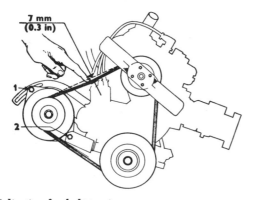

Adjusting fan belt tension

MAINTENANCE AND INSPECTION OF BRUSHES

The generator brushes should be checked every 18,000 miles.

1. Disconnect the negative battery cable, then remove cables connected to DF and D+ terminals.

2. Remove the cover band over the commutator. Always disconnect the cables before removing the cover band.

3. Lift the brush springs using a wire

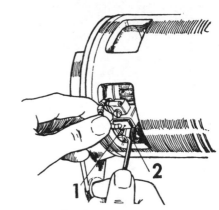

Removing carbon brushes

1. Brush   2. Spring

hook, and make sure the brushes slide freely in the holders.

4. If a brush does not slide freely in its holder, lift it out and clean both holder and brush with solvent. Do not wipe the contact surface of the brush.

5. After cleaning, install the brush in exactly the same position.

6. If a brush is damaged, or so worn so as to allow the spring to rest against the stop, a new brush must be installed. Always use genuine Bosch brushes for best results.

7. When installing, take care to prevent the spring from hitting the brush.

8. Replace the cover band, being careful not to short circuit the DF and D+ terminals.

9. Connect the DF and D+ terminal wires and the negative battery cable.

COMMUTATOR

The commutator should have a dark gray, smooth surface where the brushes contact and its surface should be free of oil and grease. If dirty, clean with a suitable solvent and dry carefully. A commutator which is scored or out-of-round must be turned down and reconditioned.

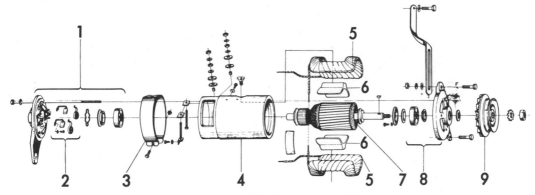

DC generator components—typical

1. Commutator frame with bearing
2. Carbon brushes with springs
3. Cover band
4. Coil housing
5. Field winding
6. Terminals
7. Armature
8. Drive end Frame
9. Belt pulley

TESTING THE GENERATOR

Check the voltage by connecting a voltmeter between D+ and D— terminals, after having connected DF to the chassis ground. At a maximum 2,050 rpm (1,900 rpm up to 1965), the voltmeter should read 12 volts. Check the current with an ammeter, connected in series with a rheostat (approximately 1 ohm) between D+ and D—. Increase the engine speed to 3,150 rpm (not more than 2,600 rpm up to 1965) and adjust the voltage to 12 volts. The current should not be less than 17 Amps (13.3 Amps up to 1965).

Alternator for Monte Carlo 850 from 1966, SAAB 95 and 96 from 1967

The SAAB Monte Carlo 850 (from 1966) and the SAAB 95 and 96 (from 1967) all are equipped with an alternator. There are some important advantages of the alternator compared to the DC generator. For example, the charging current begins earlier with an alternator and supplies the battery and electrical components at engine idle speed. Return current relays and current regulators are not used; only a voltage regulator is required. The alternator requires very little maintenance, because carbon brushes and commutators are not needed. Repair of the alternator should be done by a specialized shop.

PRECAUTIONS

The battery always must be connected when the alternator is running. Do not mix up the battery leads, because serious damage will result.

If electric welding is to be done on a car with an alternator, the ground cable should be disconnected. If this is not done, the diode rectifiers may be damaged.

DESIGNATION

The Bosch designation of the alternator is
K1 ↔ 14U35A20
The interpretation of the type designation is:

20	x 100 = 2000 rpm (rpm for 2/3 of maximum current output)
35A	Maximum current
14U	Maximum voltage
←→	Direction of rotation
1	Design of alternator
K	Pole housing diameter

DESCRIPTION—INTERNAL WIRING

The 12-volt alternator K1 ↔ 14U35A20 is internally air cooled, has a 12-pole, fork-type rotor and is equipped with six silicon diodes for rectification. An exciter diode is connected to each of the three internal windings. Their common junction constitutes the terminal D+/61. The six rectification diodes are arranged in an AC bridge network, i.e., three diodes are connected for normal polarity (anode to housing). According to polarity (positive or negative), the diode carrier is insulated from ground or connected directly to a ground contact, respectively. The insulated carrier of the exciter diode is located between these two carriers.

The stator windings are star-coupled, while the rotor carries the ring-shaped exciter coil and is of fork execution type, one

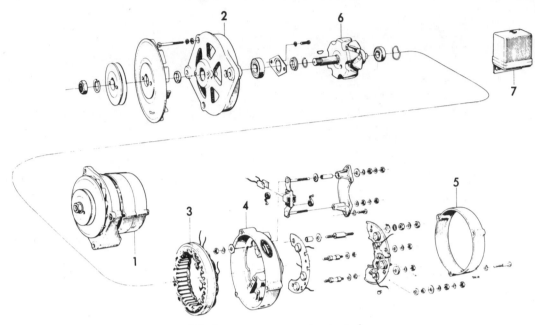

AC alternator components—typical

1. Alternator assembly
2. Bearing, gear side

3. Stator
4. Slip ring bearing

5. Protective ring
6. Rotor
7. Voltage regulator

fork having "north" polarity (six poles), and the other "south" polarity (six poles). The two forks then give the assembled rotor, alternately, a south and a north pole.

The exciter coil ends are connected to the slip rings, from which they receive the excitation current.

TERMINALS

D+/61:Output of exciter diodes, connection of regulator D+ and of charge indicator light.

DF:Input of exciter coil, connection of regulator DF.

B+:Battery connection.

D—:Ground, connection to regulator D—.

ALTERNATOR BEARING REPLACEMENT

1. Hold the pulley with a suitable tool and loosen the nut with a 22 mm. open end wrench. Loosen the pulley.

2. Mark the location of the attachment ear on the drive end plate. Remove the cover ring and the brush holder plate.

3. Loosen the bolts on the drive end plate, then remove the rotor and drive end plate.

4. Place the drive end plate on a suitable support and press out the rotor. It is now possible to remove the bearing.

5. Remove the ball bearing at the slip ring end, using a suitable puller.

Terminal end of alternator

ALTERNATOR ASSEMBLY

1. Fill the ball bearing with Bosch grease Ft 1.33 or suitable alternate grease. Press the ball bearing into the drive end plate, the enclosed side facing the drive side, using a bench vise and sockets.

2. Ease the drive end plate onto the rotor.

3. By pressing, fasten the ball bearing to the slip ring end.

4. Install the rotor and assemble the alternator. Make sure that the drive end plate

Removing brush holder plate

Soldering carbon brush connection

Pressing in slip ring end bearings

is properly positioned with relation to the slip ring end plate. Install the brush holder plate and cover ring. Torque the pulley nut to 25–29 ft. lbs.

CARBON BRUSH REPLACEMENT

Remove the brush holder plate, along with the carbon brushes. Remove the wire connections, using a soldering iron. When soldering the wire brush connections, take care to prevent solder flow into the cable. The minimum length of the brush is approximately 0.34″.

TESTING

Diodes may be tested with DC voltages of less than 24 volts.

Glow lamps (110 volt or 220 volt) may *not* be used for insulation or short circuit tests if the diodes are in the circuit.

The 80-volt, 40 Watt test voltage for the stator winding insulation test may *not* be used unless the diodes are disconnected.

While the engine is running, battery terminals may *not* be disconnected to check the charging current.

Semiconductors (diodes) are extremely sensitive to heat. To prevent damage from heat when soldering, use a pair of longnose pliers as a heat sink on the supply wire near the diode. Use a hot iron and solder as quickly as possible. Mechanical damage to the diode wires must be avoided.

The battery must be switched off or disconnected before any work is done to the alternator, either in the car or on the bench.

Only instruments having less than an 8-volt power supply may be used to measure resistance on the assembled alternator.

On the test bench, the alternator must be driven using its own pulley. All connections must be made with the correct size cable. Do not jury rig an inadequate battery connection.

A 12-volt battery must be connected parallel to the alternator before any testing begins, except during the regulating voltage, the nominal voltage and speed tests. The battery acts as a buffer and smoothes off any peak voltages arising from switching the load on or off.

Peak voltages exceeding the maximum allowable value (50 volts) will damage the diodes.

EXCITATION

As opposed to DC generators, alternators can lose their self-excitation properties after long storage; therefore, a 12-volt, 2-Watt charge indicator light must be connected between terminals 61 and B+ according the wiring diagram. The pre-exciting current then will flow through the charge indicator light, D+/61 on the alternator, D+/61 on the regulator, the closed regulator contacts and DF to the exciter coil fitted to the rotor. It is most important that the charge indicator light be a minimum 2 Watts. Self-excitation begins as soon as the exciter diodes are conducting at about 1–2 volts.

From there on, the voltage increases rapidly, the voltage drop across the charge indicator bulb decreases, and the bulb goes out as soon as battery voltage is achieved.

Voltage Regulator—DC Generator

The voltage regulator serves to keep the generator voltage constant within narrow limits, regardless of the generator speed and load. The regulator must prevent overcharging of the battery and limit the current take-off so that the maximum generator load is not exceeded, since this would damage the generator. To prevent the battery from being discharged through the generator when charging stops, the regulator incorporates a reverse current relay which interrupts the charging circuit when the reverse current has reached a certain point.

FUNCTION

The voltage regulator is of the variode type, meaning that it consists partly of a semiconductor regulating device called a *variode* by Bosch. This variode senses the temperature variations in the cable due to the intensity of the charging current and ambient temperature.

Regulation is achieved by varying the current through field winding (1). This is done, in three stages, at contact (4) of the regulator armature and at contacts (3) and (5).

Stage 1: Field winding grounded, armature (6) in upper position.

Stage 2: Field winding grounded through resistor (2), armature (6) in middle position.

Stage 3: Field winding shorted with part of the D+ cable, armature (6) in lower position.

Contact (4) will stand vibrating in one of the outer positions, depending on the voltage through the battery and connected electrical units, on the intensity of the extracted current and on the speed of the generator. All of these factors influence the force acting on the regulator armature (6), where the contact is located. The charging rate can be adjusted by changing the spring tension on armature (6)—more force gives a greater charge and vice-versa.

The variode (9) and its pilot winding (7) are connected in parallel with part of the D+ cable from the generator. The connection points are located inside the regulator casing.

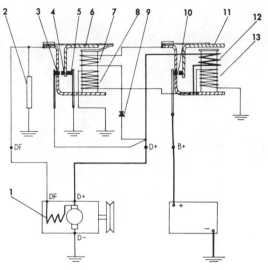

Wiring diagram—voltage regulator with variode

1. Field winding, generator
2. Resistor for field winding
3. Contact through which the field-winding can be shorted
4. Contact, armature, regulator relay
5. Contact through which the field-winding can be grounded
6. Armature, regulator relay
7. Variode pilot winding
8. Voltage winding, regulator relay
9. Variode
10. Contacts, reverse current relay
11. Armature, reverse current relay
12. Current winding, reverse current relay
13. Voltage winding, reverse current relay

The voltage over the variode and pilot winding thus will be the same as that between the connection points on the D+ cable. The resistance between the coupling points is constant for all practical purposes and the voltage is influenced only by the intensity of the generator current, which is tapped at B+.

The variode acts as a voltage-actuated and, to some extent, temperature-influenced current valve, and this feature is utilized in the voltage regulator.

When the voltage on the charging current is not high enough to open the variode, the regulator is not actuated by the pilot winding and voltage regulation is achieved with voltage winding (8) only.

If the charging current increases so much that the voltage across the variode becomes high enough to open it, part of the charging current will pass through the pilot winding, whereupon armature (6) will be attracted by the regulator coil and the field winding will be shorted through contact (3), whereupon the charging current undergoes a marked decrease. As a result, the voltage through the variode, the pilot winding and the regulator coil decreases, the armature returns and the current in the field winding increases again, thus providing a greater charging current and repeating the entire cycle. The variode thus acts as a current-limiting device in the regulator. As can be seen from the diagram, a higher voltage is required to open a cold variode. This implies that charging current will be higher when the regulator is cold (immediately after starting).

TESTING

To test *closing voltage,* connect a voltmeter between ground and D+ on the regulator. Allow engine to idle and switch on the parking lights. Increase engine rpm gradually—at the instant the voltage drops slightly, then resumes its increase as rpm rises, note the voltage. The voltage immediately prior to the drop is the closing voltage—it should be 12.4–13.1 volts except for regulator RS/VA200/12/A2, which should be 12.3–13.3 volts.

To test the *no-load voltage* with a cold voltage regulator, first disconnect the battery cable, then disconnect the B+ regulator wire. This B+ wire *must not* touch ground during this test. Connect a voltmeter between ground and the B+ regulator *terminal* and increase *generator speed* to 5,000 rpm. The voltmeter should read 13.8–14.8 volts, except for regulator RS/TBA160/12/1, which should be 14.3–15.3 volts.

To test *load voltage,* switch on the headlights (high beam), windshield wipers, and heater fan. Connect a voltmeter between ground and the regulator B+ terminal (with its wire still connected). Increase *generator speed* to 5,000 rpm—voltmeter should read 13.4–14.3, except for regulator RS/TBA160/12/1, which should be 13.5–14.5.

To test the *cut-out relay* for discharge current, disconnect the B+ terminal wire and connect an ammeter between the B+ terminal and the wire just disconnected from that terminal. Increase *generator speed* to about 2,000 rpm (but less than 2,600 rpm), then slowly reduce speed to idle. During this test, the ammeter will swing from charge to discharge—the maximum ammeter minus reading should be 2.0–7.5 Amps. (except regulator RS/TBA160/12/1, which should be 3.0–9.0 Amps.).

Starter

The starter is an electric motor, which, at the moment of starting, turns the flywheel through a pinion and ring gear. The starter pinion can slide on the armature shaft and is designed to mesh with the ring gear through operation of a solenoid. As soon as the engine has started, the pinion, driven by the flywheel ring gear, is released from the armature shaft by a freewheel mechanism, but remains in mesh with the ring gear as long as the solenoid is kept activated by the ignition key. The pinion is returned by a a spring as soon as the current for the solenoid is cut off with the key.

REMOVAL

1. Disconnect the negative battery cable.
2. Disconnect the starter motor wires.
3. Loosen the two bolts which hold the starter to the crankcase lower half. (Use a short, open end 1/2″ wrench with two ends, one at 15° and the other at 60° with relation to the handle.)
4. Pull back the starter until it's clear, then lift it out of the engine compartment.

INSTALLATION

1. Hold the starter in place and install the two bolts.
2. Reconnect the starter wires.
3. Reconnect the negative battery cable.

DISASSEMBLY

1. Remove the cover band.
2. Lift the brush springs and remove them using a wire hook.
3. If the commutator end frame is to be removed, disconnect the brush wires and the field winding wires.
4. Separate the solenoid from the pinion housing by removing the three bolts and jumper bar from the solenoid. Lift the solenoid upwards and out.
5. Remove the solenoid lever by pulling its pivot pin.
6. Loosen and remove the two through bolts which hold the three parts of the starter assembly together.
7. Separate the starter assembly at the rear end frame and remove the armature and pinion. Retrieve the brake washers located on the commutator and the adjustment washers from the pinion.
8. Remove the starter pinion from the armature by pressing in the collar using a

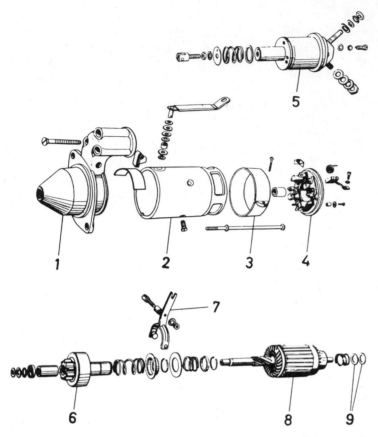

1. Pinion housing
2. Starter housing
3. Cover band
4. Commutator end frame
5. Operating solenoid
6. Starter pinion
7. Solenoid lever
8. Armature
9. Armature brake washers

Starter motor and solenoid

sleeve arbor, then removing the spring from inside the locating ring.

9. Clean the parts with compressed air and wash with solvent. Brushes, starter pinion and windings must *not* be washed with solvent.

ASSEMBLY

1. Relocate the starter pinion on the armature shaft and fasten using spring and locating ring. Lubricate the pinion, the shaft and the locating collar with special Bosch grease.

2. Insert the adjustment washers into the pinion housing, then install the solenoid lever and the armature.

3. Install the lever pivot pin.

4. Install the armature brake washers at the commutator. (The insulating washer goes between the two steel washers.) Lubricate using special Bosch grease.

5. If the commutator end frame was removed, attach it to the housing. Connect the wires from the carbon brushes and field windings.

6. Lubricate the bearings with oil, then assemble the armature, pinion housing and starter housing, together with the end frame, and tighten the two through bolts. The armature must have an axial clearance of 0.004–0.012″. This is adjusted with shims at the pinion housing. If new bearing bushings are to be installed, soak them in warm oil for an hour beforehand.

7. Install the solenoid and connect the jumper bar to the terminal bolt.

8. Install the brushes and cover band.

SOLENOID

The solenoid has two windings, a powerful winding to attract and a weaker winding to hold. If the hold winding is defective, the solenoid will repeatedly switch on and off when starting is attempted. In such cases, a new solenoid must be installed. The distance between the pin for the lever and the operating solenoid operating flange must be adjusted according to the illustration.

Coil

Two different ignition coils are used, both made by Bosch. One of these is of standard

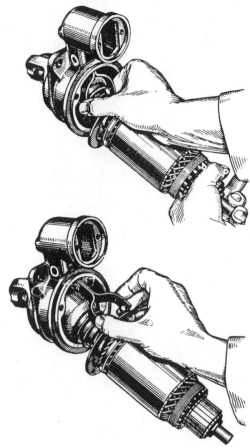

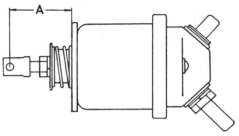

Adjusting starter solenoid yoke length, core fully extended. A=1.142 ±0.004"

Disconnecting starter solenoid yoke

design and is used on the SAAB 95 and 96 up to 1965, the other is a high output unit and is used on the SAAB Sport, Monte Carlo 850 and 95 and 96 models from 1966. The high output coil requires a ballast resistor in order to prevent its being damaged when the engine is running at low speeds or when the ignition is switched on. The ignition coil is located on the right-hand wheel well.

Distributor

The principal differences between distributors involve the vacuum advance governors. One, JFU3 (R), a vacuum distributor, is connected to a vacuum take-off on the carburetor. When setting the ignition with a stroboscope, the vacuum governor always must be disconnected by removing the line from the distributor.

REMOVAL

1. Disconnect the battery ground cable and the distributor primary lead.
2. Remove the distributor cover and, if applicable, remove the line at the vacuum chamber.
3. Loosen the locking bolt on the retainer under the distributor.
4. Pull the distributor up and out of the engine. NOTE: *With VJU3BR1T and VJU3BR2T, the generator bracket must be moved.*
5. Disconnect the spark plug wires from the distributor cap.

INSTALLATION

1. Remove the spark plugs and turn the crankshaft so that the mark on the pulley faces the centermost mark on the engine block.
2. a. *Distributors 0 231 144 002/JFU 3, VJU3BR1T, and VJU3BR2T:* Install the distributor into the engine so that the vacuum chamber faces the rear with a clearance of about 0.4–0.6" between it and the engine block. At the same time, the marks on the rotor and distributor housing should coincide.
   b. *Distributor JF 3 (R), VJ3BR7T, and VJ3BR8T:* Install the distributor into the engine so that the oil cup points forward and slightly to the right. At the same time, the marks on the rotor and distributor housing should coincide.
   c. *Distributors 0 231 144 003/JFU3 and 0 231 144 004/JFU3.*
   Install the distributor into the engine so that the vacuum chamber faces forward and slightly to the right. At the same time, the marks on the rotor and distributor housing should coincide.
3. Reconnect the distributor primary wire and the battery ground cable.
4. Install the distributor cap. The spark plug wire for the No. 2 cylinder must be installed into the tower opposite the distributor rotor when the mark on the pulley faces the centermost mark on the engine block. The two remaining spark plug wires are

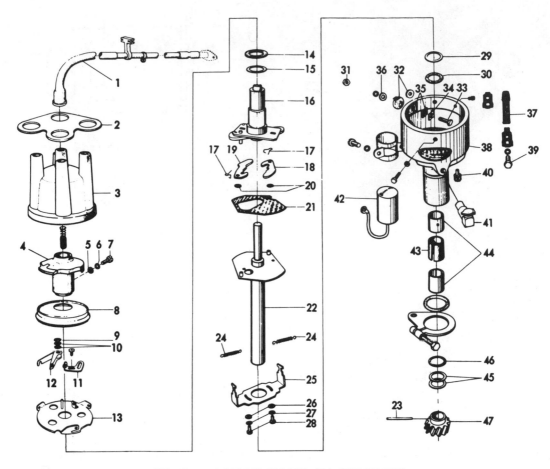

Distributor 0 231 120 023/JF3 (R) (VJ3 BR11T)

1. Ventilation hose
2. Retainer, ventilation hose
3. Distributor cap
4. Distributor arm (rotor)
5. Washer
6. Spring washer
7. Screw, distributor arm
8. Condensation shield
9. Clip
10. Shim
11. Contact plate
12. Breaker arm
13. Contact breaker plate
14. Fiber washer
15. Shim
16. Breaker arm
17. Damping spring
18. Fly weight
19. Fly weight
20. Fiber washer
21. Fiber plate
22. Distributor shaft
23. Slotted pin
24. Spring
25. Clamp
26. Washer
27. Spring washer
28. Screw
29. Shim
30. Fiber washer
31. Nut for contact screw
32. Insulating washer
33. Contact screw
34. Contact washer
35. Insulating washer
36. Washer
37. Retaining spring
38. Distributor housing
39. Screw for retaining spring
40. Bleed nipple
41. Lubricator
42. Capacitor
43. Felt bushing
44. Bushing
45. Shim
46. Fiber washer
47. Distributor pinion

installed clockwise. The one for the No. 3 cylinder first and for No. 1 cylinder afterwards.

5. Adjust the timing and, if applicable, reconnect the hose to the vacuum chamber. The vacuum hose must be installed so that its highest point is higher than the float chamber.

DISTRIBUTORS 0 231 120 023/JF3 (R), VJ3BR7T, AND VJ3BR8T DISASSEMBLY

1. Remove the rotor 4, which is fastened to the cam by means of the stop screw 7.
2. Lift off the condensation shield.
3. Loosen the nut 31 for the condenser wire.

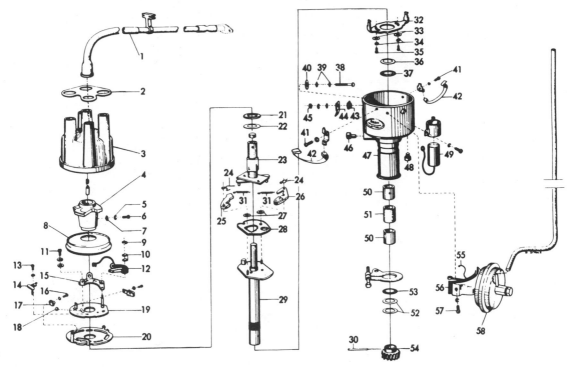

Distributor 0 231 144 002/ JFU3 (VJU3 BR2T)

1. Ventilation hose
2. Retainer, ventilation hose
3. Distributor cap
4. Distributor arm (rotor)
5. Spring washer
6. Screw, distributor arm
7. Washer
8. Condensation trap
9. Clip
10. Shim
11. Screw for contact plate
12. Breaker arm
13. Screw for pivot
14. Pivot
15. Contact-breaker plate
16. Screw for ball retainer
17. Ball retainer
18. Ball
19. Self-adjusting breaker plate

20. Stationary breaker plate
21. Fiber washer
22. Shim
23. Breaker cam
24. Locking spring
25. Fly weight
26. Fly weight
27. Fiber washer
28. Fiber plate
29. Distributor shaft
30. Pin
31. Regulator spring
32. Clamp
33. Washer
34. Spring washer
35. Screw for clamp
36. Shim
37. Fiber washer
38. Contact screw
39. Contact washer

40. Fiber washer
41. Screw, retaining spring
42. Retaining spring
43. Insulating washer
44. Connection
45. Nut, contact screw
46. Lubricator
47. Distributor housing
48. Bleeder nipple
49. Capacitor
50. Bushing
51. Felt bushing
52. Shim
53. Fiber washer
54. Distributor pinion
55. Earthing connection,
     vacuum chamber
56. Sealing strip
57. Screw, vacuum chamber
58. Vacuum chamber

4. Remove clip 9 and lift breaker arm 12.

5. Remove screw 33, together with contact washer 34, insulating washer and insulating strip 35. Retrieve the insulating washers 32.

6. Loosen the screw and remove contact plate 11.

7. Loosen and remove the three screws 39 which hold breaker plate 13. Two of these screws also hold the retaining springs 37.

8. Remove the retaining springs and lift up breaker plate 13.

9. File off and drive out the riveted slotted pin 23 which holds the distributor pinion 47 to the shaft 22.

10. Lift out the distributor shaft, together with the vacuum advance governor. Collect washers 29 and 30, as well as any shims 45.

11. Unhook the two springs 24 from spring holder 25 and lift off breaker cam 16. Collect the spacers 15 and the fiber washer 14.

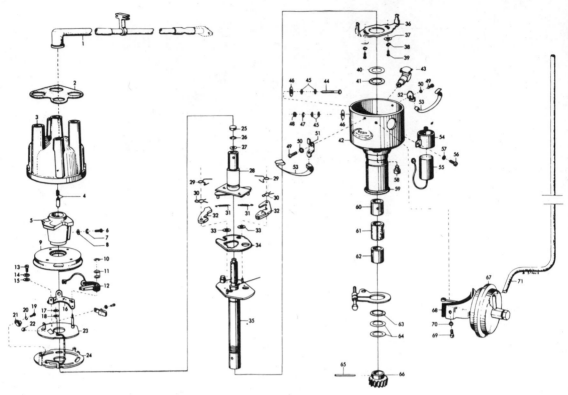

Distributor 0 231 144 003/JFU3, 0 231 144 004/JFU3

1. Ventilation hose
2. Retainer, ventilation hose
3. Distributor cap
4. Center carbon brush with spring
5. Rotor
6. Screw for rotor
7. Spring washer
8. Flat washer
9. Condensation shield
10. Clip
11. Shim
12. Breaker arm
13. Screw for contact plate
14. Spring washer
15. Flat washer
16. Contact-breaker plate
17. Clip
18. Flat washer
19. Screw for ball holder
20. Spring washer
21. Ball holder
22. Ball
23. Self-adjusting (moving) breaker plate
24. Stationary breaker plate

25. Lubricating felt
26. Retaining washer
27. Washer
28. Breaker cam
29. Damping spring (Monte Carlo 850)
30. Locking spring (Saab 95/96)
31. Governor spring
32. Governor weight
33. Fiber washer
34. Fiber plate
35. Distributor shaft
36. Clamp
37. Flat washer
38. Spring washer
39. Screw for clamp
40. Spacer
41. Fiber washer
42. Distributor housing
43. Lubricator
44. Contact screw
45. Contact washer
46. Insulating washer
47. Spring washer
48. Nut for contact screw

49. Screw for retaining-spring holder
50. Spring washer
51. Retaining-spring holder with lug
52. Retaining-spring holder without lug
53. Retaining spring
54. Capacitor clip
55. Capacitor
56. Screw for capacitor clip
57. Spring washer
58. Bleed nipple
59. Rubber ring
60. Upper bushing
61. Felt bushing
62. Lower bushing
63. Fiber washer
64. Shim
65. Serrated pin
66. Distributor pinion
67. Vacuum chamber
68. Sealing strip
69. Screw for vacuum chamber
70. Spring washer
71. Vacuum hose

Distributor Specifications

Distributor Model (Bosch Designation Plus Factory Parts No.)	Used on SAAB Models	Point Gap (in.)	Distributor Dwell Angle (deg.)	Contact Pressure (oz.)	Direction of Rotation	Condenser Type	Dynamic Timing (deg.)	Basic Timing (deg.) ▲	Ignition Coil Designation
VJ3BR7T	GT-750	.012–.016	80–84	38–42	CW	LMKO Z30Z	22B†°	2B°	ZS/KZ 2/12 A or TK 12 A 10
VJ3BR8T	95 (up to 4836) 96 (up to 148268)	.012–.016	77–83	14–19	CW	LMKO 1Z30Z	20B†	10B	ZS/KZ 1/12A, TK 12 A 4 or K–12
VJ3BR9T	GT-850 (up to Sport 96 1965)	.012–.016	80–84	39–42	CW	LMKO 1Z30	20B†	10B	ZS/KZW 1/12 (1/6), E3LC–134 or TKW 12 (1/6)
VJ3BR10T VJ3BR11T	{GT–850 (up to Sport 96 1965)	.012–.016	77–83	14–19	CW	LMKO 1Z30	20B†	10B	KW12V
VJU3BR1T	95 (from 4837) 96 (from 148269)	.012–.016	77–83	14–19	CW	LMKO 1Z42Z	17B†⊙	7B	K–12
VJU3BR2T JFU3 (R) 0 231 144 002	{95 (from 10801) 96 (from 201401)	.012–.016	77–83 (VJU3) 80–84 (JFU3)	14–19	CW	LMKO 1Z42	17B†⊙	7B	K–12
JF3 (R) 0 231 120 023	Sport 96 (up to 1965) Sonett 2-stroke	.014–.018	75–82	14–19	CW	LMKO 1Z30	20B†	10B	KW12V
JFU3 0 231 144 004	GT–850 (from 1966)	.014–.018	75–82	18–22	CW	LMKO 1Z42	20B†⊙	10B	KW12V
JFUR4 0 231 146 044 JFUR4 0 231 146 024	{95 (1967-68) 96 (1967-68)	.016	50±2	14–19	CW	1 237 330 091	6B†⊙	6B	K–12
JFUR4 0 231 146 033 JFUR4 0 231 146 073	{95 (1967-68) 96 (1967-68) Sonett V4	.016	50±2	14–19	CW	1 237 330 091 1 237 330 113°°	6B†⊙ 10B†‡	6B	K–12
JFUR4 0 231 146 084	95 (1969-70) 96 (1969-70)	.016	50±2	14–19	CW	1 237 330 091	6B†⊙	6B	K–12

▲ With test light, engine not running.
† At 3,000 rpm.
‡ At 500 rpm.
⊙ With vacuum line disconnected and plugged.
° If equipped with dual carburetor and open exhaust −20° (22 mm. below upper mark) and TDC (upper mark).
°° Sonett V4
‡‡ At 1,000 rpm (Sonett V4).

Distributor Advance Specifications

Distributor Type or Designation	Centrifugal Advance (degrees @ dist. rpm)						Vacuum Advance		
	Range (deg.)	Begins (rpm)	5° (rpm)	10° (rpm)	15° (rpm)	Stops (rpm)	Range (deg.)	Begins (in. Hg.)	Stops (in. Hg.)
VJ3 BR7 T	18–22	400–800	700–1,000	900–1,250	1,150–1,500	1,500–2,000	—	—	—
VJ3 BR8 T	17–21	900–1,300	1,200–1,600	1,400–4,700	4,600–5,300	5,300–6,000	—	—	—
VJU3 BR1 T	17–21	900–1,300	1,200–1,600	1,400–4,700	4,600–5,300	5,300–6,000	8.5–11.5	4.73–5.51°	5.51–6.30
VJU3 BR2 T	17–21	900–1,300	1,200–1,600	1,400–4,700	4,600–5,300	5,300–6,000	8.5–11.5	4.73–5.51°	5.51–6.30
JFU3 0 231 144 002	20	900–1,300	1,100–1,500	3,800–4,300	4,400–4,900	5,000–5,500	10	4.73–5.51°	5.51–6.30
JFU3 0 231 144 003	15	900–1,300	1,100–1,500	3,800–4,300	4,200–4,700	4,500–5,000	15	2.36–3.15	4.73–5.51
JF3 (R) 0 231 120 023	10	800–1,200	1,100–1,500	—	—	1,400–1,800 (@ 10°)	—	—	—
JFU3 0 231 144 004	10	800–1,200	1,100–1,500	—	—	1,400–1,800 (@ 10°)	15	2.36–3.15	4.73–5.51
0 231 146 044	12–14	375–425	450–500	1,025–1,400	—	1,800	7.7–9.0	6.69–8.67	16.9–18.1
0 231 146 024	12–14	375–425	450–500	1,025–1,400	—	1,800	7.7–9.0	6.69–8.67	16.9–18.1
0 231 146 033	12.5–14.5	300–400	450–500	950–1,250	—	1,650	7.7–9.0	6.69–8.67	16.9–18.1
0 231 146 073	12.5–14.5	300–400	450–500	950–1,250	—	1,650	7.7–9.0	6.69–8.67	16.9–18.1
0 231 146 084	11.5–13.5	500–615	790–910	1,300–1,800	—	2,400	6.5–8.5	3.54–5.51	9.68

° Should return to zero before 3.94 in. Hg. (100 mm. Hg.) is reached.

12. Unhook the springs from the breaker cam. If necessary, bend the spring holders carefully.

13. Remove the damping springs 17 and lift off the governor weights 18 and 19. Remove the fiber washers 20 from beneath the weights.

14. Remove the fiber plate 21. Note the screws 28 under the distributor shaft plate. If these screws are loosened, the spring holder 25 can be turned to adjust the tension of the governor springs. This tension is correctly set at the factory and should not be altered.

15. Remove condenser 42 from the distributor housing.

16. Remove the rubber ring from the distributor housing.

17. If the bushings in the distributor housing are worn, press or drive them out.

ASSEMBLY

1. If new bushings are installed, press them into the housing and place the felt lubricating pad between them.

2. Attach the condenser to the distributor housing.

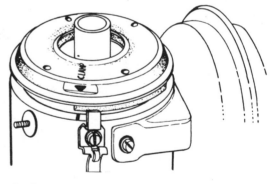

Condensation trap

3. Install a new rubber ring.

4. Place the fiber plate 21 on the distributor shaft steel plate; align it so that its oblong cut-out faces the round hole in the steel plate.

5. Place the fiber washers 20 on the stubs of the governor weights and smear a little grease on the stubs. Any grease applied to bearings or sliding surfaces must be applied in small quantities.

6. Put the governor weights 18 and 19 on the stubs. The weights must be positioned

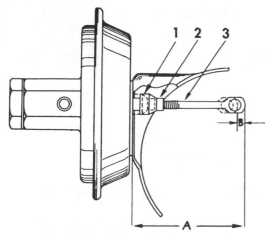

Checking length of vacuum chamber control arm. To adjust length, hold nut (1) and loosen locknut (2), then screw the arm in or out until correct length is obtained.

$$A=1.68 \pm 0.008'' \atop B=0.137 \pm 0.0059''\Big\} \text{ Up to 1965}$$

$$A=1.68 \pm 0.008'' \atop B\pm0.197 = 0.0059''\Big\} \text{ From 1966}$$

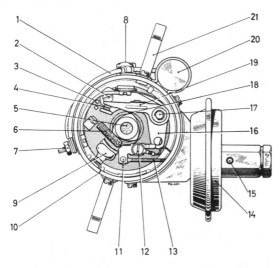

Breaker points and components—distributor JFU 3

1. Condenser cable
2. Locking screw
3. Adjusting lug for breaker points
4. Breaker points
5. Lubricating felt pads
6. Lubricating felt pads
7. Connection for low tension cable
8. Lubricator
9. Bearing
10. Ignition setting mark
11. Pivot (SAAB 95/96 1965 model)
12. Pivot screw (SAAB 95/96, 1965 model)
13. Control arm
14. Vacuum chamber
15. Vacuum-hose connection
16. Contact plate with stationary breaker point
17. Stub for breaker arm
18. Fiber lug
19. Breaker arm
20. Condenser
21. Retaining spring

with the slide projections facing downwards towards the fiber plate.

7. Secure the weights with the damping springs 17.

8. Hook the governor springs 24 onto the holders on the breaker cam 16 and bend the holders down to prevent the springs from loosening during assembly.

9. Grease the distributor shaft, then install the breaker cam onto it. The pins on the bottom of the breaker cam must fit into the grooves in the governor weights. Make sure the longer pin is fitted into the corresponding hole in the distributor shaft plate. Note that the pins of the breaker cam must be inserted properly in order to stretch the damping springs.

10. Hook the governor springs onto the spring holders on clamp 25.

11. Check that the ignition advance mechanism functions properly by turning the breaker cam clockwise.

12. Install spacer 29, followed by fiber washer 30, onto the distributor shaft.

13. Grease the shaft and slide it into the distributor housing.

14. Mount the shim 15, followed by the fiber washer 14, on the breaker cam.

15. Install the breaker plate 13 into the distributor housing and secure the retaining springs 37 with screws 39.

16. Install contact plate 11; loosely turn down the screw.

17. Install screw 33 for the primary wire connection, along with the contact and insulating washers, then connect the condenser.

18. Grease the bearing pin and install the breaker arm. Adjust axial play and height in relation to the breaker contact, using shims 10. Secure using the clip 9 and tighten the nut 31 on the screw 33.

19. Install the distributor pinion onto the shaft, after having adjusted the axial play of the latter using the shims 45. The permissible axial play is 0.004–0.008″. Note that the fiber washer 46 is placed above the shim, against the distributor housing. When driving in and riveting the slotted shaft pin, take care not to damage the shaft, pinion, or the shaft bearing. The height of the rivet bead must not exceed 0.02″.

20. Adjust the point gap to 0.014–0.018″. Tighten the screw for the contact plate. If

the gap is adjusted using a dwellmeter tester, the dwell angle should be 75–82°.

21. Install the condensation shield over the breaker mechanism so the arrow points toward the mark on the distributor housing.

22. Screw on the rotor.

DISASSEMBLY AND ASSEMBLY OF DISTRIBUTORS 0 231 144 002/JFU3 (VJU3BR2T), 0 231 144 003/JFU3, AND VJU3BR1T

Follow the same general procedure as outlined for 0 231 120 023/JF3 (R). Use the part identification and location number from the corresponding illustrations. See the chart for setting clearances and dwell.

Ignition Timing

The firing order is 1–2–3. No. 1 cylinder is the rear cylinder. Ignition setting is done with No. 2 cylinder at TDC.

The ignition timing should be checked and adjusted using a strobe timing light at an engine speed of 3,000 rpm. This is more reliable than setting static timing using a test lamp.

At the front end of the engine there are four marks: one mark on the pulley and three on the engine block. These marks are used as follows:

a. When the mark on the pulley coincides with the upper mark on the engine block, No. 2 piston should be at TDC. This upper mark is used to determine if the pulley mark is in the correct position, and when remarking the pulley after installing a new crankshaft or pulley.

b. When the mark on the pulley coincides with the middle mark on the engine block, it shows the basic ignition setting for No. 2 cylinder. It is used when adjusting the static ignition timing on a stationary engine using a test lamp and when installing the distributor.

c. When the mark on the pulley coincides with the lower mark on the engine block, it shows the ignition position for No. 2 cylinder at an engine speed of approximately 3,000 rpm. This mark is utilized for ignition setting using a strobe timing light. Note that the engine revolutions must be within the limits shown after the first step on the timing curve. If the engine is equipped with a vacuum advance distributor, always remove the hose to the vacuum chamber before setting ignition timing.

Degrees on the Crankshaft	Distance on Pulley from Upper Mark
1°	0.04″
7°	0.30″
10°	0.43″
15°	0.65″
17°	0.74″
20°	0.87″

NOTE: *Mark is TDC for No. 2 cyl. Pulley dia. = 4.961″.*

DYNAMIC TIMING USING STROBE LIGHT

1. Check the breaker points and arm and adjust to the correct gap. When installing the rotor, always use a new spring washer to prevent the screw from working loose. Inspect all wires, cap, spark plugs and connections and be certain everything is in good condition.

2. Turn the crankshaft in the normal direction of rotation until the mark on the pulley coincides with the middle mark on the engine block.

3. Turn the distributor so that the mark on the rotor is opposite the mark on the edge of the distributor housing and the vacuum chamber points rearwards on the SAAB 95 and 96 (1965) and that the distributor housing lubricator points forward and a little to the right on the SAAB Sport (1965). From 1966, the distributor must be turned so that the vacuum chamber points forward and a little to the right.

4. Connect the strobe light to the spark plug wire or cap tower of No. 2 cylinder and start the engine. Gradually increase the engine speed. A noticeable change in the ignition setting will be observed somewhere between 1,000 and 2,000 rpm; a further increase in engine speed should result in no change. Adjust the timing within this rpm range by loosening the locking bolt and turning the distributor housing; in the normal direction of rotation to retard, against to advance. When the mark on the pulley coincides with the lower mark on the engine block, secure the distributor by tightening the locking bolt.

STATIC TIMING USING TEST LIGHT

If a strobe light is not available, the ignition timing can be adjusted using a small 12-volt test light between the chassis ground and the primary wire on the distributor.

Bosch designation	0 231 144 002/JFU3 (VJU3 BR2T)	0 231 120 023/JF3 (R) (VJ3 BR11T)	0 231 144 003/JFU3	0 231 144 004/JFU3
Model	Saab 95/96, model 1965	Saab Sport model 1965	Saab 95/96 as from model 1966	Saab Monte Carlo 850 as from model 1966
Ignition timing	Centrifugal and vacuum regulation	Centrifugal regulation	Centrifugal and vacuum regulation	Centrifugal and vacuum regulation
Breaker gap	0,012–0,016 in. (0,3–0,4 mm)	0,014–0,018 in. (0,35–0,45 mm)	0,014–0,018 in. (0,35–0,45 mm)	0,014–0,018 in. (0,35–0,45 mm)
Dwell angle	80–84°	75–82°	75–82°	75–82°
Basic setting of ignition with the aid of a test lamp with engine standing still, and when fitting a distributor Ignition position in degrees on pulley B.T.D.C.	7°	10°	10°	10°
Stroboscope setting of ignition at approx. 3000 r/m Ignition position in degrees on pulley B.T.D.C.	17° Set the ignition, with the vacuum hose disconnected	20°	15° Set the ignition, with the vacuum hose disconnected	20° Set the ignition, with the vacuum hose disconnected
Checking the mark on pulley. The piston in cyl. 2 shall be at T.D.C. The mark on the pulley shall now coincide with the upper mark on the engine block.				

Ignition timing settings

1. Remove the distributor cap, rotor, and condensation trap. Examine the points and adjust the gap.

2. Reinstall the condensation trap and rotor.

3. Turn the crankshaft until the mark on the pulley coincides with the middle mark on the engine block.

4. Turn the distributor as in Step 3 of the preceding section.

5. Connect a test light between the chassis and the terminal for the primary wire on the distributor; switch on the ignition.

6. Turn the distributor housing a little to find the position in which the test light comes on. Check that the weights of the centrifugal governor are in the inner position by turning the rotor counterclockwise. Now, secure the distributor with the locking bolt.

7. Check that the ignition timing is correct by turning the crankshaft one complete turn clockwise. When the mark on the pulley again coincides with the middle mark on the engine block, the test light should come on. While in this position, check that the marks on the rotor and distributor hous-

Distributor Bosch designation	VJ3 BR7T	VJ3 BR8T	1. VJU3 BR1T 2. VJU3 BR2T
Model	Saab GT 750	Saab 95 up to chassis No. 4836 Saab 96 up to chassis No. 148268	1. Saab 95 from chassis No. 4837 2. Saab 95 from chassis No. 10801 1. Saab 96 from chassis No. 148269 2. Saab 96 from chassis No. 201401
Ignition advance	centrifugal reg.	centrifugal reg	centrifugal and vacuum reg.
Breaker gap	0.3—0.4 mm	0.3—0.4 mm	0.3—0.4 mm
Dwell angle	80°—84°	77°—83°	77°—83°
Basic setting of ignition with aid of test lamp stationary engine — Ignition position in degrees on crankshaft B.T.D.C.	S 203 2° (see note*)	S 204 10°	S 205 7°
Stroboscope setting at 3.000 r.p.m. approx — Ignition position in degrees on crankshaft B.T.D.C.	S 206 22° (see note**)	S 206 20°	S 207 17° NB with disconnected vacuum hose
Check that the mark on the pulley tallies — The 2nd cylinder shall be at T.D.C.	S 208	S 208	S 209

The following applies for GT 750 if equipped with double carburetors and special exhaust system:
* Basic setting = 0° (uper setting mark)
**Stroboscope setting = 20° (22 mm below the upper setting mark)

Ignition timing settings

ing coincide and that the centrifugal weights are in the inner position.

8. Switch off the ignition and remove the test light. Clean and inspect all wires, spark plugs and the distributor cap.

Spark Plugs

Spark plugs should be chosen according to the type of driving done. While "cold" plugs may be good for racing and high-speed, cross-country driving, they will quickly foul in a short-trip, city-driving situation. On the other hand, "hot" plugs definitely are not suited to high-speed driving condition—plug life will be short and, with a two-stroke engine, generated heat must be dissipated rapidly or ignition by incandescence will result. In short, it is best

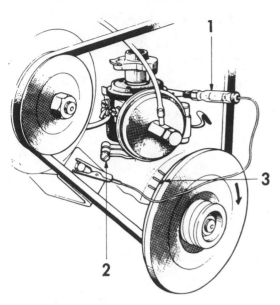

Setting ignition timing using the test light method

1. Test light
2. Lock screw
3. Timing marks

to use only approved spark plug types in the SAAB.

In the SAAB 95 and 96, conventional type spark plugs are used; in the SAAB Sport (for hard driving), Bosch MGV 260 T31S surface gap plugs are used. These plugs have no side electrode and the spark gap is the space between the center electrode and the lower part of the plug. This plug remains relatively cold and is therefore especially suitable for hard driving.

MGV 260 T31S plugs have a big pre-sparking (booster) gap inside the insulator to give a better spark effect. This reduces the risk of missing and fouled plugs. The booster gap requires a special ignition system having high ignition voltage (i.e., a special ignition coil having series resistance).

Bosch MGV 260 T31S plugs should *not* be sand blasted; clean only with a wire brush. As the gap is not adjustable, the plug must be replaced when the gap reaches 0.05″. The tightening torque is 14 ft. lbs. Other plugs should be gapped to 0.022–0.024″.

MAINTENANCE

The spark gap should be checked and adjusted to 0.030″ every 3,000 miles (except UK-16 surface gap type). Plugs with large gaps require an abnormally high ignition voltage, which involves the risk of cross-firing in the distributor cap, ignition coil and plug wires. Spark plugs in two-stroke engines normally last about 6,000 miles.

Table of Approved Spark Plugs

Type of Car	Spark Plug Make and Type	Type of Driving
SAAB 95 and 96	AC M83	Easy
	AC M82	Hard
	AC 82-S-COM	Normal
	Bosch M 175T1	Easy
	Bosch M 225T1	Normal
	Bosch M 240T1	Hard
	Champion UK-10	Easy
	Champion K-9	Normal, hard
	NGK A7	Easy, normal
SAAB Sport, Sonett, and Monte Carlo	Bosch MGV 260 T31 S	Normal, hard, easy
GT-750	Bosch M 240T1	Easy
	Bosch M 270T16	Hard

Spark Plug Wires

The spark plug wires are equipped with resistors to suppress the interference produced by the electrical discharge at the spark plugs, which could be picked up on television and radio sets. These resistors consist of a core of graphite-impregnated plastic wire covered with an insulating sheath.

Because of the high ignition voltage, the wires of the SAAB Sport should not be placed closer to any grounded parts than about 0.4″. It is extremely important that the wires be properly connected to the plugs, distributor cap and ignition coil, to avoid bad contact and resultant radio static.

Check the resistance in cables and connections if fouled spark plugs are a common occurrence. The total resistance between the ignition coil, the distributor and spark plugs should be a maximum 35,000–40,000 ohms; a minimum of 8,000 ohms.

Suppression of Interference

The SAAB 95 and 96, SAAB Sport and Monte Carlo models are equipped with suppressed ignition cables to prevent radio and television interference. When a radio is installed in the car, no separate resistors may be installed on the distributor and spark plugs, nor may suppressed spark plugs be used with suppression wiring. The total permissible resistance then would be exceeded, resulting in a reduction of the strength of the spark.

The following table shows some further methods that can be used to suppress static; make sure the front panel and grill is grounded with a multi-braid cable.

Part II—Four-Stroke (V4) Models

The V4 electrical system differs only slightly from that used on the two-stroke models. The main differences are the starter and the distributor.

The starter, up to and including the 1968 model, has a rated output of 0.8 horsepower, while the latest models are rated at 1.0 horsepower.

Distributor

The distributor, Bosch JFUR 4, is installed at the rear of the engine; it rotates in a clockwise direction. It is equipped with both centrifugal and vacuum advance; centrifugal advance regulating ignition timing with relation to engine speed and vacuum advance regulating ignition timing with relation to load.

Suppression Measures

Degree of Necessity	Location	Description
2	Generator	Condenser 0.5 mfd. between D+ and ground D−.
2	AC alternator	Condenser between B+ and ground. In the pole housing of the alternator, there is a screw hole (146) for mounting the condenser.
2	Charging regulator DC generator	Condenser between B+ and ground.
1	Charging regulator DC generator	The regulator is suppressed by factory.
2	Ignition coil	Condenser between 15 or + and ground. Grounding of the ignition coil cover.
3	Spark plug	Shielded cable terminal with built-in wound resistance 1,000 ohms.
3	Engine compartment	Multi-braided ground lead between hood and battery grounding point.
3	Wheels	In certain cases, a connection may be needed between the wheels and ground. This is provided by a coil spring between the grease cover and spindle.
1	Spark plug wires	Suppressed wires between ignition coil, distributor, spark plugs are standard squipment. Total resistance max. 35,000–40,000 ohms, min. 8,000 ohms.

Degrees of Necessity:
    1—Basic suppression (fitted as standard at the factory).
    2—If interference occurs, suppress according to 2.
    3—If interference persists, proceed according to 3.

Distributors Used

Bosch Designation	Chassis No. up to and Including	Remarks
0 231 146 044	95/ 46.137	Semi enclosed crankcase ventilation
0 231 146 024	96/ 434.173	
0 231 146 033	95/ 46.138 96/ 434.174	Fully enclosed crankcase ventilation
0 231 146 072	95/ 47.504 96/ 444.942	Fully enclosed crankcase ventilation
0 231 146 073	95/ 49.093 96/ 453.130	Fully enclosed crankcase ventilation
0 231 146 084	95/ 65.001 96/ 520.001	Fully enclosed crankcase ventilation

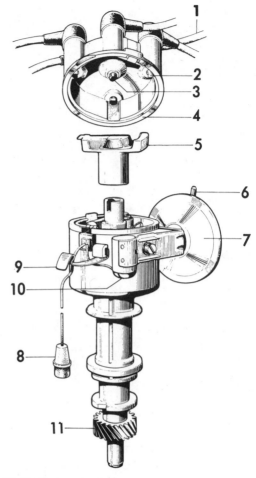

V4 distributor—typical

1. Spark plug wire
2. Contact
3. Center carbon button
4. Distributor cap
5. Rotor
6. Vacuum hose connection
7. Vacuum chamber
8. Ignition primary wire
9. Retaining spring
10. Condenser
11. Drive gear

REMOVAL

1. Remove wires from spark plugs.
2. Release retaining springs and remove cap.
3. Remove primary wire.
4. Remove the vacuum hose.
5. Crank engine until the mark on the rotor and the mark on the distributor housing are directly opposite each other. This is the firing position for No. 1 cylinder (6° BTDC).
6. Unscrew the retaining clamp screw and remove the clamp.
7. Remove the distributor from engine.

INSTALLATION

1. Turn the distributor until the rotor is directly opposite the assembly mark.
2. Insert the distributor into the engine.
3. See that the gears mesh properly. Rock the engine back and forth until the distributor shaft engages the oil pump driveshaft properly.
4. Check that the mark on the pulley coincides with the 6° mark on the transmission cover (firing position for No. 1 cylinder).
5. Turn the distributor housing so that the mark on the rotor is directly opposite the mark on the edge of the distributor housing.
6. Adjust the ignition timing.
7. Tighten retaining clamp slightly with the screw so that the distributor still can be turned.

8. Connect the primary wire.
9. Connect dwellmeter and adjust dwell angle at starter rpm with switch "on."
10. Install cap (correct position is indicated by rear retaining spring). Secure it with retaining springs and connect spark plug wires.
11. Connect a strobe light and adjust ignition timing at starter rpm, or start engine and let it run at 500 rpm. At higher engine speeds, the centrifugal governor begins to operate and invalidates the reading.
12. Tighten the distributor clamp.
13. Adjust the idle speed rpm.

V4 distributor internal parts

1. Vacuum chamber
2. Adjustment mark
3. Adjustment rod
4. Ground lead
5. Lubricating felt
6. Assembly mark
7. Retaining spring
8. Bearing
9. Condenser
10. Primary cable
11. Fiber peg
12. Adjuster-fixed
     point
13. Breaker points
14. Locking Screw
15. Fixed breaker
     point
16. Movable breaker
     point

Breaker Points

REMOVAL

1. Release retaining springs and remove cap.

2. Remove rotor.

3. Disconnect breaker arm lead.

4. Remove clip and washers from breaker pivot (applies to distributors 0 231 146 044 and 0 231 146 024).

5. Press leaf spring out of hole in contact support and remove breaker arm. Collect any shims (applies to distributors 0 231 146 044 and 0 231 146 024).

6. Remove retaining screw that secures the fixed breaker point.

7. Remove breaker point (breaker unit on distributor 0 231 146 033).

INSTALLATION

1. Insert the fixed breaker point or breaker unit and insert retaining screw without tightening it fully.

2. Lubricate pivot and bearing bushing on breaker arm using Bosch Ft1v 22 grease or equivalent. Do not get any oil or grease on contact surfaces, because oxidation will result.

3. Place breaker arm leaf spring in hole in contact support (applies to distributors 0 231 146 044 and 0 231 146 024). The contact surfaces of the points must be parallel to each other. Correct any misalignment with shims or by bending the fixed breaker point.

4. Install shims and clip onto the pivot (applies to distributors 0 231 146 044 and 0 231 146 024).

5. Smear the breaker arm and fiber rubbing block with Bosch Ft1v 22 grease or equivalent.

6. Connect the breaker arm lead.

7. Adjust point gap and dwell angle.

a. *Point Gap:* Crank engine until breaker arm is the greatest distance away from the fixed breaker point. Insert a screwdriver between the two adjusting lugs and slot; turn screwdriver to adjust gap. Tighten retaining screw and recheck gap.

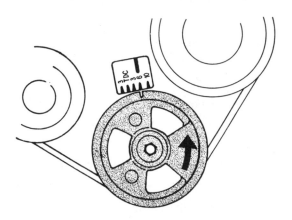

Ignition timing marks—V4 engine

b. *Dwell Angle:* Connect a dwellmeter between the primary coil wire and ground, then turn on ignition and crank engine with starter. Compare indicated value with specified value. Correct, if necessary, by adjusting the fixed breaker point. Tighten retaining screw and recheck gap.

8. Soak the lubricating felt in the distributor shaft with oil and install the rotor.

9. Install the distributor cap and secure with the two retaining springs.

10. Connect a strobe timing light and check the ignition timing at starter speed or with the engine running at 500 rpm, vacuum hose removed.

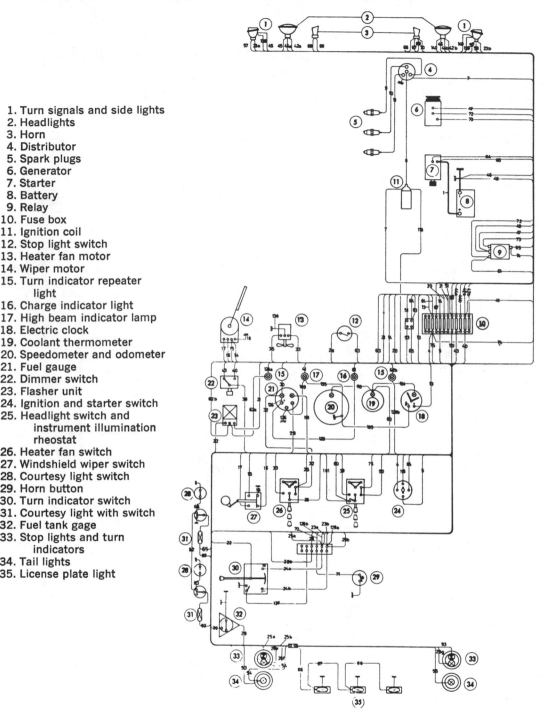

1. Turn signals and side lights
2. Headlights
3. Horn
4. Distributor
5. Spark plugs
6. Generator
7. Starter
8. Battery
9. Relay
10. Fuse box
11. Ignition coil
12. Stop light switch
13. Heater fan motor
14. Wiper motor
15. Turn indicator repeater light
16. Charge indicator light
17. High beam indicator lamp
18. Electric clock
19. Coolant thermometer
20. Speedometer and odometer
21. Fuel gauge
22. Dimmer switch
23. Flasher unit
24. Ignition and starter switch
25. Headlight switch and instrument illumination rheostat
26. Heater fan switch
27. Windshield wiper switch
28. Courtesy light switch
29. Horn button
30. Turn indicator switch
31. Courtesy light with switch
32. Fuel tank gage
33. Stop lights and turn indicators
34. Tail lights
35. License plate light

Wiring diagram—SAAB 95 (station wagon) 1965

Black: 1, 7, 18, 19, 45, 46, 47, 49, 71, 105, 109, 135, 136, 139, 140.

Red: 5, 8, 9, 10, 11, 21, 28, 28e, 28f, 28g, 32, 39, 61, 63, 65, 67, 68 72, 92, 126, 129.

Green: 16, 22, 50, 51, 53, 54, 55, 57, 58, 60, 86, 87, 88, 101, 104, 110.

Gray: 4, 25b, 29, 35, 44a, 62a, 62b, 64, 69, 70, 74, 75, 85, 93.

White: 20, 23b, 24b, 40, 42b, 66, 82, 83, 118, 128a.

Yellow: 17, 23a, 24a, 33, 43, 44b, 73, 84, 128b.

Brown: 14, 15, 30, 137.

Blue: 13, 25a, 41, 42a.

1. Turn signal indicators and side lights
2. Headlights
3. Horn
4. Distributor
5. Spark plugs
6. Generator
7. Starter
8. Battery
9. Voltage regulator
10. Fuse box
11. Ignition coil
12. Series resistance
13. Stop light switch
14. Heater fan motor
15. Wiper motor
16. Direction indicator repeater light
17. Charge indicator light
18. High beam indicator light
19. Electric clock
20. Coolant thermometer
21. Speedometer and odometer
22. Fuel gauge
23. Dimmer switch
24. Flasher
25. Ignition and starter switch
26. Headlight switch and instrument
26. Headlight switch and instrument illumination rheostat
27. Warning flasher switch with control lamp
28. Heater fan switch
29. Windshield wiper switch
30. Courtesy light switch
31. Horn button
32. Direction indicator switch
33. Courtesy light with switch
34 Fuel tank gauge
35. Stop light and turn indicators
36. Tail lights
37. License plate light

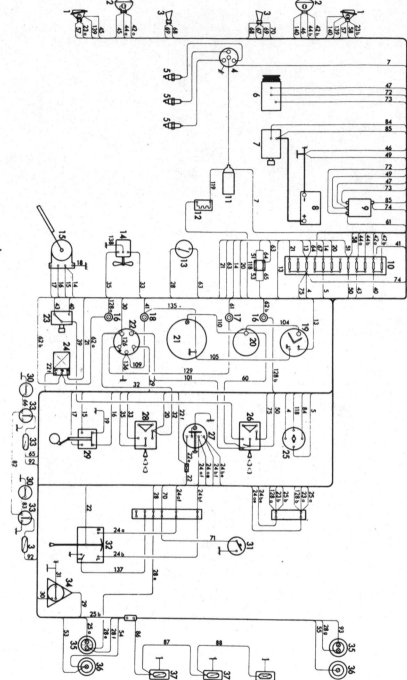

Wiring diagram—SAAB 95 (station wagon) 1966 USA version

Black: 7, 18, 19, 45, 46, 47, 49, 71, 105, 109, 135, 136, 138, 139, 140.

Red: 5, 21, 28, 28e, 28f, 28g, 32, 39, 61, 63, 65, 67, 68, 72, 92, 126, 129.

Green: 16, 22, 22e, 22f, 50, 51, 53, 54, 55, 57, 58, 60, 86, 87, 88, 101, 104, 110, 119.

Grey: 4, 25b, 29, 35, 44a, 62a, 62b, 64, 69, 70, 74, 75, 85, 93.

White: 20, 23b, 24b, 24be, 24bf, 40, 42b, 66, 82, 83, 118, 128a.

Yellow: 17, 23a, 24a, 24ae, 24af, 33, 43, 44b, 73, 84, 128b.

Brown: 14, 15, 30, 137.

Blue: 13, 25a, 41, 42a.

1. Turn signal indicators and side lights
2. Headlights
3. Horn
4. Distributor
5. Spark plugs
6. Voltage regulator
7. Alternator
8. Starter
9. Battery
10. Fuse box
11. Ignition coil
12. Stop light switch
13. Heater fan motor
14. Wiper motor
15. Direction indicator repeater light
16. Charge indicator light
17. High beam indicator light
18. Electric clock
19. Temperature gauge
20. Speedometer with odometer
21. Fuel gauge
22. Dimmer switch
23. Flasher
24. Ignition and starter switch
25. Headlight switch and instrument illumination rheostat
26. Warning flasher switch with control lamp
27. Heater fan switch
28. Windshield wiper switch
29. Courtesy light switch
30. Courtesy light with switch
31. Horn button
32. Direction indicator switch
33. Fuel tank gauge
34. Stop lights and direction indicators
35. Tail lights
36. License plate light

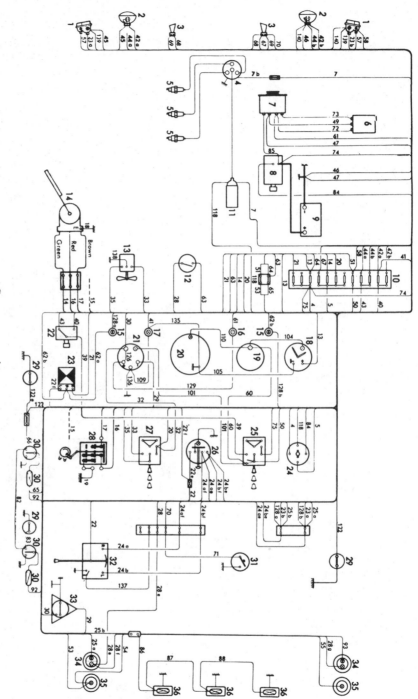

Wiring diagram—SAAB 95 (station wagon) 1967 USA version

Black: 7, 7b, 18, 19, 45, 46, 47, 49, 71, 105, 109, 135, 136, 138, 139, 140.

Red: 5, 21, 28, 28e, 28f, 28g, 32, 39, 61, 63, 65, 67, 68, 72, 92, 126, 129.

Green: 16, 22, 22e, 22f, 50, 51, 53, 54, 55, 57, 58, 60, 86, 87, 88, 101, 104, 110.

Grey: 4, 25b, 29, 35, 44a, 62a, 62b, 64, 69, 70, 74, 75, 85, 93.

White: 20, 23b, 24b, 24be, 24bf, 40, 42b, 66, 82, 83, 118, 122, 122e, 128a.

Yellow: 17, 23a, 24a, 24ae, 24af, 33, 43, 44b, 73, 84, 128b.

Brown: 14, 15, 30, 137.

Blue: 13, 25a, 41, 42a.

1. Turn signal indicators and side lights
2. Headlights
3. Horn
4. Distributor
5. Spark plugs
6. Generator
7. Starter
8. Battery
9. Relay
10. Fuse box
11. Ignition coil
12. Stop light switch
13. Heater fan motor
14. Wiper motor
15. Direction indicator repeater light
16. Charge indicator light
17. High beam indicator light
18. Electric clock
19. Coolant thermometer
20. Speedometer and odometer
21. Fuel gauge
22. Dimmer switch
23. Flasher
24. Ignition and starter switch
25. Headlight switch and instrument illumination rheostat
26. Heater fan switch
27. Windshield wiper switch
28. Courtesy light switch
29. Horn button
30. Direction indicator switch
31. Courtesy light with switch
32. Fuel tank gauge
33. Stop lights, turn indicators and tail lights
34. License plate light
35. Trunk light

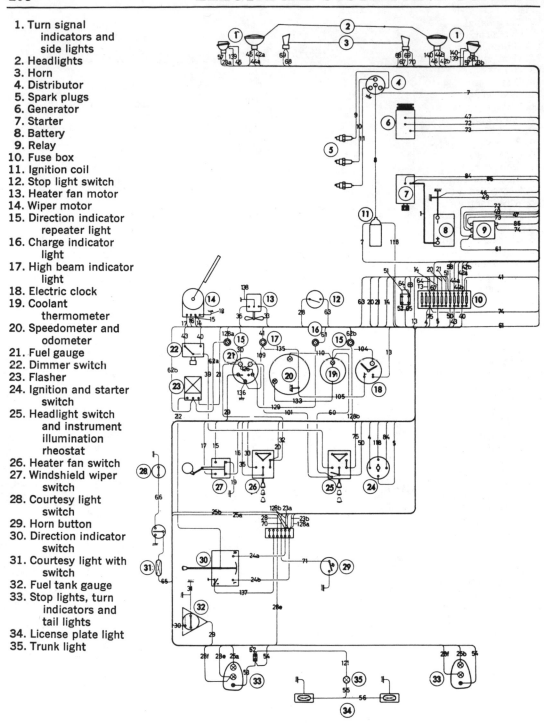

Wiring diagram—SAAB 96 1965

Black: 1, 7, 18, 19, 45, 46, 47, 49, 71, 105, 109, 135, 136, 139, 140.

Red: 5, 8, 9, 10, 11, 21, 28, 28e, 28f, 32, 39, 61, 63, 65, 67, 68, 72, 126, 129.

Green: 16, 22, 50, 51, 52, 53, 54, 55, 56, 57, 58, 60, 69, 70, 85, 101, 104, 110, 121, 133.

Grey: 4, 25b, 29, 35, 44a, 62a, 62b, 64, 74, 75.

White: 20, 23b, 24b, 40, 42b, 66, 118, 128a.

Yellow: 17 23a, 24a, 33, 43, 44b, 73, 84, 128b.

Brown: 14, 15, 30, 137.

Blue: 13, 25a, 41, 42a.

1. Turn signal indicators and side lights
2. Headlights
3. Horn
4. Distributor
5. Spark plugs
6. Generator
7. Starter
8. Battery
9. Voltage regulator
10. Fuse box
11. Ignition coil
12. Series resistance
13. Stop light switch
14. Heater fan motor
15. Wiper motor
16. Direction indicator repeater light
17. Charge indicator light
18. High beam indicator light
19. Electric clock
20. Coolant thermometer
21. Speedometer and odometer
22. Fuel gauge
23. Dimmer switch
24. Flasher
25. Ignition and starter switch
26. Headlight switch and instrument illumination rheostat
27. Warning flasher switch with control lamp
28. Heater fan switch
29. Windshield wiper switch
30. Courtesy light switch
31. Horn button
32. Direction indicator switch
33. Courtesy light with switch
34. Fuel tank gauge
35. Stop lights, turn indicators and tail lights
36. License plate light
37. Trunk light

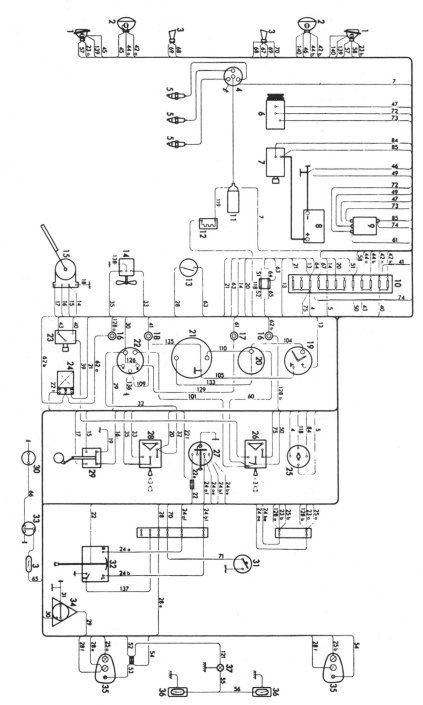

Wiring diagram—SAAB 96 1966 USA version

Black: 7, 18, 19, 45, 46, 47, 49, 71, 105, 109, 135, 136, 138, 139, 140.

Red: 5, 21, 28, 28e, 28f, 32, 39, 61, 63, 65, 67, 68, 72, 126, 129.

Green: 16, 22, 22e, 22f, 50, 51, 52, 53, 54, 55, 56, 57, 58, 60, 101, 104, 110, 121, 133.

Grey: 4, 25b, 29, 35, 44a, 62a, 62b, 64, 69, 70, 74, 75, 85.

White: 20, 23b, 24b, 24be, 24bf, 40, 42b, 66, 118, 128a.

Yellow: 17, 23a, 24a, 24ae, 24af, 33, 43, 44b, 73, 84, 128b.

Brown: 14, 15, 30, 137.

Blue: 13, 25a, 41, 42a.

1. Turn signal indicators and side lights
2. Headlights
3. Horn
4. Distributor
5. Spark plugs
6. Voltage regulator
7. Alternator
8. Starter
9. Battery
10. Fuse box
11. Ignition coil
12. Back-up light switch
13. Stop light switch
14. Heater fan motor
15. Wiper motor
16. Direction indicator repeater light
17. Charge indicator light
18. High beam indicator light
19. Electric clock
20. Temperature gauge
21. Speedometer with odometer
22. Fuel gauge
23. Dimmer switch
24. Flasher
25. Ignition and starter switch
26. Headlight switch and instrument illumination rheostat
27. Warning flasher switch with control lamp
28. Heater fan switch
29. Windshield wiper switch
30. Courtesy light switch
31. Courtesy light with switch
32. Horn button
33. Direction indicator switch
34. Fuel tank gauge
35. Back-up lights
36. Stop lights, direction indicators and tail lights
37. License plate light
38. Trunk light

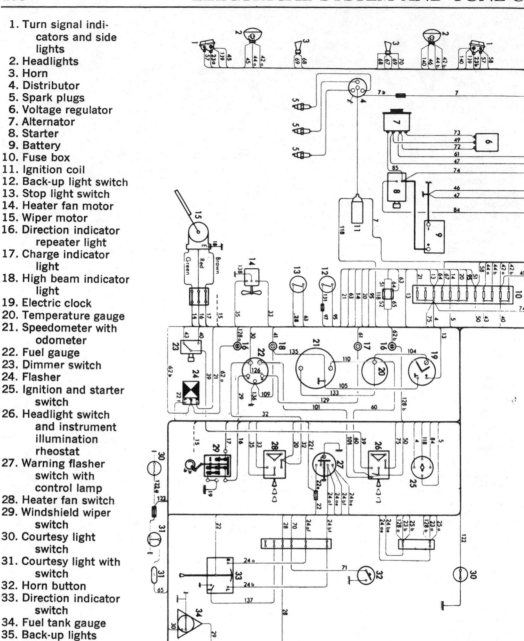

Wiring diagram—SAAB 96 1967 USA version

Black: 7, 7b, 18, 19, 45, 46, 47, 49, 71, 105, 109, 135, 136, 138, 139, 140.

Red: 5, 21, 28, 28e, 28f, 32, 39, 61, 63, 65, 67, 68, 72, 126, 129.

Green: 16, 22, 22e, 22f, 50, 51, 52, 53, 54, 55, 56, 57, 58, 60, 101, 104, 110, 121, 133.

Grey: 4, 25b, 29, 35, 44a, 62a, 64, 69, 70, 74, 75, 85.

White: 20, 23b, 24b, 24be, 24bf, 40, 42b, 66, 95, 97, 98, 118, 122, 122e, 128a, 131.

Yellow: 17, 23a, 24a, 24ae, 24af, 33, 43, 44b, 73, 84, 128b.

Brown: 14, 15, 30, 137.

Blue: 13, 25a, 41, 42a.

1. Turn signal indicators and side lights
2. Headlights
3. Horn
4. Foglight and spotlight
5. Distributor
6. Spark plugs
7. Voltage regulator
8. Generator
9. Starter
10. Battery
11. Fuse box
12. Ignition coil
13. Series resistance
14. Oil warning relay
15. Oil gauge
16. Back-up light switch
17. Stop lamp switch
18. Heater fan motor
19. Temperature meter
20. Windshield-washer pump
21. Wiper motor
22. Direction indicator repeater light
23. Charge indicator light
24. Indicator light, oil pressure
25. High beam indicator light
26. Indicator light, fuel
27. Ignition and starter switch
28. Electric clock
29. Speedometer, odometer and tripmeter
30. Coolant thermometer
31. Fuel gauge
32. Tachometer
33. Flasher
34. Maneuvre relay, light
35. Dimmer relay
36. Dimmer switch
37. Cigarette lighter
38. Spotlight switch
39. Foglight switch
40. Headlight switch and instrument illumination rheostat
41. Heater fan switch
42. Windshield wiper and washer switch
43. Courtesy light switch
44. Courtesy light with switch
45. Horn button
46. Direction indicator switch
47. Fuel tank gauge
48. Back-up lights
49. Stop lights, direction indicators and tail lights
50. License plate light
51. Trunk light

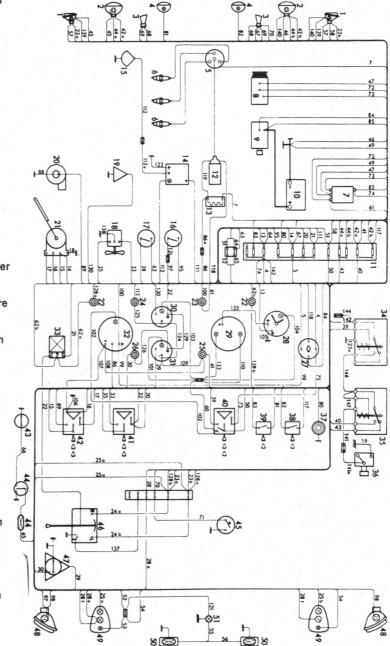

Wiring diagram—SAAB Monte Carlo 850 1965 USA version

Black: 7, 18, 19, 45, 46, 47, 49, 71, 80, 88, 105, 106, 107, 108, 109, 123, 123e, 124, 125, 135, 138, 139, 140.

Red: 5, 21, 28, 28e, 28f, 32, 39, 61, 63, 65, 67, 68, 72, 83, 86, 86e, 111, 126, 129.

Green: 16, 22, 50, 51, 52, 53, 54, 55, 56, 57, 58, 60, 82, 101, 102, 103, 104, 110, 119, 121, 133, 146, 147.

Grey: 4, 25b, 29, 35, 44a, 62a, 62b, 64, 69, 70, 74, 75, 85, 89, 113, 117, 142, 144.

White: 20, 23b, 24b, 40, 42b, 66, 95, 97, 98, 118, 128a, 131.

Yellow: 17, 23a, 24a, 33, 43, 44b, 73, 81, 84, 99, 100, 112, 112e, 128b, 130.

Brown: 14, 15, 30, 137, 141, 141e.

Blue: 3, 25a, 41, 42a.

1. Turn signal indicators and side lights
2. Headlights
3. Horn
4. Foglight and spotlight
5. Distributor
6. Spark plugs
7. Voltage regulator
8. Generator
9. Starter
10. Battery
11. Fuse box
12. Ignition coil
13. Series resistance
14. Oil warning relay
15. Oil gauge
16. Back-up light switch
17. Stop lamp switch
18. Heater fan motor
19. Temperature meter
20. Windshield-washer pump
21. Wiper motor
22. Direction indicator repeater light
23. Charge indicator light
24. Indicator light, oil pressure
25. High beam indicator light
26. Indicator light, fuel
27. Ignition and starter switch
28. Electric clock
29. Speedometer, odometer and trip meter
30. Coolant thermometer
31. Fuel gauge
32. Tachometer
33. Flasher
34. Maneuvre relay, light
35. Dimmer relay
36. Dimmer switch
37. Cigarette lighter
38. Spotlight switch
39. Foglight switch
40. Headlight switch and instrument illumination rheostat
41. Warning flasher switch
42. Heater fan switch
43. Windshield wiper and washer switch
44. Courtesy light switch
45. Courtesy light with switch
46. Horn button
47. Direction indicator switch
48. Fuel tank gauge
49. Back-up lights
50. Stop lights, direction indicators and tail lights
51. License plate light
52. Trunk light

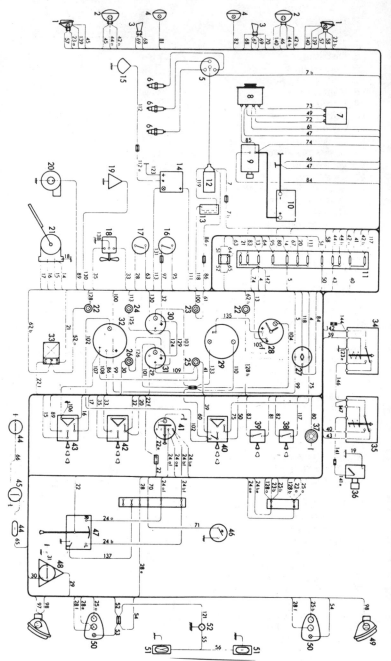

Wiring diagram—SAAB Monte Carlo 850 1966 USA version

Black: 7, 7b 18, 19, 31, 45, 46, 47, 49, 71, 80, 88, 105, 106, 107, 108, 109, 123, 123e, 124, 125, 135, 138, 139, 140.

Red: 5, 21, 28, 28e, 28f, 32, 39, 61, 63, 65, 67, 68, 72, 83, 86, 86e, 111, 126, 129.

Green: 16, 22, 22e, 22f, 50, 51, 52, 53, 54, 55, 56, 57, 58, 60, 82, 101, 102, 103, 104, 110, 119, 121, 133, 146, 147.

Grey: 4, 25b, 29, 35, 44a, 62a, 62b, 64, 69, 70, 74, 75, 85, 89, 113, 117, 142 144.

White: 20, 23b, 24b, 24be, 24bf, 40, 42b, 66, 95, 97, 98, 118, 128a, 131.

Yellow: 17, 23a, 24a, 24ae, 24af, 33, 43, 44b, 73, 81, 84, 99, 100, 112, 112e, 128b, 130.

Brown: 14, 15, 30, 137, 141, 141e.

Blue: 3, 25a, 41, 42a.

1. Parking and turn signal indicator lights
2. Headlights
3. Horns
4. Ignition coil
5. Spark plugs
6. Distributor
7. Voltage regulator
8. Alternator
9. Starter motor
10. Battery
11. Fuse box
12. Temperature gauge sending unit
13. Oil pressure switch
14. Stop light switch
15. Heater motor
16. Windshield wiper motor
17. Turn signal indicator warning lights
18. Charge indicator light
19. High beam indicator light
20. Oil pressure warning light
21. Electric clock
22. Temperature gauge
23. Speedometer with odometer
24. Fuel gauge
25. Foot dimmer switch
26. Flasher
27. Cigarette lighter
28. Ignition and starter switch
29. Headlight and parking light switch with instrument illumination rheostat
30. Warning flasher switch with control light
31. Heater switch
32. Windshield wiper switch
33. Automatic door switch for dome light
34. Dome light with switch
35. Horn ring
36. Direction indicator switch
37. Fuel tank sending unit
38. Stop light and direction indicator light
39. Tail lights
40. License lights

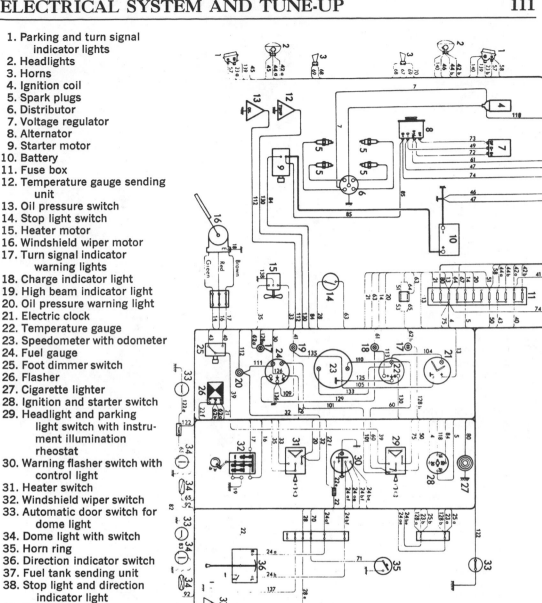

Wiring diagram—SAAB 95 (station wagon) 1967 USA version

Black: 7, 18, 19, 45, 46, 47, 49, 71, 80, 105, 109, 125, 135, 136, 138, 139, 140.

Red: 5, 21, 28, 28e, 28f, 28g, 32, 39, 61, 63, 65, 67, 68, 72, 92, 111, 113, 126, 129.

Green: 16, 22, 22e, 22f, 50, 51, 53, 54, 55, 57, 58, 60, 86, 87, 88, 101, 104, 110, 133.

Grey: 4, 25b, 29, 35, 44a, 62a, 62b, 64, 69, 70, 74, 75, 85, 93.

White: 20, 23b, 24b, 24be, 24bf, 40, 42b, 66, 82, 83, 118, 122, 122e, 128a.

Yellow: 17, 23a, 24a, 24ae, 24af, 33, 43, 44b, 73, 84, 128b.

Brown: 14, 30, 130, 137.

Blue: 13, 25a, 41, 42a, 112.

1. Turn signals and side lights
2. Headlights
3. Horn
4. Ignition coil
5. Spark plugs
6. Distributor
7. Voltage regulator
8. Alternator
9. Starter
10. Battery
11. Fuse box
12. Temperature gauge sending unit
13. Oil pressure switch
14. Back-up light switch
15. Stop light switch
16. Brake warning contact
17. Heater fan motor
18. Windshield washer pump
19. Wiper motor
20. Charge indicator light
21. Direction indicator repeater light
22. Brake warning light
23. High beam indicator light
24. Oil pressure warning light
25. Temperature gauge
26. Speedometer with odometer
27. Fuel gauge
28. Dimmer switch
29. Flasher
30. Ignition and starter switch
31. Headlight switch
32. Instrument illumination rheostat
33. Heater fan switch
34. Warning flasher switch
35. Courtesy light switch
36. Courtesy light with switch
37. Switch for windshield wiper, washer and signal horn
38. Direction indicator switch with headlight flasher
39. Fuel tank gauge
40. Stop lights and direction indicators
41. Tail lights
42. Back-up lights
43. License plate light

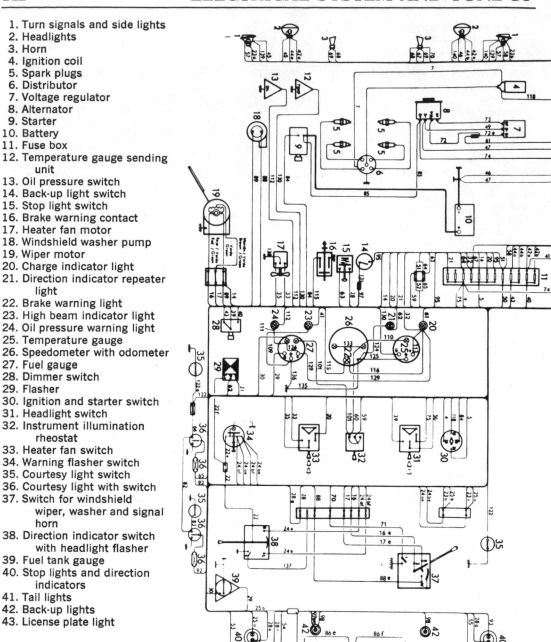

Wiring diagram—SAAB 95 (station wagon) 1968 USA version

Black: 7, 45, 46, 47, 49, 69, 70, 88, 88e, 109, 124, 125, 135, 136, 138, 139, 140.

Red: 5, 21, 28, 28e, 28f, 28g, 32, 39, 61, 63, 65, 67, 68, 72, 72e, 92, 111, 113, 116, 126, 129.

Green: 22, 22e, 22f, 50, 51, 53, 54, 55, 57, 58, 59, 60, 86, 86e, 86f, 101, 110.

Grey: 4, 16, 16e, 25b, 29, 35, 44a, 62, 64, 74, 75, 85, 93.

White: 20, 23b, 24b, 24be, 24bf, 40, 40c, 42b, 66, 82, 83, 95, 97, 97ae, 98, 118, 112, 122e, 131.

Yellow: 23a, 24a, 24ae, 24af, 33, 43, 44b, 73, 84, 115.

Brown: 14, 15, 30, 89, 130, 137.

Blue: 17, 17e, 25a, 41, 42a, 112.

1. Parking light and turn signals
2. Headlights
3. Horn
4. Ignition coil
5. Spark plugs
6. Distributor
7. Voltage regulator
8. Alternator
9. Starter
10. Battery
11. Fuse box
12. Temperature transmitter
13. Oil pressure switch
14. Back-up light switch
15. Stop light switch
16. Brake warning contact
17. Heater fan motor
18. Windshield washer pump
19. Windshield wiper motor
20. Charge indicator light
21. Direction indicator repeater light
22. Brake warning light
23. High beam indicator light
24. Oil pressure warning light
25. Electric clock (Extra equipment)
26. Temperature gauge
27. Speedometer and odometer
28. Fuel gauge
29. Flasher unit
30. Dimmer relay
31. Ignition and starter switch
32. Headlight switch
33. Instrument illumination rheostat
34. Heater fan switch
35. Warning flasher switch
36. Courtesy light switch
37. Courtesy light with switch
38. Switch for windshield wiper,
      washer and signal horn
39. Direction indicator switch with
      headlight flasher and dimmer
      switch
40. Fuel transmitter
41. Back-up light and direction
      indicators
42. Tail light and stop light
43. License plate light

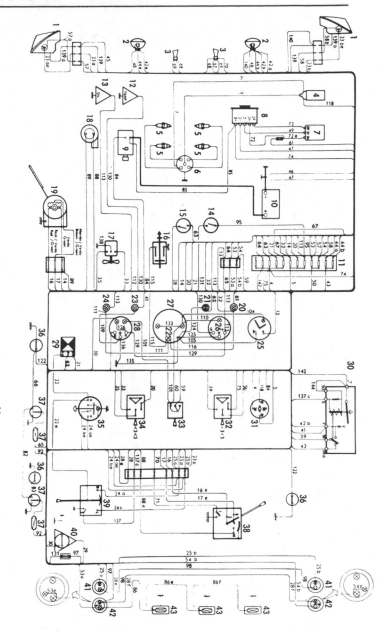

Wiring diagram—SAAB 95 (station wagon) 1969 USA version

4 grey	24a yellow	42b white	58 green	73 yellow	101 green	131 white
5 red	24ae yellow	43 yellow	58b green	74 grey	104 green	133 green
7 black	24b white	44a grey	59 green	75 grey	105 black	135 black
13 blue	24be white	44b yellow	60 green	82 white	109 black	136 black
14 brown	25a blue	45 black	61 red	83 white	110 green	137 brown
16 grey	25b grey	46 black	62 grey	84 yellow	111 red	137c brown
16e grey	28 red	47 black	63 red	85 grey	112 blue	138 black
17 blue	28e red	49 black	64 grey	86 green	113 white	139 black
17e blue	28f red	50 green	65 red	86e green	115 yellow	139a black
20 white	29 grey	53 blue	66 white	86f green	116 red	139b black
21 red	30 brown	53a blue	67 red	88 black	118 white	140 black
22 green	32 red	53e green	68 red	88e black	122 white	142 grey
22e green	33 yellow	54 green	69 black	89 brown	124 black	144 grey
23a yellow	35 grey	54b green	70 black	92 red	125 black	
23ae yellow	39 red	54e green	71 black	95 white	126 white	
23b white	41 blue	57 blue	72 red	97 white	129 white	
23be white	42a blue	57a blue	72e red	98 white	130 brown	

1. Parking and turn signal
    lights
2. Headlights
3. Horns
4. Ignition coil
5. Spark plugs
6. Distributor
7. Voltage regulator
8. Alternator
9. Starter motor
10. Battery
11. Fuse box
12. Temperature gauge,
    sending unit
13. Oil pressure switch
14. Back-up light switch
15. Stop light switch
16. Heater motor
17. Windshield wiper motor
18. Direction indicator warning
    lights
19. Charge indicator light
20. High beam indicator light
21. Oil pressure warning light
22. Electric clock
23. Temperature gauge
24. Speedometer with
    odometer
25. Fuel gauge
26. Foot dimmer switch
27. Flasher
28. Cigarette lighter
29. Ignition and starter switch
30. Headlight and parking light
    switch with instrument
    illumination rheostat
31. Warning flasher switch with
    control light
32. Heater switch
33. Windshield wiper switch
34. Automatic door switch for
    dome light
35. Dome light with switch
36. Horn ring
37. Direction indicator switch
38. Fuel tank sending unit
39. Back-up lights
40. Stop lights, direction
    indicator and tail lights
41. License lights
42. Trunk light

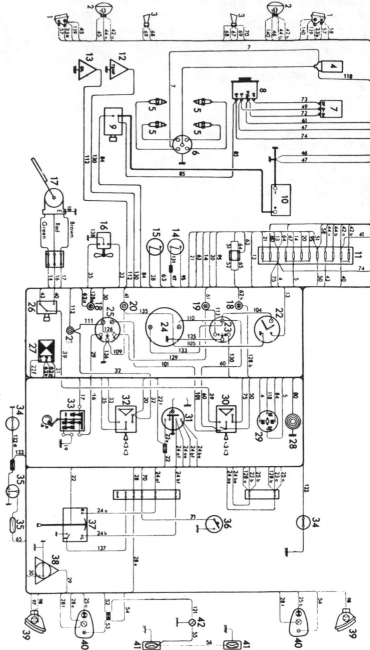

Wiring diagram—SAAB 96 1967 USA version

Black: 7, 18, 19, 45, 46, 47, 49, 71, 80, 105,
    109, 125, 135, 136, 138, 139, 140.

Red: 5, 21, 28, 28e, 28f, 32, 39, 61, 63, 65, 67,
    68, 72, 111, 113, 126, 129.

Green: 16, 22, 22e, 22f, 50, 51, 52, 53, 54, 55,
    56, 57, 58, 60, 101, 104, 110, 121, 133.

Grey: 4, 25b, 29, 35, 44a, 62a, 62b, 64, 69, 70,
    74, 75, 85.

White: 20, 23b, 24b, 24be, 24bf, 40, 42b, 66, 95,
    97, 98, 118, 122, 122e, 128a, 131.

Yellow: 17, 23a, 24a, 24ae, 24af, 33, 43, 44b,
    73, 84, 128b.

Brown: 14, 30, 130, 137.

Blue: 13, 25a, 41, 42a, 112.

1. Turn signals and side lights
2. Headlights
3. Horn
4. Ignition coil
5. Spark plugs
6. Distributor
7. Voltage regulator
8. Alternator
9. Starter
10. Battery
11. Fuse box
12. Temperature gauge, sending unit
13. Oil pressure switch
14. Back-up light switch
15. Stop light switch
16. Brake warning contact
17. Heater fan motor
18. Windshield washer pump
19. Wiper motor
20. Charge indicator light
21. Direction indicator repeater light
22. Brake warning light
23. High beam indicator light
24. Oil pressure warning light
25. Temperature gauge
26. Speedometer with odometer
27. Fuel gauge
28. Dimmer switch
29. Flasher
30. Ignition and starter switch
31. Headlight switch
32. Instrument illumination rheostat
33. Heater fan switch
34. Warning flasher switch
35. Courtesy light switch
36. Courtesy light with switch
37. Switch for windshield wiper, washer and signal horn
38. Direction indicator switch with headlight flasher
39. Fuel tank gauge
40. Back-up light
41. Stop lights, direction indicators and tail lights
42. License plate light
43. Trunk light

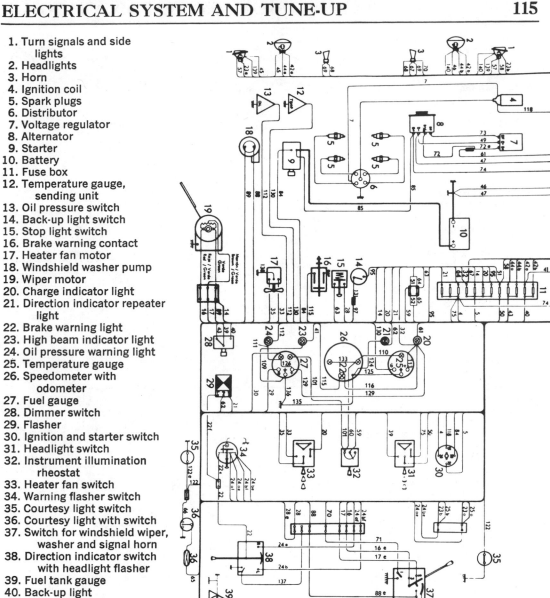

Wiring diagram—SAAB 96 1968 USA version

Black: 7, 45, 46, 47, 69, 70, 71, 88, 88e, 109, 124, 125, 135, 136, 138, 139, 140.

Red: 5, 21, 28, 28e, 28f, 32, 39, 61, 63, 65, 67, 68, 72, 72e, 111, 113, 116, 126, 129.

Green: 22, 22e, 22f, 50, 51, 52, 53, 54, 55, 56, 57, 58, 59, 60, 101, 110, 121, 133.

Grey: 4, 16, 16e, 25b, 29, 35, 44a, 62, 64, 74, 75, 85.

White: 20, 23b, 24b, 24be, 24bf, 40, 42b, 66, 95, 97, 98, 118, 122, 122e, 131.

Yellow: 23a, 24a, 24ae, 24af, 33, 43, 44b, 73, 84, 115.

Brown: 14, 30, 89, 130, 137.

Blue: 17, 17e, 25a, 41, 42a, 112.

1. Parking light and direction indicators
2. Headlights
3. Horn
4. Ignition coil
5. Spark plugs
6. Distributor
7. Voltage regulator
8. Alternator
9. Starter
10. Battery
11. Fuse box
12. Temperature transmitter
13. Oil pressure switch
14. Stop light switch
15. Back-up light switch
16. Brake warning contact
17. Heater fan motor
18. Windshield washer pump
19. Windshield wiper motor
20. Charge indicator light
21. Direction indicator repeater light
22. Brake warning light
23. High beam indicator light
24. Oil pressure warning light
25. Electric clock (Extra equipment)
26. Temperature gauge
27. Speedometer with odometer
28. Fuel gauge
29. Flasher unit
30. Dimmer relay
31. Ignition and starter switch
32. Headlight switch
33. Instrument illumination rheostat
34. Heater fan switch
35. Warning flasher switch
36. Courtesy light switch
37. Courtesy light with switch
38. Switch for windshield wiper washer and signal horn
39. Direction indicator switch with headlight flasher and dimmer switch
40. Fuel transmitter
41. Back-up lights
42. Stop lights, direction indicators and tail light
43. License plate light
44. Trunk light

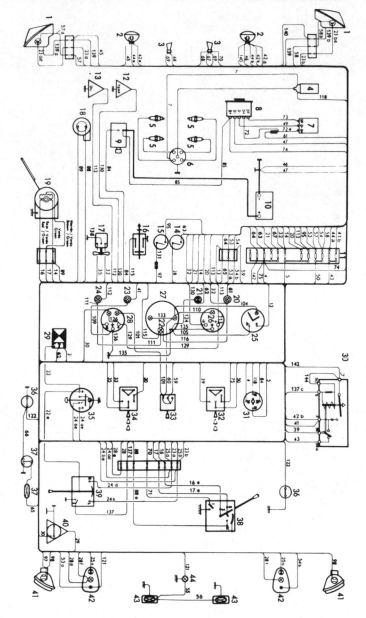

Wiring diagram—SAAB 96 1969 USA version

4 grey	24ae yellow	44a grey	60 green	85 grey	121 green	142 grey
5 red	24b white	44b yellow	61 red	88 black	122 white	144 grey
7 black	24be white	45 black	62 grey	88e black	124 black	
13 blue	25a blue	46 black	63 red	89 brown	125 black	
14 brown	25b grey	47 black	64 grey	95 white	126 white	
16 grey	28 red	49 black	65 red	97 white	129 white	
16e grey	28e red	50 green	66 white	98 white	130 brown	
17 blue	28f red	53 blue	67 red	101 green	131 white	
17e blue	29 grey	53a blue	68 red	104 green	133 green	
20 white	30 brown	54 green	69 black	105 black	135 black	
21 red	32 red	54b grey	70 black	109 black	136 black	
22 green	33 yellow	55 green	71 black	110 green	137 brown	
22e green	35 grey	56 green	72 red	111 red	137c brown	
23a yellow	39 red	57 blue	72e red	112 blue	138 black	
23ae yellow	41 blue	57a blue	73 yellow	113 white	139 black	
23b white	42a blue	58 green	74 grey	115 yellow	139a black	
23be white	42b white	58b green	75 grey	116 red	139b black	
24a yellow	43 yellow	59 green	84 yellow	118 white	140 black	

1. Turn signals and side lights
2. Headlights
3. Horn
4. Foglight and spotlight
5. Ignition coil
6. Spark plugs
7. Distributor
8. Voltage regulator
9. Alternator
10. Starter
11. Battery
12. Fuse box
13. Temperature meter
14. Oil gauge
15. Back-up light switch
16. Stop light switch
17. Heater fan motor
18. Windshield-washer pump
19. Wiper motor
20. Direction indicator repeater
    lights
21. Charge indicator light
22. Indicator light, oil pressure
23. High beam indicator light
24. Indicator light, fuel
25. Ignition and starter switch
26. Electric clock
27. Speedometer, odometer
    and trip meter
28. Temperature gauge
29. Fuel gauge
30. Tachometer
31. Flasher
32. Maneuvre relay, light
33. Dimming relay
34. Dimming switch
35. Cigarette lighter
36. Spotlight switch
37. Fog light switch
38. Headlight switch and
    instrument illumination
    rheostat
39. Warning flasher switch
40. Heater fan switch
41. Windshield wiper and
    washer switch
42. Courtesy light switch
43. Courtesy light with switch
44. Horn button
45. Direction indicator switch
46. Fuel tank gauge
47. Back-up lights
48. Stop lights, direction
    indicators and tail lights
49. License plate lights
50. Trunk light

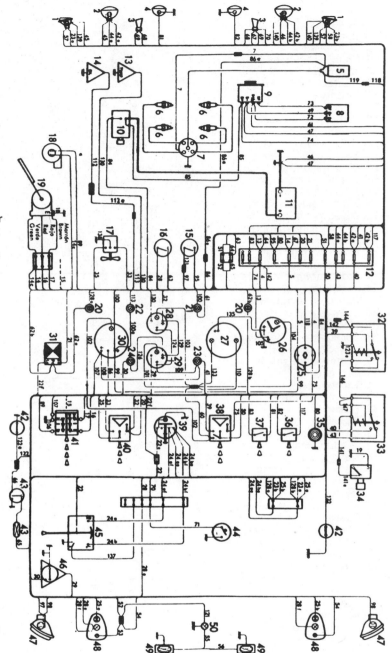

Wiring diagram—SAAB Monte Carlo 1967 USA version

Back: 7, 7b, 18, 19, 45, 46, 47, 49, 71, 80, 105, 106, 107, 108, 109, 123e, 124, 135, 138, 139, 140.

Red: 5, 21, 28, 28e, 28f, 32, 39, 61, 63, 65, 67, 68, 72, 83, 86, 86e, 126, 129.

Green: 16, 22, 22e, 22f, 50, 51, 52, 53, 54, 55, 56, 57, 58, 60, 82, 101, 102, 103, 104, 110, 119, 121, 133, 146, 147.

Grey: 4, 25b, 29, 35, 44a, 62a, 62b, 64, 69, 70, 74, 75, 85, 89, 113, 117, 142, 144.

White: 20, 23b, 24b, 24be, 24bf, 40, 42b, 66, 95, 97, 98, 118, 122, 122e, 128a, 131.

Yellow: 17, 23a, 24a, 24ae, 24af, 33, 43, 44b, 62b, 73, 81, 84, 99, 100, 100e, 112, 112e, 128b, 130.

Brown: 14, 14c, 15, 30, 137, 141, 141e.

Blue: 13, 25a, 41, 42a.

1. Turn signals and side lights
2. Headlights
3. Horn
4. Ignition coil
5. Spark plgs
6. Distributor
7. Voltage regulator
8. Alternator
9. Starter
10. Battery
11. Fuse box
12. Temperature gauge, sending unit
13. Oil pressure switch
14. Back-up light switch
15. Stop light switch
16. Brake warning contact
17. Heater fan motor
18. Windshield-washer pump
19. Wiper motor
20. Direction indicator repeater light
21. Brake warning light
22. Charge indicator light
23. Indicator light, oil pressure
24. High beam indicator light
25. Indicator light, fuel
26. Ignition and starter switch
27. Electric clock
28. Speedometer, odometer and trip meter
29. Temperature gauge
30. Fuel gauge
31. Tachometer
32. Dimmer switch
33. Flasher
34. Cigarette lighter
35. Switches for extra equipment
36. Headlight switch
37. Instrument illumination rheostat
38. Heater fan switch
39. Warning flasher switch
40. Courtesy light switch
41. Courtesy light with switch
42. Switch for windshield wiper, washer and signal horn
43. Direction indicator switch with headlight flasher and dimmer switch
44. Fuel tank gauge
45. Back-up lights
46. Stop lights, direction indicators and tail lights
47. License plate light
48. Trunk light

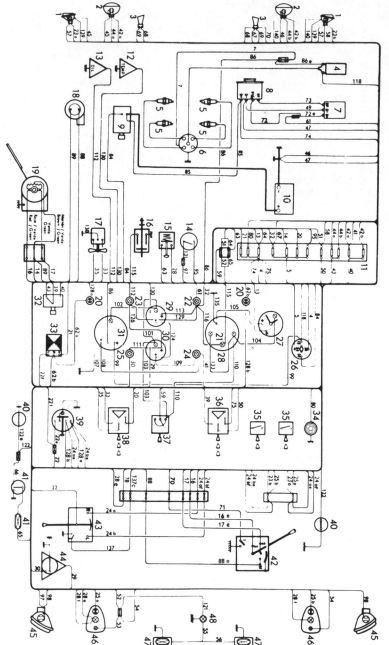

Wiring diagram—SAAB DeLuxe 1968 USA version

Black: 7, 23a, 45, 46, 47, 49, 71, 80, 88, 88e, 105, 107, 108, 109, 124, 135, 138, 139, 140.

Red: 5, 21, 28, 28e, 28f, 32, 39, 61, 63, 65, 67, 68, 72, 72e, 86, 86e, 111, 113, 116, 126, 129.

Green: 22, 22e, 22f, 50, 51, 52, 53, 54, 55, 56, 57, 58, 59, 101, 102, 103, 104, 110, 121, 133.

Grey: 4, 16, 16e, 25b, 29, 35, 44a, 62a, 62b, 64, 69, 70, 74, 75, 85.

White: 20, 23b, 24b, 24be, 24bf, 40, 42b, 66, 95, 97, 98, 99, 118, 122, 122e, 128a, 131.

Yellow: 24a, 24ae, 24af, 33, 43, 44b, 73, 84, 115, 128b.

Brown: 14, 30, 89, 130, 137, 137c.

Blue: 13, 17, 17e, 25a, 41, 42a, 112.

1. Parking light and direction indicators
2. Headlights
3. Horn
4. Ignition coil
5. Spark plugs
6. Distributor
7. Voltage regulator
8. Alternator
9. Starter
10. Battery
11. Fuse box
12. Temperature transmitter
13. Oil pressure switch
14. Back-up light switch
15. Stop light switch
16. Brake warning contact
17. Heater fan motor
18. Windshield washer pump
19. Windshield wiper motor
20. Direction indicator repeater light
21. Brake warning light
22. Charge indicator light
23. Oil pressure warning light
24. High beam indicator light
25. Indicator light, fuel
26. Ignition and starter switch
27. Electric clock
28. Speedometer, odometer and trip meter
29. Temperature gauge
30. Fuel gauge
31. Tachometer
32. Flasher unit
33. Dimmer relay
34. Cigarette lighter
35. Switches for extra equipment
36. Headlight switch
37. Instrument illumination rheostat
38. Heater fan switch
39. Warning flasher switch
40. Courtesy light switch
41. Courtesy light with switch
42. Switch for windshield wiper, washer and signal horn
43. Direction indicator switch with headlight flasher and dimmer switch
44. Fuel transmitter
45. Back-up lights
46. Stop lights, direction indicators and tail lights
47. License plate light
48. Trunk light

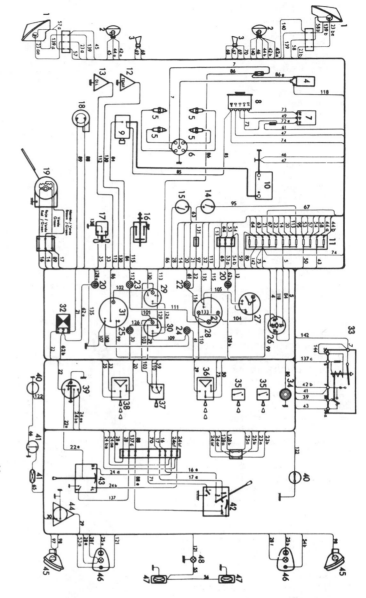

Wiring diagram—SAAB DeLuxe 1969 USA version

4 grey	23b white	32 red	53 blue	68 red	98 white	124 black
5 red	23be white	33 yellow	53a blue	69 black	99 white	126 white
7 black	24a yellow	35 grey	54 green	70 black	101 green	128a white
13 blue	24ae yellow	39 red	54b green	71 black	102 green	128b yellow
14 brown	24af yellow	41 blue	55 green	72 red	103 green	129 white
16 grey	24b white	42a blue	56 green	72e red	104 green	130 brown
16e grey	24be white	42b white	57 blue	73 yellow	105 black	131 white
17 blue	24bf white	43 yellow	57a blue	74 grey	107 black	133 green
17e blue	25a blue	44a grey	58 green	75 grey	108 black	135 black
20 white	25b grey	44b yellow	58b green	80 black	109 black	137 brown
21 red	28 red	45 black	59 green	84 yellow	110 green	137c brown
22 green	28e red	46 black	61 red	85 grey	111 red	138 black
22e green	28f red	47 black	62a grey	86 red	112 blue	139 black
23a yellow	29 grey	49 black	62b grey	86e red	113 white	139a black
23ae yellow	30 brown	50 green	63 red	88 black	115 yellow	139b black
			64 grey	88e black	116 red	140 black
			65 red	89 brown	118 white	142 grey
			66 white	95 white	121 green	144 grey
			67 red	97 white	122 white	

1. Parking light and direction indicators
2. Headlights
3. Horn
4. Ignition coil
5. Spark plugs
6. Distributor
7. Voltage regulator
8. Alternator
9. Starter
10. Battery
11. Fuse box
12. Temperature transmitter
13. Oil pressure switch
14. Back-up light switch
15. Stop light switch
16. Brake warning contact
17. Heater fan motor
18. Windshield washer pump
19. Windshield wiper motor
20. Cigarette lighter
21. Contact for warning buzzer
22. Buzzer
23. Clock
24. Speedometer and odometer
25. High beam indicator light
26. Direction indicator repeater light
27. Brake warning light
28. Temperature and fuel gauges
29. Indicator light, fuel amount
30. Oil pressure warning light
31. Charge indicator light
32. Flasher unit
33. Dimmer relay
34. Ignition and starter switch
35. Hazard warning flasher switch
36. Instrument illumination rheostat
37. Headlight switch
38. Heater fan switch
39. Dome lamp switch
40. Dome lamp with switch
41. Switch for windshield wiper, and washer
42. Signal horn contact
43. Direction indicator switch with headlight flasher and dimmer switch
44. Fuel transmitter
45. Back-up light and direction indicators
46. Tail light and stop light
47. License plate light

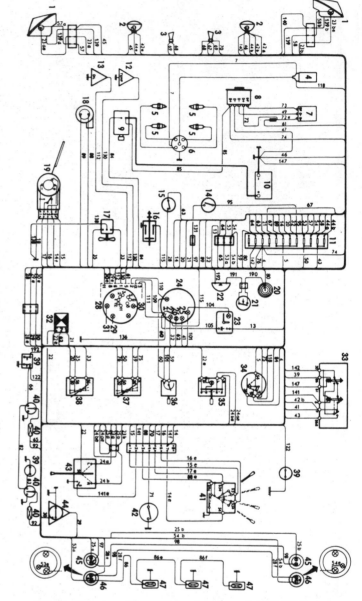

Wiring diagram—SAAB 95 (station wagon) 1970 USA version

4 grey	22e green	30e brown	53a blue	67 red	86e green	118 white
5 red	23a yellow	32 red	53e green	68 red	86f green	122 white
7 green	23ae yellow	33 yellow	54 green	69 black	88 black	130 brown
13 blue	23b white	35 grey	54b green	70 black	88e black	131 white
14 brown	23be white	39 yellow	54e green	71 black	89 brown	136 black
14e brown	24a yellow	41 blue	57 blue	72 red	92 red	138 black
14f brown	24ae yellow	42a blue	57a blue	72e red	95 white	139 black
15 red	24b white	42b white	58 green	73 yellow	97 white	139a black
15e red	24be white	43 yellow	58b green	74 grey	98 white	139b black
16 grey	25a blue	44a grey	59 green	75 red	101 green	140 black
16e grey	25b grey	44b yellow	60 green	76 grey	104 green	141 brown
17 blue	28 red	45 black	61 red	80 black	105 black	141e brown
17e blue	28e red	46 black	62 grey	82 white	109 black	142 grey
18 black	28f red	47 black	63 red	83 white	110 green	147 black
20 white	29 grey	49 black	64 grey	84 yellow	111 red	190 yellow
21 red	29e green	50 green	65 red	85 grey	112 blue	191 grey
22 green	30 brown	53 blue	66 white	86 green	115 yellow	192 black

1. Parking light and direction indicator
2. Headlights
3. Horn
4. Ignition coil
5. Spark plugs
6. Distributor
7. Voltage regulator
8. Alternator
9. Starter
10. Battery
11. Fuse box
12. Temperature transmitter
13. Oil pressure switch
14. Back-up light switch
15. Stop light switch
16. Brake warning contact
17. Heater fan motor
18. Windshield washer pump
19. Windshield wiper motor
20. Cigarette lighter
21. Contact for warning buzzer
22. Buzzer
23. Clock
24. Speedometer with odometer
25. High beam indicator light
26. Direction indicator repeater light
27. Brake warning light
28. Temperature and fuel gauges
29. Indicator light, fuel amount
30. Oil pressure warning light
31. Charge indicator light
32. Flasher unit
33. Dimmer relay
34. Ignition and starter switch
35. Hazard warning flasher switch
36. Instrument illumination rheostat
37. Headlight switch
38. Heater fan switch
39. Dome lamp switch
40. Dome lamp with switch
41. Switch for windshield wiper, and
    washer
42. Signal horn contact
43. Direction indicator switch with
    headlight flasher and dimmer
    switch
44. Fuel transmitter
45. Back up light
46. Stop lights, direction indicators
    and tail light
47. License plate light
48. Trunk light

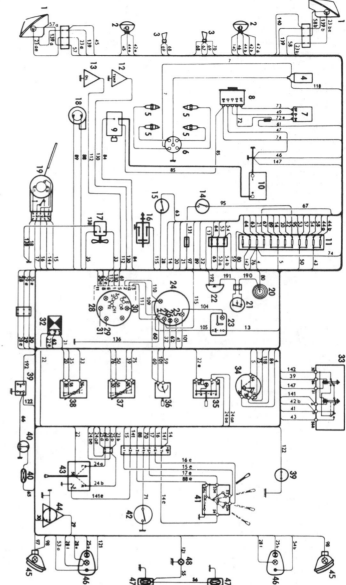

Wiring diagram—SAAB 96 1970 USA version

4 grey	22e green	30e brown	53a blue	67 red	95 white	138 black
5 red	23a yellow	32 red	54 green	68 red	97 white	139 black
7 green	23ae yellow	33 yellow	54b green	69 black	98 white	139a black
13 blue	23b white	35 grey	55 green	70 black	101 green	139b black
14 brown	23be white	39 yellow	56 black	71 black	104 green	140 black
14e brown	24a yellow	41 blue	57 blue	72 red	105 black	141 brown
14f brown	24ae yellow	42a blue	57a blue	72e red	109 black	141e brown
15 red	24b white	42b white	58 green	73 yellow	110 green	142 grey
15e red	24be white	43 yellow	58b green	74 grey	111 red	147 black
16 grey	25a blue	44a grey	59 green	75 red	112 blue	190 yellow
16e grey	25b grey	44b yellow	60 green	76 grey	115 yellow	191 grey
17 blue	28 red	45 black	61 red	80 black	118 white	192 black
17e blue	28e red	46 black	62 grey	84 yellow	121 green	
18 black	28f red	47 black	63 red	85 grey	122 white	
20 white	29 grey	49 black	64 grey	88 black	130 brown	
21 red	29e green	50 green	65 red	88e black	131 white	
22 green	30 brown	53 blue	66 white	89 brown	136 black	

1. Turn signals and side lights
2. Headlights
3. Horn
4. Foglight and spotlight
5. Distributor
6. Spark plugs
7. Voltage regulator
8. Generator
9. Starter
10. Battery
11. Fuel pumps
12. Fuse box
13. Ignition coil
14. Series resistance
15. Oil warning relay
16. Oil gauge
17. Cooling fan
18. Thermostat contact
19. Temperature transmitter
20. Back-up light switch
21. Stop lamp switch
22. Heater fan motor
23. Wiper motor
24. Windshield-washer pump
25. Charge indicator light
26. Indicator light oil pressure
27. Indicator light fuel
28. Direction indicator repeater light
29. High beam indicator light
30. Ignition and starter switch
31. Tachometer
32. Coolant thermometer
33. Fuel gauge
34. Speedometer, odometer and trip meter
35. Electric clock
36. Cigarette lighter
37. Flasher
38. Maneuver relay, headlight flasher
39. Maneuver relay, light
40. Dimmer relay
41. Dimmer switch
42. Spotlight switch
43. Fog light switch
44. Headlight switch and instrument illumination rheostat
45. Windshield wiper and washer switch
46. Map reading light with switch
47. Map reading light switch
48. Fuel tank gauge
49. Heater fan switch
50. Cooling fan switch
51. Warning flasher switch
52. Direction indicator switch with headlight flasher
53. Horn button
54. Stop lights and direction indicator lights
55. Tail lights
56. Back-up lights
57. License plate light

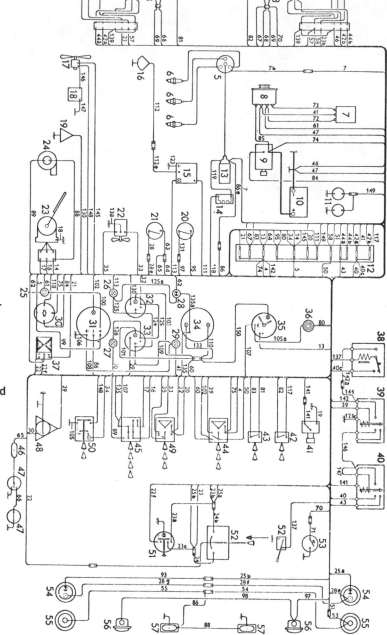

Wiring diagram—SAAB Sonnet with two-stroke engine (Sonnet II)

Black: 1, 7, 7b, 18, 19, 41, 46, 47, 71, 80, 105, 105a, 106, 107, 108, 109, 123, 123c, 124, 125, 125a, 135, 135a, 138, 138, 147

Red: 5, 21, 28, 28e, 28f, 28g, 32, 34, 39, 61, 63, 65, 67, 68, 72, 83, 86, 86e, 111, 126, 129

White: 20, 23a, 23b, 24b, 40, 40c, 42b, 95, 97, 98, 118, 131

Green: 16, 22, 22f, 50, 51, 53, 54, 55, 57, 58, 60, 82, 86, 88, 101, 102, 103, 110, 119, 133, 145, 146, 147, 148, 150

Yellow: 17, 23, 23c, 24a, 33, 43, 44b, 62, 66, 73, 81, 84, 99, 100, 112, 112e, 130

Blue: 13, 25a, 41, 42a, 64, 149

Grey: 4, 25b, 29, 35, 44a, 69, 70, 74, 75, 85, 89, 93, 113, 117, 142, 142a, 144

Brown: 14, 30, 88, 137c, 141

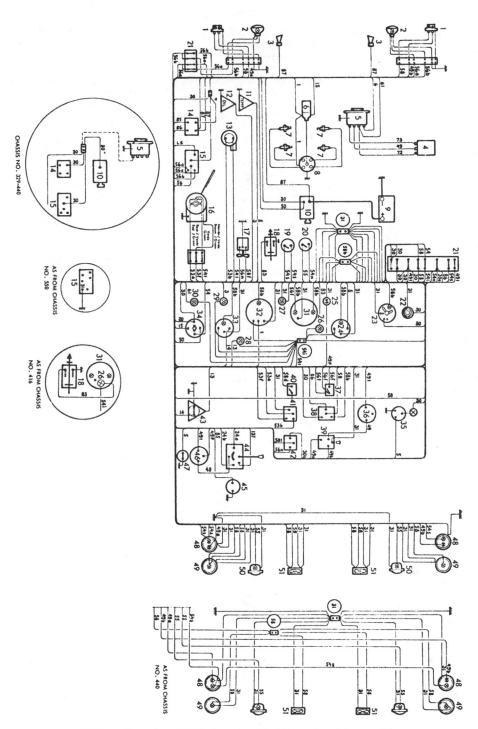

Wiring diagram—SAAB Sonnet with V4 engine (Sonnet II)

Black: 31, 85, LS.

Red: 1, 6, 15, 30, 30a, 49t, 50, 54, 54i, 54n, 54r, 54s, 54t, 61, 72, 86, 87.

White: 24b, 49b, 55, 56a.

Green: 49, 53a, 58, 58b, 58d.

Yellow: 8, 24a, 49p, 53f, 54h, 56b, 73.

Blue: 49b, 56a, 56f.

Grey: 14, 49a, 53b, 56, 58t.

Brown: 3, 5, 13, 83, 137.

Wiring diagram—SAAB Sonnet with V4 engine (Sonnet II)

1. Turn signals and side lights
2. Headlights
3. Horn
4. Voltage regulator
5. Alternator
6. Ignition coil
7. Spark plugs
8. Distributor
9. Battery
10. Starter
11. Temperature transmitter
12. Oil pressure switch
13. Windshield-washer pump
14. Relay, signal
15. Maneuver relay, light
16. Wiper motor
17. Heater fan motor
18. Brake warning contact
19. Stop lamp switch
20. Back-up light switch

21. Fuse box
22. Cigarette lighter
23. Electric clock
24. Temperature gauge
25. Direction indicator repeater light
26. Brake warning light
27. High beam indicator light
28. Indicator light fuel
29. Indicator light oil pressure
30. Charge indicator light
31. Speedometer, odometer and trip meter
32. Tachometer
33. Fuel gauge
34. Ignition and starter switch
35. Map reading light with switch
36. Warning flasher relay
37. Spotlight switch

38. Headlight switch and instrument illumination rheostat
39. Warning flasher switch
40. Fog light switch
41. Windshield wiper and washer switch
42. Heater fan switch
43. Fuel tank gauge
44. Direction indicator switch with headlight flasher and dimmer switch
45. Horn button
46. Flasher relay
47. Map reading light switch
48. Stop lights and direction indicator lights
49. Tail lights
50. Back-up lights
51. License plate light

1. Parking and turn signal lights
2. Headlights
3. Horns
4. Distributor
5. Spark plugs
6. Generator
7. Fuel pump
8. Starter motor
9. Battery
10. Voltage regulator
11. Fuse box
12. Ignition coil
13. Heater fan motor
14. Windshield wiper motor
   a. SWF
   b. Bosch
15. Stop-light switch
16. Instruments cluster
17. Dip switch
18. Door switch for roof light
19. Road-light switch
20. Heater fan switch
21. Instrument-lighting switch
22. Turn indicator repeater light
23. Ignition and starting switch
24. Windshield-wiper switch
25. Cigar lighter
26. Turn indicator switch
27. Horn button
28. Fuel-gauge sender unit
29. Roof light and switch
30. Rear roof light
31. Stop lights and turn indicator lights
32. Parking lights
33. License light
34. Door switch for roof light

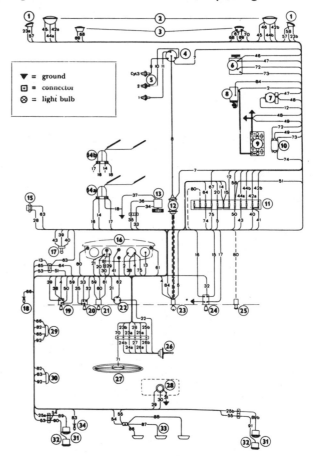

Wiring diagram—SAAB 95 (station wagon) up to chassis No. 10,800

Grey: 4, 12, 13, 25b, 26b, 29, 35, 36, 38, 44a, 62, 64, 69, 70, 74, 75, 76.

White: 23b, 24b, 40, 41, 42b.

Yellow: 17, 25a, 26a, 30, 43, 44b, 66, 73, 81, 82, 83, 84, 89a, 89b.

Blue: 42a.

Black: 1, 7, 18, 19, 23a, 24a, 32, 37, 45, 46, 47, 48, 49, 71, 77, 78, 79, 80.

Red: 2, 5, 8, 9, 10, 11, 14, 15, 20, 21, 27, 28, 33, 34, 39, 63, 65 67, 72, 92.

Green: 16, 22, 50, 5, 52, 53, 54, 55, 56, 57, 58, 59, 60, 61, 86, 87, 88, 90, 91.

NOTE: Saab 95 cars up to chassis No. 1700 have the same wiring as the Saab 93 from chassis No. 49801, except for leads to rear lights.

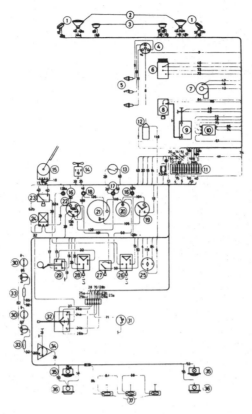

Wiring diagram—SAAB 95 (station wagon) from
chassis No. 10,801

1. Parking and turn signal lights
2. Headlights
3. Horns
4. Distributor
5. Spark plugs
6. Generator
7. Fuel pump
8. Starter motor
9. Battery
10. Voltage regulator
11. Fuse box
12. Ignition coil
13. Stop-light switch
14. Heater fan motor
15. Windshield-wiper motor
16. Turn-indicator repeater light
17. Charge indicator light
18. High beam indicator light
19. Electric clock

20. Coolant thermometer (lighting)
21. Speedometer and odometer
22. Fuel gauge
23. Dip switch
24. Turn indicator flasher
25. Ignition and starter switch
26. Headlight switch
27. Instrument-lighting rheostat
28. Heater fan switch
29. Windshield-wiper switch
30. Door switches for courtesy light
31. Horn button
32. Turn indicator switch
33. Courtesy lights with switch
34. Fuel gauge sender unit
35. Stop lights, and turn indicator lights
36. Tail lights
37. License lights

Black: 1, 7, 18, 19, 23a, 24a, 45, 46, 47, 48, 49,
   71, 105, 109, 135, 136.

Red: 5, 8, 9, 10, 11, 14, 20, 21, 27, 28, 32, 39,
   61, 63, 65, 67, 68, 72, 92, 126, 129.

Green: 16, 22, 50, 51, 53, 54, 55, 58, 59, 60,
   86, 87, 88, 101, 104, 110.

Grey: 4, 12, 25b, 26b, 29, 35, 44a, 62a, 62b, 64,
   69, 70, 74, 75, 85, 93.

White: 23b, 24b, 40, 42b, 66, 82, 83, 118, 128a.

Yellow: 17, 26a, 33, 43, 44b, 73, 84, 128b.

Brown: 15, 30.

Blue: 13, 25a, 41, 42a.

1. Parking and turn signal lights
2. Headlights
3. Horns
4. Extra lights
5. Distributor
6. Spark plugs
7. Generator
8. Fuel pump
9. Starter motor
10. Battery
11. Voltage regulator
12. Fuse box
13. Resistance
14. Ignition coil
15. Heater fan motor
16. Windshield-wiper motor
17. Windshield-washer pump
18. Stop-light switch
19. Dimmer switch
20. Instruments
21. Halda Speed Pilot
22. Door switch
23. Light switch
24. Heater fan switch
25. Flasher unit
26. Windshield wiper switch
27. Ignition and starter switch
28. Cigar lighter
29. Back-up light switch with ind.
    light
30. Switch for optional lights
31. Instrument illumination switch
32. Extra switch
33. Turn indicator switch
34. Horn button
35. Courtesy light with switch
36. Fuel gauge, sender unit
37. Tail, stop and turn indicator signal
    lights
38. Back-up lights
39. License plate lights

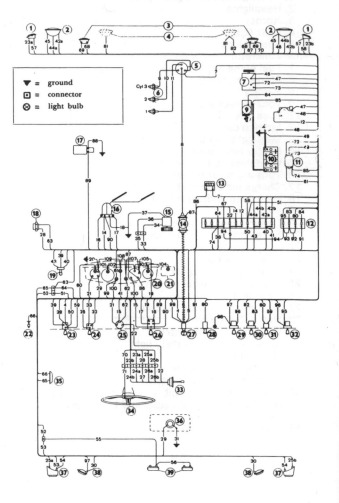

Wiring diagram—SAAB GT-750

Black: 1, 7, 18, 19, 20, 23a, 24a, 32, 37, 45, 46, 47, 48, 49, 71, 80, 88, 89, 91, 105, 107, 108, 109.

Red: 5, 8, 9, 10, 11, 14, 15, 21, 27, 28, 33, 34, 39, 61, 63, 65, 67, 68, 72, 86, 90.

Yellow: 17, 25a, 26a, 43, 44b, 66, 73, 84, 99, 100.

Green: 16, 22, 50, 51, 52, 53, 54, 55, 56, 57, 58, 59, 60, 81, 82, 83, 101, 102, 103, 104.

Blue: 12a, 62.

Grey: 4, 12, 25b, 26b, 29, 35, 36, 38, 44a, 64, 69, 70, 74, 85, 87, 92, 93, 94.

White: 23b, 24b, 30, 40, 41, 42b, 95, 96, 97, 98.

Chapter 7

Brakes and Suspension

Part I—Brakes

The SAAB has used three separate and distinct brake systems, although some minor differences between them exist. The first type (Type I) is a four-wheel drum system having self-energizing front shoes, each shoe having a single wheel cylinder. The rear shoes are actuated by a single cylinder, but the cylinder is movable—the pushing action against one shoe resulting in an opposite reaction to move the other shoe against the drum.

The second type (Type II) is also a four-wheel drum system. It, however, has standard double-ended wheel cylinders at the rear, fixed to the backing plate.

The third type (Type III) is a four-wheel, dual-circuit system utilizing either a front drum/rear drum or a front disc/rear drum configuration. With this type system, the master cylinder controls the left front and the right rear independently of, and simultaneously with, the right front and left rear wheels. If hydraulic fluid leakage occurs, braking effort will be lost only on one diagonal pair of wheels. Leakage manifests itself by long pedal travel and by a tendency for the car to swerve toward the side where brake pressure is the greatest. A warning light system is used after 1968, consisting of a light in the speedometer housing and a switch on the pedal mechanism.

Brake System Application

System	Model	Serial No.
Type I	95	Up to 3130
	96	Up to 134999
	GT-750	Up to 134999
Type II	95	3131 to 10800
	96	135000 to 201400
	GT-750	135000 to 201400
Type III	95	From 10801
	96	From 201401
	96 Sport (GT-850)	From 201401
	Sonett	All

Up to and including the 1966 model, pressure regulating valves are installed in the lines to the rear brakes on the SAAB 96, SAAB Sport and Monte Carlo 850. The pressure regulating valves are to prevent premature lock-up of the rear wheels.

The mechanical handbrake acts on the rear wheels and the brake level is located between the front seats.

Master Cylinder

The tandem master cylinder includes a

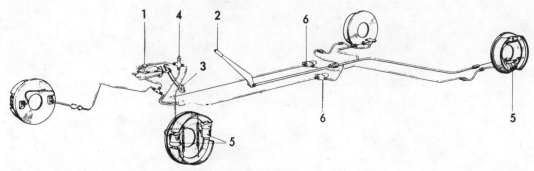

Two-circuit braking system used up to and including 1967

1. Master cylinder
2. Handbrake lever
3. Brake pedal

4. Stop light contact
5. Wheel cylinders

6. Pressure regulating valve
   (SAAB 96 and Monte Carlo
   850 up to and including
   1966 model.)

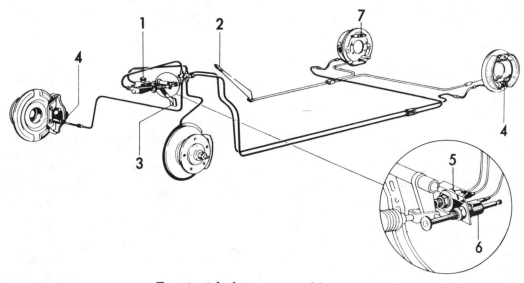

Two-circuit braking system used from 1968-70

1. Master cylinder
2. Handbrake lever
3. Brake pedal

4. Wheel cylinder
5. Stop light switch

6. Brake warning light contact
7. Adjusting screw, rear brake

body housing, a primary piston (10) and a secondary piston (14), which is actuated by a pushrod (31) from the brake pedal. The pistons are held apart by a spring (18), the distance between them being determined by a clip (17) and the retaining pin (19). The secondary piston has a primary cup (12) and a secondary cup (15). Fitted behind the primary cup is a dished piston washer (13), which prevents the cup from being extruded into the feed holes in the flange. The primary cup of the primary piston (21) also has a dished piston washer

(22) and a secondary cup (26), which bears against the piston rod and prevents leakage of brake fluid. The spring (9) returns the pistons to the initial position. One-way valves are fitted in the two outlets (1 and 2).

When the brake pedal is depressed, the pushrod (31) actuates the primary piston, the thrust being transmitted by the spring (18) to the secondary piston, which forces brake fluid out through the one-way valve to one brake circuit. As the secondary chamber rises, the spring force between the

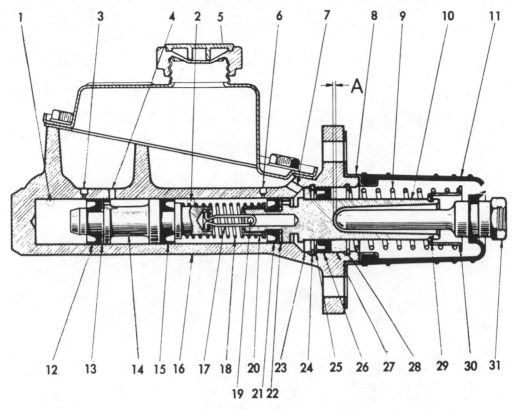

Cross-sectional view of master cylinder. A=0.024-0.047"

1. Outlet to one circuit
2. Outlet to other circuit
3. Bypass port
4. Feed hole
5. Brake fluid reservoir
6. Bypass port
7. Feed hole
8. Retaining plate
9. Spring
10. Primary piston
11. Rubber boot

12. Primary piston
13. Piston washer
14. Secondary piston
15. Secondary cup
16. Body
17. Clip
18. Spring
19. Retaining pin
20. Spring holder
21. Primary cup

22. Piston washer
23. Piston stop ring
24. Circlip
25. Washer
26. Secondary cup
27. Guide bearing
28. Circlip
29. "Spirol ox" circlip
30. Spring retainer
31. Pushrod

pistons is overcome, and further effort on the brake pedal compresses the spring slightly, causing brake fluid to be forced to the second brake circuit. The pressure in front of the primary piston also reacts on the back of the secondary piston. Consequently, the latter froms a partition and balances the pressures until they are equal in both brake circuits.

Upon removal of the load from the brake pedal, the return spring (9) returns the pistons to the initial position faster than the fluid is able to flow back from the wheel cylinders. The front (or primary) cups therefore move forwards a little and the dished washers uncover the feed holes behind the cups and admit brake fluid from the reservoir. Meanwhile, the brake shoe return springs pull back the brake pistons, whereupon brake fluid flows back through the one-way valves. The brake fluid then flows back to the reservoir via the bypass ports (3) and (6), which also compensate for contraction or expansion of the brake fluid due to temperature changes. When the brake shoes have been returned, the one-way valve closes, and any residual pressure is relieved through the hole (43) in the valve. The purpose of the one-way valve is to prevent entry of brake fluid from the wheel cylinders when bleeding the brake system. This ensures that a fresh charge of brake fluid, completely free of air, will pass from the reservoir and through the systems at each stroke of the brake pedal. In the event of a leak occurring in the system

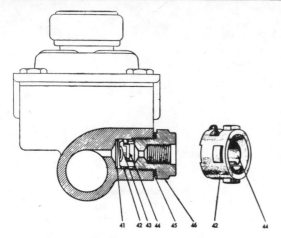

One-way valve in master cylinder

41. Spring   44. Spring clip
42. Valve body   45. Gasket
43. Equalizing hole   46. Adapter

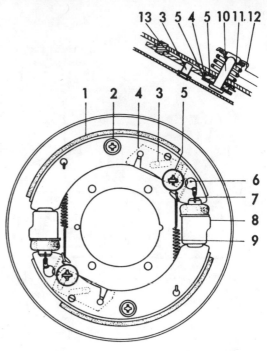

Front brake components

1. Brake shoe   7. Piston-locking
2. Steady pin with   spring
   spring   8. Wheel cylinder
3. Back plate peg   9. Return spring
4. Adjuster lever   10. Retaining pin
5. Friction washers   11. Spring
6. Hole for locking   12. Spring retainer
   spring   13. Peg

operated by the primary piston, the spring (18) is compressed until the primary piston strikes the secondary piston. The latter can then function normally. If leakage occurs in the circuit operated by the secondary piston, the secondary piston will be thrust forward by the primary piston and spring until it touches the bottom of the cylinder bore, whereupon the brake fluid can be forced out into the remaining circuit. The Sonett master cylinder is similar to the ones used on other SAAB models, with the exception of the remote mounted fluid reservoir.

Front Brakes—SAAB 95 and 96 up to 1966

The front brake shoes are of the self-energizing type and each one is operated by its own single-acting wheel cylinder. The shoes are engaged in slots in the wheel cylinder piston and opposing wheel cylinder, where they are free to slide and thus to center in relation to the drum. Each shoe carries its own automatic adjustment device, consisting of an adjuster lever (4), secured to the brake shoe by a peg (13) at one end, with serrations at the other end. The lever is held to the brake shoe by two retaining washers (5), a retaining pin (10), loaded by a spring (11), and a spring retainer (12). One end of the brake shoe return spring (9) is designed as a pawl, which engages in the serrations of the adjuster lever. On the backing plate, a peg (3) is provided, which slides in a groove in the center of the lever. The brake shoes are held against the backing plate by a spring, a washer and anchor

pin (2). They are also held to the wheel cylinder piston by means of a piston locking spring (7).

The backing plate peg (3) always has a certain amount of clearance in the adjuster lever slot; this determines how much free-play will exist between the brake linings and the brake drums when the shoes are "off." Upon application of the brake, the shoe is forced out against the drum by the piston and is accompanied by the adjuster lever, so that the peg takes up a new position in the slot. As the brake linings wear down, the automatic adjustment device becomes effective. Further travel of the brake shoe, together with the adjuster lever, results in the detention of the lever in the middle by the peg (3). However, since the lever is carried in a bearing (2) at one end, it turns there and slides between the retaining washers (4) at the other end. The friction of these retaining washers is sufficient to hold the adjuster lever in this new position when the brake shoes return to the "off"

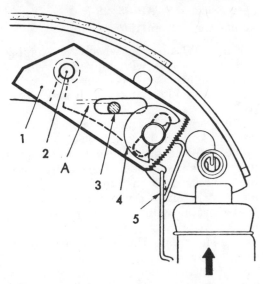

Brake shoe with worn lining, showing in applied position

A. Clearance
1. Adjuster lever
2. Bearing
3. Backing plate peg
4. Friction washers
5. Return spring with pawl catch

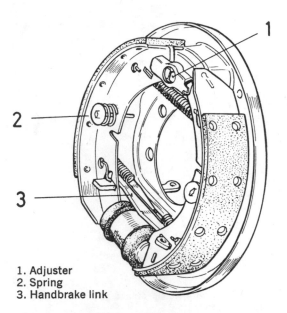

1. Adjuster
2. Spring
3. Handbrake link

REAR BRAKES

position. When the adjuster lever has traveled far enough, the pawl on the return spring drops into the next serration and thus ensures positive retention of the adjuster lever. When the brake shoe returns to the "off" position, it will move only as much as is allowed by the free-play at the peg, which is just enough to ensure that the brake shoe clears the drum. In order to prevent any variation in the brake pedal travel due to the piston's working back into the cylinder on its own, the piston is connected to the brake shoe by a piston locking spring.

Rear Wheel Brakes and Handbrake

The rear wheel brakes and handbrake are, in principle, identical for all models. All have a wheel cylinder mounted in the backing plate. The cylinder is fitted with two pistons, with the exception of early 95, 96 and GT-750 models, each of which acts on one brake shoe. The shoes are adjusted manually. SAAB Sport and Monte Carlo up to and including 1966 are equipped with pressure regulating valves for the rear brakes in order to provide a proper distribution of braking effort. The handbrake operates through sealed Bowden cables by a lever located between the front seats.

Disc Brakes—SAAB Sport and Monte Carlo 850 up to and Including 1966

The front wheel disc brakes consist of a disc attached to the front hub which rotates with the wheel. On each side of the disc is a friction pad which, when the brakes are applied, is forced against the brake disc by a brake piston. The brake pistons are located in a split caliper housing which encases the brake disc. In the caliper housing, the fluid is distributed to the two brake cylinders, and a bleed screw is fitted at the highest point. The caliper housing is screwed to a holder, which is fastened to the steering knuckle. The brake pistons are 2″ in diameter. The piston seals are located in grooves in the cylinders; the pistons have a completely smooth surface. The outer seals serve to keep out dust and dirt, while the inner seals prevent leakage of brake fluid. The brake pistons act directly on the friction pads, the latter being held in position by means of two springs and cotter pins. Pads can be changed by removing the springs and pins. There are no return springs for the pads, which means that the disc brakes are self-adjusting. When the brakes are applied, brake fluid is forced from the master cylinder to the brake cylinders, and the brake pistons press the friction pads against the disc. When the pressure is removed from the brake pedal, the pistons are returned a few thousandths of an inch because of the flexibility of the

Front axle assembly, showing disc brakes used up to and including 1966

1. Brake disc   3. Caliper housing
2. Wheel hub   4. Friction pads

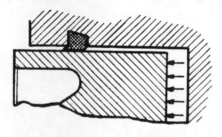

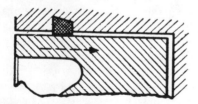

The brake piston is moved back under influence of piston seal

piston seal. This is sufficient to prevent the friction pads from bearing on the disc. Wear on the pads is compensated for in this manner, as the piston gradually moves farther out. Excessive wear on the pads is, therefore, not revealed by excessive pedal travel with this type brake.

Disc Brakes—SAAB 95, 96 and Monte Carlo from 1967

From 1967, the front wheels are equipped with disc brakes with only one cylinder. The main parts are the support bracket, caliper assembly, cylinder body and friction pads.

The support bracket is bolted to the steering knuckle housing, which keeps the brake in place and transmits the braking force to the suspension. The caliper assembly is secured to the support bracket by means of a hinge pin and a friction unit. It is movable with relation to the support bracket, the torsional center being provided by the hinge pin. The brake cylinder is the same type as previously used with the addition of an outer wiper seal to prevent the entry of dirt, plus an inner fluid seal. The friction pads are wedge-shaped in order to compensate for the irregular wear which occurs because of the movement around the hinge pin. The outer friction pad is mounted in the caliper assembly; the inner pad rests against the brake piston and is held in position by the support bracket and caliper assembly.

Hydraulic pressure from the master cylinder actuates the brake piston, causing it to move outwards and press the friction pad against the disc. The movable brake unit then is influenced so that the outer friction pad is also pressed against the brake disc. The flexibility of the piston seals is sufficient to provide clearance between the friction pads and the disc when the brake pedal pressure is released.

As the friction pads wear, the brake body assembly rotates around the hinge pin, thus causing the angle of wear to be changed continuously. When the linings have become so worn as to need replacement, the angle has become so small that the lining is almost parallel to the disc.

Drum Brake Service

Because the front shoes are self-adjusting, it is not possible to detect worn linings by excessive pedal travel. It is, therefore, important to remove the wheels at regular intervals in order to check lining wear through the inspection holes in the drum. If the linings are less than 1.0 mm. (.040″) thick, replacement is necessary.

Front axle assembly, showing disc brakes used from 1967

1. Brake disc   3. Caliper housing
2. Wheel hub   4. Friction pads

BRAKE DRUM REMOVAL

1. Remove the cotter pin and spindle nut.
2. Jack up the car.
3. Remove the wheel.
4. a. *Rear wheels:* Release the handbrake and adjust the rear shoes with the adjusting screw.

b. *Front wheels:* The front shoes must be adjusted in the following manner.

Insert a screwdriver into the extra hole in the brake drum, then into the hole (6) in the brake shoe. Then, with another screwdriver or bar bearing against the hub nut, press the brake drum and shoe against the normal direction of rotation, until a grating sound is heard, indicating that the shoe has been forced back and the pawl has released. Readjust both shoes before removing the brake drum.

5. Remove the brake drum, using puller No. 784002 for SAAB 95 and 96 and No. 784201 for SAAB Sport and Monte Carlo models. If the proper puller is not available, a standard wheel puller will do if used carefully. Never hammer on drums.

6. Examine the linings on all the shoes. If they are worn below inspection limits, cracked, burned, charred or worn unevenly, or covered with grease, new linings must be installed. Never install new linings on only one side.

Inspection hole in brake drum

Adjusting brake shoes

7. If linings are replaced, they must be ground in a special machine to a radius of about 0.010–0.012″ less than that of the drum for perfect contact. The edges of the linings must *not* be chamfered, they should be left as sharp as possible.

FRONT BRAKE SHOES DISASSEMBLY

1. Remove the locking springs (7) that hold the brake piston to the brake shoe. (Unhook the spring from the piston first.)
2. Remove the anchor springs (2) for the brake shoes.

3. Ease the heel of the lower shoe out of the wheel cylinder, then move the shoe carefully outwards a little way to disengage the backing plate peg (3) from the adjuster lever groove. The toe of the shoe then can be removed from the brake piston. Use only the fingers and do not touch the return springs. Also, take care not to distort the return springs and pawl mechanism catches.

4. Remove the upper shoe in the same manner. Use a small piece of wire or some suitable device around the cylinders to prevent the pistons from falling out.

5. Remove the retaining washers, the spring and pin, then the adjuster lever from the brake shoe.

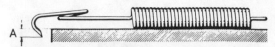

Checking return spring pawl mechanism. A=0.157″

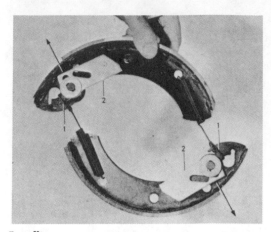

Installing return springs

mechanism catches are correctly positioned in the retaining washers.

4. Remove the wires used to retain the pistons.

5. Refit the upper shoe first, making sure that the backing plate (3) engages the oval hole in the adjuster lever.

6. Next install the lower shoe in the same manner, using the hands only, taking care not to touch the springs. It is most important that the pawl catches on the return springs are not distorted during assembly.

7. Refit the piston locking springs and the anchor springs, with retaining pins and washers.

8. Center the shoes and install the drums.

9. Adjust the front brakes by applying the brakes hard several times. Do not drive the car until this is done.

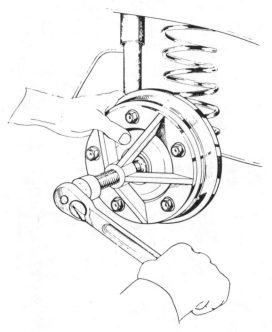

Using puller No. 784002 to remove brake drum

ASSEMBLY

1. If the adjuster lever and retaining washers have been removed, check them for wear, then locate the adjuster lever in its slot in the brake shoe. Install the retaining washers on either side of the adjuster lever and install the spring, retaining pin, and spring retainer. Do *not* lubricate the retaining washers.

2. Check the return springs and, if necessary, adjust the pawl mechanism catches to the correct dimension.

3. Push the adjuster levers over as far as possible towards the shoe table. Refit both return springs, making sure that their pawl

REAR BRAKE SHOES DISASSEMBLY

1. Use a piece of wire or clamp to keep the brake pistons in the wheel cylinder.

2. Remove the springs which hold the shoes to the backing plate.

3. Remove the shoes from the cylinder and handbrake levers; first the top, then the bottom.

ASSEMBLY

1. Hook the springs between the shoes.

2. Install the front shoe, with the handbrake lever in the oblong hole.

3. Lift the rear shoe with the handbrake lever into the large hole. Make sure the spring presses against the lever as illustrated.

4. Remove the wire or clamp used to keep the brake pistons in place.

5. Adjust the shoes approximately in the center of the backing plate. Install the springs that hold the shoes against the backing plate.

6. Install the wheel hub and wheel.

7. Adjust the brakes.

BRAKE ADJUSTMENT

Brake wear is revealed by excessive travel of the brake pedal or handbrake lever before brakes take effect. The distance between the fully depressed pedal and the floor board

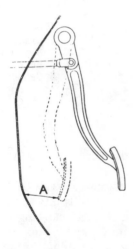

Measuring distance between brake pedal and floorboard. A=2.5″

should be not less than 2.5″. Since the front brakes are self-adjusting, only the rear brakes require adjustment.

1. Jack up the car so that the rear wheels clear the ground. It is possible to adjust the brakes without removing the wheels.

2. Release the handbrake and make sure that the brake levers return all the way. If the cable seems to bind, the levers must be returned by hand.

3. Press the brake pedal hard several times to center the brake shoes.

4. The adjusting screw for the rear brakes is the square peg located on the rear of the backing plate. Turn this adjuster, using the special wrench included in the tool kit of the car, until the wheel no longer rotates. Back off one or more notches until the wheel again rotates freely.

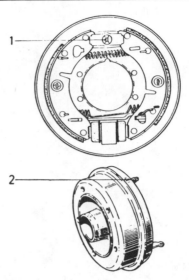

Rear brake adjusting screw (2) and adjusting device (1)

5. After adjusting, make sure that the free movement of the brake pedal is 0.12–0.24″. If the clearance is less, the brake shoes are not returning when the brake pedal is released.

6. If the adjusting screw cannot be tightened enough to lock the wheel, the brake linings are worn and must be replaced. Always change linings on both wheels at the same time. This is to be certain that braking is even. After adjusting the brakes, make sure the rear wheels turn freely.

BRAKE DRUM TURNING

If the brake drums are only moderately and equally scored, braking will not be affected to any great degree. If, on the other hand, only one drum is scored, or if both drums are severely scored, they should be replaced or machined. Replacement or machining is also necessary if the brake drum is out-of-round, a condition which manifests itself by a jerky pedal action when braking. The front drums may be machined to a maximum diameter of 9.059″ and the rear to a maximum 8.059″.

Disc Brake Service

BRAKE DISC REPLACEMENT UP TO 1966 MODELS

If the brake disc shows signs of heavy wear, it must be replaced. Moderate scoring, on the other hand, does not necessitate replacement. Never separate the two caliper

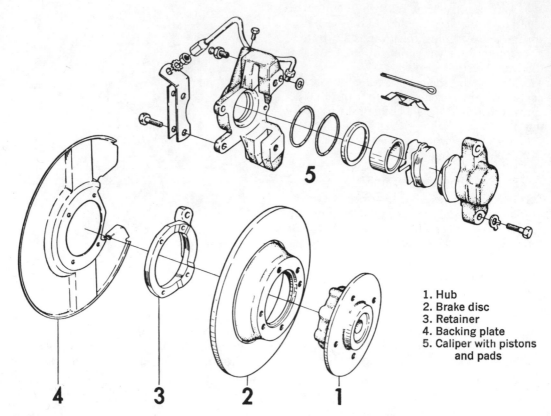

Disc brake components up to and including 1966

1. Hub
2. Brake disc
3. Retainer
4. Backing plate
5. Caliper with pistons and pads

halves except when absolutely essential. In any case, normal service can be done without dismantling the caliper.

1. Remove the hubcap and loosen the spindle nut.

2. Jack up the front of the car, take off the wheel, and remove the spindle nut.

3. Back off and remove the two bolts that hold the caliper to the steering knuckle. These bolts are accessible from inside the brake disc.

4. Lift the caliper away from the brake disc; *do not disconnect* the brake hose. Take care not to scratch the friction pads. Wire the caliper assembly to the suspension to avoid damaging the brake hose.

5. Pull off the wheel hub, with brake disc attached, using a wheel puller.

6. Remove the brake disc from the hub. Reassemble in the reverse order. Always use new tab lock plates when installing the caliper bolts.

BRAKE SQUEAL ELIMINATION—SPORT AND MONTE CARLO UP TO 1966

1. Remove the friction pads and make sure that the grooved faces of the brake pistons are pointing downwards. If they are not, rotate the pistons into the correct position using a pair of snap-ring pliers. Place the pliers inside the piston so as not to damage the outer contact surface.

2. If the noise still persists, obtain the proper shims from the dealer (anti-squeak plates), then install a shim between each brake piston and friction pad. The shim has two recesses, which should be placed downwards so as to align with the ends of the relieved faces of the pistons.

BRAKE DISC REPLACEMENT FROM 1967 MODELS

1. Remove hubcap and loosen the spindle nut.

2. Jack up the front of the car, take off the wheel and remove the spindle nut.

3. Remove the two bolts that hold the brake to the steering knuckle housing. These bolts are accessible from inside the brake disc. Lift the caliper clear of the brake disc. *Do not disconnect* the brake hose; wire the brake in such a way that the hose is not damaged.

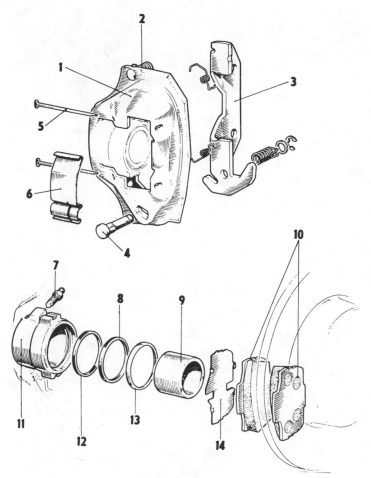

1. Brake body assembly
2. Spring-loaded steady pin
3. Support bracket
4. Hinge pin
5. Split pins
6. Spring clip
7. Bleedscrew
8. Wiper seal
9. Piston
10. Friction pad assemblies
11. Cylinder body
12. Fluid seal
13. Retainer
14. Shim

Disc brake components from 1967

4. Pull off the wheel hub, with disc attached, using a wheel puller.

5. Detach the brake disc from the wheel hub. Reassemble in reverse order. When installing the caliper bolts, always use a new tab lock plate. After assembly, pump the pedal a few times to seat the brake pistons.

FRICTION PAD REPLACEMENT—GENERAL

As the disc brakes on the SAAB Sport, Monte Carlo and SAAB 95 and 96 from 1967 are self-adjusting, it is not possible to decide by the length of the pedal stroke whether or not the linings are worn. It is, therefore, important that the wheels be removed at regular intervals to check the thickness of the linings. The friction pads should be replaced when the thickness is less than 0.06″.

PAD REPLACEMENT—SPORT AND MONTE CARLO UP TO 1966

1. Jack up the car and remove the wheel.

2. Remove the cotter pins and springs that hold the friction pads. Remove one friction pad, twisting slightly to ease removal.

3. Clean the protruding part of the brake piston with brake fluid. Make sure there is no rust or dirt in the recesses for the friction pad.

4. Drive the piston back into the caliper, using tool No. 784132 or a suitable small C-clamp. When the brake pistons are forced back into the cylinders, the brake fluid in the reservoir will be displaced; therefore the surplus should be drained.

5. Make sure that the brake piston is correctly positioned with the recess in the contact face towards the friction pad, aligned downwards. If you have to twist the brake piston into the proper position, take care not to damage its sealing surface.

6. Clean the brake disc thoroughly with a solvent which will leave no residue, such as trichloroethylene.

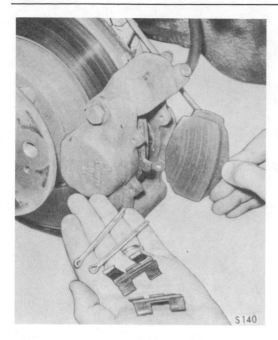

Replacing friction pads—disc brakes up to and including 1966

7. Install the new friction pad, making sure it moves easily in its recess in the caliper. Protruding parts of the friction pads can be trimmed with a file.

8. Change the other pads in the same manner.

9. Install new springs and cotter pins.

10. Pump the brake pedal a few times to seat the pads.

11. Top up brake fluid in the reservoir.

Pad Replacement—Monte Carlo and 95 and 96 Models from 1967

1. Jack up the car and remove the wheel.

2. Remove the cotter pins and the springs that hold the friction pads. Remove the friction pads.

3. Clean the exposed part of the piston, making sure there is no rust or dirt on the friction pad surfaces which contact the bracket and yoke. When cleaning, use only brake fluid or methylated spirits.

4. Drive the piston back into the brake housing, using tool No. 786043 or a small C-clamp. When the piston is forced back, the fluid in the reservoir will be displaced and it may be necessary to drain off the excess.

5. Clean the brake disc with a solvent which leaves no residue, such as Trichloroethylene.

Pressing back brake piston using tool No. 786043

6. Turn the movable brake component towards the wheel and install the outer friction pad. Make sure it moves easily in its yoke. Protruding pad parts can be trimmed with a file. If used friction pads are installed, they must be placed in their original positions.

7. Turn the movable brake component backwards as far as possible.

8. Fit anti-squeak shims to the back of the friction pads, making sure they don't exceed the contours of the pressure plate.

9. Make sure the shims are installed with the two recesses directed downwards in such a way that they are centered on the ends of the piston recess. Install the inner friction pad. Make sure that the recess in the piston is directed downwards.

10. Install the spring. The recess in the spring should be as near as possible to the outer friction pad. Install new cotter pins, the upper cotter pin first. To install the lower cotter pin, press the spring upwards using a screwdriver.

11. Pump the brake pedal a few times to seat the pads.

12. Top up the brake fluid deservoir.

Hydraulic System Service

If it becomes necessary to disassemble the hydraulic system, it must be done under extremely clean conditions. Remove all dirt and grease before removing any parts. Do not use gasoline, kerosene or similar solvents, which cause damage to rubber parts. Dismantle the units on a bench covered with a sheet of clean paper. After dismantling, place all metal parts in a tray of clean brake fluid to soak. Having done this, dry off with a clean, lint-free cloth. It is recommended that all rubber parts be replaced. Parts are readily available in the form of repair kits

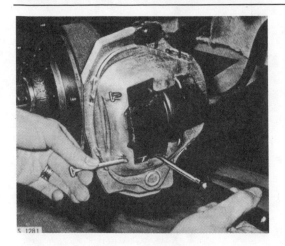

Installing friction pads

containing all the rubber parts required for each unit. When assembling, all internal parts should be dipped in brake fluid and assembled wet. When assembling rubber parts, use the fingers only, nicks caused by sharp tools will result in brake failure.

INSPECTION

For safety reasons, it is necessary to check the brake system at regular intervals as outlined in the owner's manual.

Every 6,000 Miles

1. Check the brake fluid level. (Or once every three months.)
2. Adjust the rear brakes.
3. Check the wear on brake linings and friction pads. Brake linings should be replaced when worn to a thickness of 0.06″.
4. Road test the car to check the function of the brakes.

Every 12,000 Miles

1. Check the condition of brake hoses and lines and check the master cylinder, wheel cylinders and fittings for leakage.
2. Adjust the handbrake.

Every 36,000 Miles or Every Three Years

Replace all brake hoses, rubber cups and rubber seals throughout the system; change the brake fluid.

BRAKE FLUID

Always keep the reservoir properly filled. Check the level every 6,000 miles or every three months.

Use only brake fluid meeting the minimum requirements of specification SAE 70 R 3.

For SAAB Sport and Monte Carlo 850 models, use Lockheed H D 328 brake fluid. For SAAB 95 and 96 models, use Lockheed Super Heavy Duty brake fluid.

When refilling the reservoir, always clean the cap before unscrewing it to prevent any dirt from entering the system. Be certain the air vents in the cap are not blocked.

BRAKE BLEEDING

Bleeding is not a routine procedure and is necessary only when part of the system

Location of bleedscrews, front brakes—SAAB 95 and 96 up to and including 1966

Location of bleedscrews, rear brakes—SAAB 95, 96, Sport, and Monte Carlo 850

has been disassembled or when the brake fluid has been drained. Indications that air has entered the system are excessive pedal travel, spongy pedal action or absence of braking effect until the pedal has been pumped several times.

A bleed screw is provided for each brake. Bleed screws for the disc brakes are located on the inner part of the caliper up to and including 1966, from 1967 the screws are located on the brake cylinder.

When bleeding the rear brakes on the SAAB Sport and 96 and Monte Carlo 850 up to chassis No. 400477, the pressure regulating valves will shut off the supply of brake fluid to the rear wheels if the brake pedal is depressed too hard before the bleed screw is opened.

To bleed the system, proceed as follows:

1. Check that the reservoir is full and that the air vents are not blocked.

2. Since the master cylinder has tandem pistons, it is necessary to bleed both rear wheels and both front wheels at the same time in order to purge the system. Begin with the rear wheels and bleed the front wheels afterwards.

3. Fit suitable hoses to the bleed screws.

4. Dip the hose ends into a glass jar full of clean brake fluid.

5. Back off both screws 1/2–1 turn.

6. Have another person quickly push the pedal down and allow to come up slowly.

Location of bleedscrews, front brakes—SAAB Sport and Monte Carlo up to and including 1966

Continue until escaping fluid is free of air bubbles. Keep the hose ends below the fluid level in the jars during the operation.

7. Close the bleed screws, keeping the pedal depressed.

8. Be certain the fluid in the reservoir does not run out while the system is being bled; top up as you go along.

9. Top off the reservoir after bleeding both the front and rear brakes.

CAUTION: *Discard brake fluid in the jars, as it is permeated with air.*

Master Cylinder

REMOVAL

1. Disconnect the brake outlet lines from the master cylinder.

2. Remove the rubber boot from the pushrod, or back off the locking nut and unscrew the pushrod from the clevis on the brake pedal.

3. Loosen and remove the two master cylinder retaining bolts. The lower one is a stud bolt and the nut is reached from the engine compartment. The upper one is a standard bolt, accessible from inside the car.

4. Remove the master cylinder.

INSTALLATION

1. Cover all openings to prevent the entry of dirt during installation.

2. Attach the brake cylinder to the cowl plate.

3. Install the rubber boot onto the pushrod. Reassemble the pushrod if it has been disassembled.

4. Connect the brake outlet lines and refill the system with brake fluid.

5. Adjust the brake pedal free-play.

6. Bleed the hydraulic system.

DISASSEMBLY

1. Remove the rubber boot (11) from its retaining plate (8), together with the pushrod (31). Bend the four ears of the boot retaining plate away from the mounting flange and remove it from the end of the cylinder.

2. Depress the spring retainer (30) and, using a small screwdriver, unwind the "Spirolox" circlip (29) from the groove on the primary piston, taking care not to distort the coils; remove the spring retainer (30) together with the spring (9).

3. Remove the circlip (28), taking care not to damage the surface finish of the pri-

mary piston (10). Lightly tap the mounting flange of the cylinder body on the bench and remove the nylon guide bearing (27), the secondary cup (26) and the plain washer (25).

4. Using special snap-ring pliers with long narrow jaws, tool No. 784199, remove the inner snap-ring (24), taking care not to damage the surface finish of the primary piston (10).

5. Removal of the snap-ring (24) will allow both pistons to be withdrawn together with the piston stop (23).

6. Compress the intermediate spring (18), together with spring holder (20), then drive out the retaining pin (19) using a suitable pin punch. This will separate the two pistons (10 and 14), and allow the withdrawal of spring (18) and spring holder (20).

7. Remove the primary cups (12 and 21), together with the piston washers (13 and 22), from the primary and secondary pistons. Remove the secondary cup (15) from the back of the secondary piston. Do not attempt to remove the clip (17) from the secondary piston, as it is permanently peened in position.

8. Unscrew the outlet adapters (46) and remove them with the gaskets.

9. Remove the one-way valves—the spring (41), valve body (42) and spring clip (44). Take care not to distort the spring clip (44) when removing it from the valve body.

10. Remove the six bolts that hold the cover of the brake fluid reservoir (5), then take off the cover and gasket.

Inspection

1. Make sure the cylinder bore is not scored.

2. Check the bypass holes; probe with a thin piece of steel piano wire.

3. Check all parts; replace any defective ones. Internal rubber parts should be replaced in any event.

Assembly

Before assembling, dip all parts in brake fluid.

1. Using the fingers only, stretch the secondary cup (15) over the large end of the secondary piston, with the lip pointing toward the peened clip. Gently work around the cup with the fingers to ensure correct seating.

2. Install the piston washer onto the secondary piston, as illustrated, so that the convex edge faces the rear of the cup. Using the fingers only, ease the primary cup (12) over the nose and into the groove, with the lip of the cup pointing away from the head of the piston.

3. Use the same procedure with the primary cup (21) and piston washer (22) of the primary piston. Ease the spring holder (20) into the end of the spring (18) and fit the other end of the spring over the rear of the secondary piston (14).

4. Place the retaining pin (19) in the hole in the primary piston; do not seat fully. Compress the spring until the secondary piston clip (17) is visible. Place the clip in position in the primary piston and secure it by pushing the retaining pin fully home. Release the spring and check that the spring holder (20) is correctly positioned.

5. Ease the pistons gently into the cylinder bore and slide the piston stop (23) over the primary piston. Install the snap-ring (24) into the inner groove, using snap-ring pliers. Do not damage the surface finish of the primary piston because this could cause leakage past the secondary cup.

6. Install the plain washer (25) into the cylinder bore against the snap-ring, followed by the secondary cup (26).

7. Place the nylon guide bearing (27) in position and secure the outer snap-ring (28).

8. Fit the boot retaining plate (8) in position over the mounting flange and bend the four ears over to hold it in position.

9. Mount the spring retainer (30) with the return spring (9) on the primary piston (10). Compress the spring until the piston circlip groove is visible behind the spring retainer, then install the "Spirolox" circlip. Before installing the rubber boot (11), smear the small end of the pushrod (31) and its groove with silicone grease to ensure that the rod will rotate freely when assembled.

10. Ease the pushrod into position in the rubber boot and push the boot into its groove.

11. Ease the spring clip (44) into the one-way valve body and make sure that it is correctly positioned. Install the return spring over the valve body and assemble the parts within the outlet port, inserting the spring first.

12. Screw the outlet adapter (46), together with gasket (45), into the outlet port and tighten to a torque of 28 ft. lbs. Use the same procedure for the other outlet port.

13. Place the cover of the brake fluid reservoir (5) in position, with the gasket, and secure using the six bolts, tightening them to a torque of 6 ft. lbs.

Brake Lines

The brake lines are made of 3/16″ Bundy tubing. The ends of all the lines are flanged and fitted with compression nuts, which must be pushed onto the line before the ends are flanged. All lines, rubber hoses and fittings in the brake system must be kept in good condition at all times.

New lines must fit well at both ends and at the clips. Never stretch a too short line or bend a previously installed line. Such procedures could result in stresses, which could cause leakage, line fracture or stripped threads.

Lines for connection to brake hoses are flanged as "type A"; other lines are flanged as "type B."

Brake Hoses

The brake system has two front and two rear brake hoses, providing a flexible connection between the body and the wheel cylinders. These hoses are of different lengths and must not be confused. Install the hoses with the wheels freely suspended and aligned straight ahead. When tightening the brake line, hold the brake hose (not the locknut) to prevent the hose from twisting and changing position. When installing hoses it is of extreme importance that they are correctly positioned so that they do not rub steering or suspension components or the body.

Stop Light Switch

The stop light switch is connected to the hydraulic system and is actuated by hydraulic pressure. It is found in a four-way coupling on the firewall beside the master cylinder.

From chassis No. 439334 for SAAB 96, and 46816 for SAAB 95, a mechanical stoplight switch is utilized. This switch is located on a bracket above the brake pedal.

Pressure Regulating Valve

The SAAB 96, Sport and Monte Carlo 850 up to and including the 1966 model, are equipped with two pressure regulating valves for the rear brakes.

The valves are bolted to the floor under the rear seat, and serve to limit the hydraulic pressure to the rear brakes so that the braking effect is properly distributed between the front and rear wheels. The valve is set for a given pressure and cannot be adjusted. When the pressure reaches 425–485 psi, the spring force acting on the piston is overcome, causing the piston to travel and close the passage to the rear brakes. Any additional pressure increases the effect of the front brakes, while the pressure on the rear brakes remains constant.

Wheel Cylinders

SAAB 95 AND 96 UP TO AND INCLUDING 1966—FRONT

The front wheel cylinders contain a single piston with a rubber sealing ring and an external rubber boot. The piston is forced toward the brake shoe by the fluid pressure.

Each of the rear wheel cylinders has two pistons which actuate separate brake shoes. Each piston is fitted with a rubber sealing ring and an external rubber boot.

Removal

1. Jack up the car and remove the wheel, brake drum, brake shoes, and backing plate.
2. Disconnect the brake hose from the wheel cylinder.
3. Disconnect the brake hose between the cylinders.
4. Remove the cylinder by unscrewing the bolts from the rear of the backing plate.

Disassembly

The illustration shows a dismantled wheel cylinder. Remove the rubber boot from the cylinder, withdraw the piston and take off the sealing ring.

Inspection

1. Clean all parts with brake fluid. Do not allow gasoline or oil to come into contact with the rubber sealing rings or boots.
2. Make sure the cylinder bore is not scored.
3. Check that the rubber sealing rings and boots are in good condition. The use of unsuitable brake fluids can cause rubber parts to swell up to 50%. Any rubber parts that are even slightly damaged or swollen must be replaced.

Assembly

Lubricate all parts with brake fluid before assembling. Install a cup onto the piston, taking care to align it as illustrated. Use the fingers only. Next, install the piston into the cylinder and put on the rubber boot.

Installation

1. Attach the cylinders to the backing plate with the bolts; don't forget the elastic washers.
2. Reinstall the brake line between the cylinders.
3. Secure the brake hose. Remember to insert the copper gasket.
4. Refit the backing plate, brake shoes, brake drum, and wheel.

SAAB 95 and 96, Sport and Monte Carlo 850—Rear

From chassis No. 400478, the SAAB 96 and Monte Carlo are equipped with smaller wheel cylinders at the rear than those of the SAAB 95. The location of their anchor pins differs from the 95 to prevent crossover. The anchor pin must not be removed.

Removal

1. Remove the wheel, brake drum and brake shoes.
2. Disconnect the handbrake cable from the levers.
3. Disconnect the brake line from the rear of the backing plate.
4. Remove the wheel cylinder retaining ring and the bleed screw from the rear of the backing plate.
5. Remove the wheel cylinder.

Disassembly

1. Remove the rubber boots from the cylinder.
2. Pull out the pistons.
3. Take the rubber seals off the pistons.

Inspection

1. Clean and dry all parts. Do not allow gasoline or grease to come in contact with the rubber seals.
2. Make sure the cylinder bore is not scored.
3. Check that all the rubber seals and cups are in perfect condition.

Assembly

Utmost cleanliness must be observed when assembling the wheel cylinder. Lubricate all parts with brake fluid when assembling. Assemble, as shown in the illustration, making certain the piston seal is facing the correct way; use no sharp tools.

Installation

1. Bolt the wheel cylinder to the backing plate and locate the retaining ring and bleed screw. The cylinder has an anchor pin which fits in a hole in the backing plate.
2. Connect the brake line.
3. Install the brake shoes, brake drum and wheel, taking care not to damage the axle seal.
4. Connect the handbrake cable. The handbrake lever must be installed with the bent part upwards. Bleed the system whenever a cylinder has been removed or a line disconnected.

Brake Pedal Free-Play Adjustment

In order to allow the piston in the master cylinder to return fully each time the pedal is released, there always must be clearance between the master cylinder piston and the brake pedal pushrod when the pedal is at rest. This clearance should be measured at the tip of the pedal, and should be 0.12–0.24″.

1. Loosen the locknut.
2. Turn the hexagonal section of the pushrod until the correct clearance is obtained.
3. Tighten the locknut.

Handbrake Adjustment

Adjustment of the handbrake lever travel or of the brake cables always should be preceded by adjustment of the rear brakes. If the handbrake still requires adjustment, proceed as follows:

1. Jack up the car so that both rear wheels clear the floor.
2. Remove the right front seat and move the lever to its lowest position.
3. Tighten the left-hand adjusting nut until the brake shoes contact the left brake drum.
4. Back off the nut just enough to permit the wheel to rotate, then back off one more full turn.
5. Repeat this procedure for the right-hand adjusting nut.

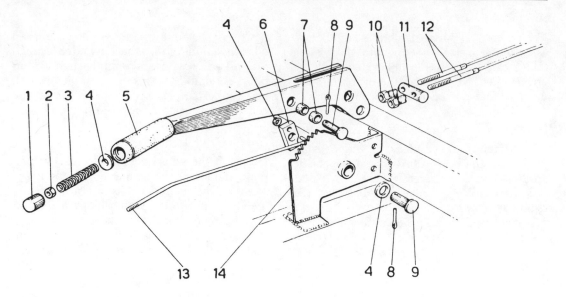

Handbrake components

1. Release button	6. Pawl	11. Cable pin
2. Nut	7. Spacer sleeve	12. Threaded wire rods
3. Return spring	8. Cotter pin or circlip	13. Pawl rod
4. Washer	9. Pin	14. Ratchet
5. Handbrake lever	10. Adjustment nut	

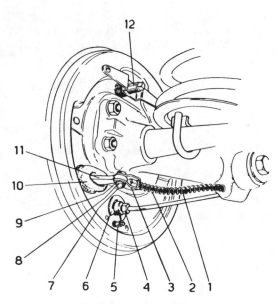

Reverse side of left-rear backing plate

1. Handbrake wire	7. Pin
2. Coil spring	8. Cotter pin
3. Clevis	9. Washer
4. Brake pipe connection	10. Rubber Boot
5. Bleed nipple	11. Brake lever
6. Lock washer	12. Adjustment device

6. Test by pulling the handbrake all the way on, then releasing it. The wheels should still rotate freely with the lever pulled up two notches from off, but should be locked at the third-notch.

7. Make sure the braking effect is equal for both wheels.

Brakes—V4

The major difference between the brakes used on the 1969–70 V4 and previous models is that a power brake unit is used. It consists of a vacuum cylinder, which is actuated by the brake pedal. A hose connects the cylinder to the intake manifold of the engine. The operation of the system is described below.

INITIAL POSITION

When "off," the return spring holds the valve piston and the pushrod in the right-hand end position in the guide housing. In this position, the atmospheric air bore is kept closed and the vacuum bore open. Since the right-hand side of the diaphragm is connected with the left-hand side via the open vacuum bore in the guide housing, the pressure is equal on both sides of the diaphragm.

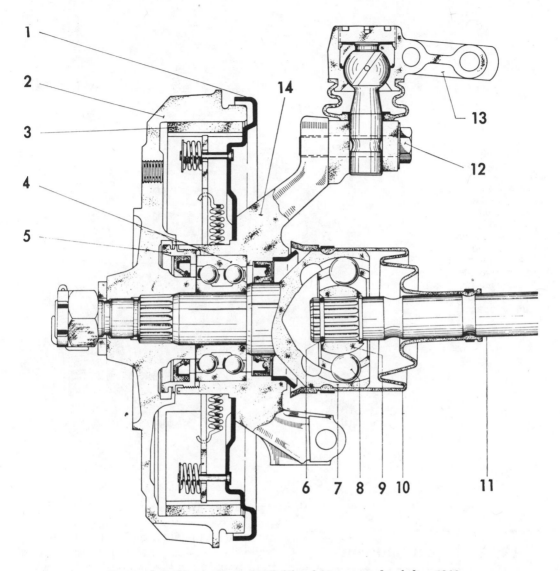

Front axle and suspension—SAAB 95 and 96 up to and including 1966

1. Backing plate	5. Nut	9. Hub	13. Ball joint
2. Brake drum	6. Lock ring	10. Rubber bellows	14. Steering knuckle
3. Brake shoe	7. Outer driveshaft	11. Inner driveshaft	housing
4. Ball bearing	8. Ball	12. Bolt	

BRAKE POSITION

When the pedal is pressed, the vacuum bore closes and the atmospheric air bore opens, overcoming the tension of the return spring. Vacuum on the left-hand side of the diaphragm, and atmospheric pressure on the right-hand side, results in servo action being obtained. The brake effect can be increased further by greater pressure on the pedal.

When the pedal pressure drops, the return spring forces the valve piston back. The vacuum bore then opens and the atmospheric air bore closes. The vacuum servo returns to its "off" position.

Should the power brake unit malfunction, the brake system in the car will still function without servo effect. CAUTION: *Individual parts are not available for the vacuum servo and the unit is not serviceable.*

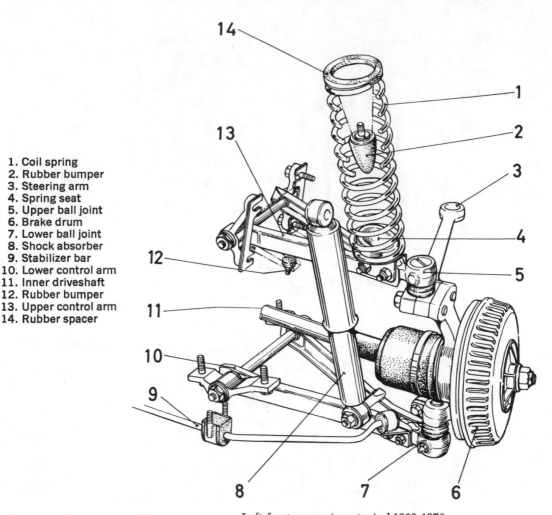

1. Coil spring
2. Rubber bumper
3. Steering arm
4. Spring seat
5. Upper ball joint
6. Brake drum
7. Lower ball joint
8. Shock absorber
9. Stabilizer bar
10. Lower control arm
11. Inner driveshaft
12. Rubber bumper
13. Upper control arm
14. Rubber spacer

Left-front suspension—typical 1960-1970

Part II—Suspension

All four wheels have coil springs. Each front wheel is attached to a steering knuckle, which is suspended on ball joints between two conventional A-frames (transverse control arms). The inner ends of these control arms are supported by rubber-clad bearings on the body and the vertical coil spring. Wheel travel is limited by rubber bumbers.

Steering Knuckle

A large, forged steering knuckle forms a frame for the front axle, its principal components being a bearing housing with two inward-inclined arms, an upper and a lower. The outer driveshaft is carried in a ball bearing enclosed in the bearing housing. The wheel hub and brake drum or disc are mounted on the outer end of the driveshaft, while the backing plate or caliper, with its front brake assembly, is bolted to the steering knuckle.

Ball joints are attached to the steering knuckle arms, where they provide flexible connections for the ends of the control arms. The steering arm, to which the tie-rod is connected, is located on the upper steering knuckle arm. The outer and inner driveshafts are interconnected through the outer universal joint, the turning center of which is on the king pin axis. A pleated rubber boot prevents dirt and foreign matter from entering the outer universal joint and contains the grease for that joint. The inner universal joint is located on the stub of the differential output shaft.

The SAAB Sport, Monte Carlo 850, and SAAB 95 and 96 from 1967 have disc brakes on the front wheels. The wheels on the

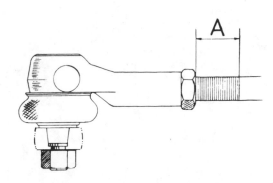

CHECKING THE LENGTH OF A TIE-ROD WITHOUT KEY GRIP

> **NOTE!**
> After adjustment of toe-in, the measurement A for a tie-rod of the old design must on no account exceed 1.57 in. (40 mm).
> For tie-rods opposed to each other, the difference between the measurements "A" must not exceed 0.08 in. (2 mm).

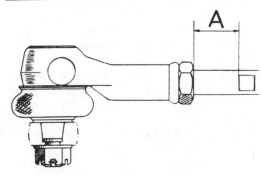

CHECKING THE LENGTH OF A TIE-ROD WITH KEY GRIP

> **NOTE!**
> After adjustment of toe-in, the measurement A for a tie-rod of the new design must on no account exceed 1.18 in. (30 mm).
> For tie-rods opposed to each other, the difference between the measurments "A" must not exceed 0.08 in. (2 mm).

latter models are different from those used on the SAAB 95 and 96 up to and including 1966. Other components, such as the control arms with their ball joints and rubber bearings, the coil springs and rubber bumpers, and the stabilizer bar, are the same as used on the 1966 model. The front wheel alignment is also identical. The Sonett suspension is identical, with the exception of the stabilizer bar, which is omitted on this model.

The SAAB Sport and Monte Carlo 850, up to and including 1966, features a special hub, to which the brake disc is bolted. The wheel is secured to the wheel hub with only four bolts. The steering knuckle, which is identical to that on the SAAB 95 and 96, carries a holder for the brake housing.

Wheel Alignment

It is of the utmost importance that the front wheels be correctly aligned, since incorrect steering geometry can cause:

1. Driver fatigue, due to impaired roadability.
2. Difficulty in keeping the car under control.
3. Increased tire and repair costs due to abnormal wear of tires and steering components.

CHECKING AND ADJUSTMENT

Before adjusting, the following items should be attended to:

1. Check that the tire pressure is correct on all wheels and that the tires are not too unevenly worn.
2. Check the front wheel bearings, control arm bushings, ball joints and tie-rod ends, adjusting or replacing as necessary to eliminate errors that can be caused by worn parts.
3. Check the steering gear and adjust any faults.
4. Check the function of the shock absorbers and renew any defective shock absorbers and rubber bushings.
5. If the car has been involved in an accident, driven into a ditch, etc., any damage incurred must be repaired before checking the front alignment. Bent steering arms must be replaced—straightening is not safe practice.
6. Immediately before checking, road test the car, without hard cornering, to seat the suspension components and provide a basis for evaluation of any changes made. During alignment, the car must be unloaded and on a flat surface.

TOE-IN

Toe-in is the difference between measurements taken at the forward extremes of the tires and the rearward extremes of the tires.

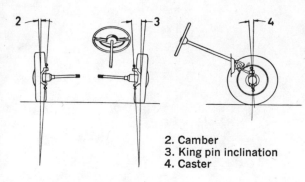

2. Camber
3. King pin inclination
4. Caster

Front wheel alignment

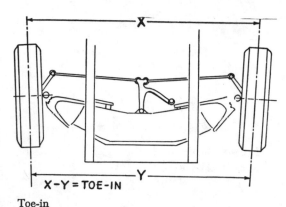

X−Y = TOE-IN

Toe-in

In the illustration, this is shown as the difference between X and Y.

The correct setting is 0.08″ ± 0.04″ (i.e., measurement Y should be 0.04–0.12″ less than measurement X). Toe-in is adjusted by changing the length of the tie-rod with the wheels in the straight-ahead position. Toe-in is 0.04″ ± 0.04″ for Sonett II models.

CAMBER

Camber is the amount, expressed in degrees, that the front wheels are inclined outward at the top. The purpose of camber is to take some of the load from the outboard spindle bearing. If the wheel is tilted outward at the top, the camber is positive; if inward, the camber is negative. The correct camber for SAAB models is $+3/4° ±1/4°$, with the exception of the Sonett II, which requires $0° ±1/4°$.

CASTER

Caster is the amount that the king pin is tilted toward the rear of the car, expressed in degrees. Positive caster means that the top of the king pin is tilted towards the rear; negative caster that the top is tilted towards the front. The correct caster setting for SAAB models, including the Sonett II, is $+2° ±1/2°$.

Chapter 8

Competition Tuning

Part I—Two-Stroke Models

To prepare a car for competition, two primary areas must be improved—power and handling. A third area—safety—also must be considered when making any modifications.

Before beginning, make sure to thoroughly investigate all the pertinent rules and regulations for the particular type of competition. Another thing to remember is that each car is different and must be prepared on an individual basis. General procedures that work for one car may not work on another; some experimentation with the following procedures may be necessary to achieve the desired results.

Power

Power can be increased by altering the cylinder head to increase compression and by modifying the intake, exhaust, and transfer ports to increase breathing efficiency. Modifying the ports on a two-stroke engine is equivalent to installing a high-performance camshaft in a four-stroke engine.

The following procedures are arranged in three groups—Stage I is a mild tuning procedure for the street or gymkhanas; Stage II is for hillclimbs, sprint races, ice races, or other events where major modifications are permitted; and Stage III is for all-out competition.

850 cc. Engine to 1965

STAGE I

Stage I tuning consists entirely of carburetor and exhaust system modifications. Re-jet the carburetor, depending on whether a GT (2.01″ diameter) exhaust system and a modified air filter is used.

	Std. Filter and Exhaust	Modified Filter and GT Exhaust
Air throat	28 mm.	31 mm.
Main jet	135	145–150
Emulsion jet	250	250
Fuel idle jet	45	45
Air idle jet	100	100

STAGE II

Increase compression by milling the cylinder head (9.5:1). After milling, check the piston crown-to-cylinder head clearance—it must be at least 0.73 mm. (0.0285″). The combustion chambers can be flycut to correct clearance. Grind the ports to the dimensions shown in the chart, then polish and smooth the surfaces. The exhaust ports are ground upwards, as are the transfer ports, while the intake ports are extended

151

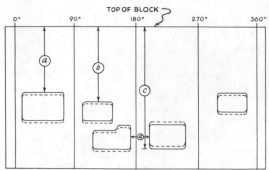

NOTE: ⓐ equals 10mm. Dotted lines are stock port positions

Engine	Exhaust ports raised ⓐ mm	Transfer ports raised ⓑ mm	Intake ports lowered ⓒ mm
850 to '65 STAGE II	47	57	96
850 to '65 STAGE III	46	56	97
750 STAGE II	46.4	57	96.2
750 STAGE III	45.7	56.8	97.8
850 1965-66	44	56	99

Port modifications—two-stroke engine

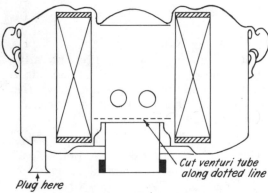

Cut venturi tube along dotted line

Plug here

Modify air intake as below

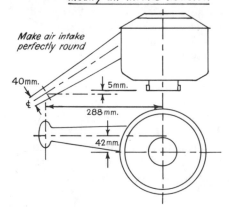

Make air intake perfectly round

40mm.

5mm.

288mm.

42mm.

Air cleaner modifications

downwards. All measurements are taken between the edge of the port and the top surface of the cylinder block.

Ignition modifications are simple—use a Bosch VJ3BR7 distributor in conjunction with copper spark plug wires and a Bosch TK12A1D ignition coil. The ignition timing can be varied, but is best set at TDC with this set-up.

Modify the air cleaner as illustrated. The 1965 air filter does not have to be modified, however. Polish the carburetor barrel, then re-jet the carburetor as follows:

Air throat	31 mm.
Main jet	150–155
Fuel idle jet	50
Fuel air jet	50

STAGE III

Increase compression by milling the cylinder head 4.5 mm. (0.177″). The combustion chambers must be flycut afterwards to maintain a piston crown-to-cylinder head clearance of 0.73 mm. (0.0285″). Grind the ports to the dimensions shown in the chart, then polish and smooth the surfaces. The exhaust ports are ground upward, as are the transfer ports, while the intake ports are extended downward. All measurements are taken between the edge of the ports and the top surface of the cylinder block. The amount of material removed in this operation requires that certain care be taken to ensure adequate wall thickness. This can be checked through the coolant passages.

Standard crankshaft

A great increase in power can be achieved by installing the GT crankshaft. This crankshaft has larger, full-diameter counterweights which take up more space in the crankcase than the stock unit. In a two-stroke engine, this decrease in crankcase

GT crankshaft—note filled counterweights

volume serves to increase compression.

Carburetion should be increased by replacing the stock unit with one of the three-carburetor systems or the single Solex dual-throat 44PII.

Use a Bosch VJ3BR7 distributor, a Bosch TK12A1 ignition coil, copper spark plug wires, and Bosch M310T1 spark plugs for best results. Set ignition timing to TDC.

It is advisable to install a Bendix electric fuel pump to prevent fuel starvation at high rpm. Install pistons at 0.0035–0.0040″ clearance to prevent galling, and use only SAAB two-stroke oil and high-test (at least 97 octane) gasoline.

Pay particular attention to the head torque sequence, after milling the head, to prevent gasket blowing. Initial tightening torque is 35 ft. lbs.—this should be rechecked at 300, 600, and 1,200 miles if the car is used on the street; or before every competition meet.

If 6,000 rpm is exceeded very often, the stock front vibration damper tends to become out-of-round. Since this quite often causes destruction of the front bearing (and crankshaft), a tachometer is recommended. The proper hook-up for the three-cylinder engine is illustrated.

750 cc. Engine

The 750 cc. engine responds to the same modifications as does the 850 cc. engine up to 1965. Port timing is shown in the chart.

850 cc. Engine—1965–66

Modify the ports, as previously described, according to the illustration and chart. An

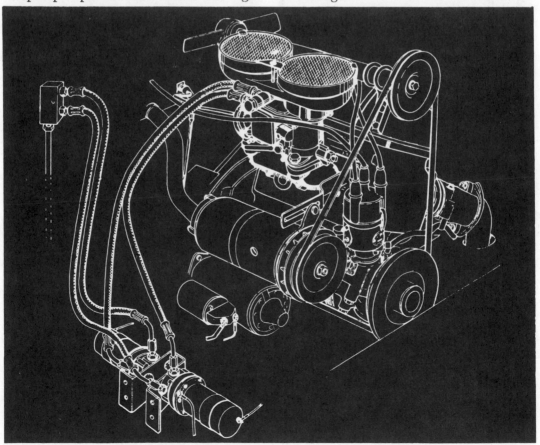

Solex dual-throat 44 PII carburetor and twin fuel pump hook-up

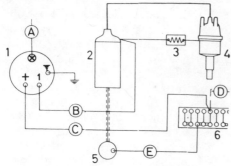

Tachometer installation schematic—two-stroke engines

1. Tachometer
2. Ignition coil
3. Resistance
4. Distributor
5. Ignition switch
6. Fuse block
A. Instrument lamp lead
B. Lead between coil and terminal 1 on Tach
C. Lead between fuse block (fuel pump) and terminal on Tach
D. Lead to fuel pump
E. Lead from ignition switch to fuse block

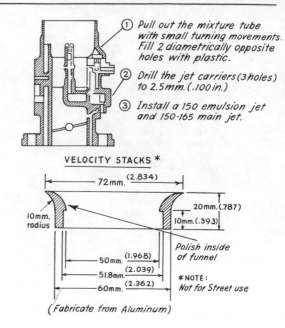

① Pull out the mixture tube with small turning movements. Fill 2 diametrically opposite holes with plastic.

② Drill the jet carriers (3 holes) to 2.5mm. (.100 in.)

③ Install a 150 emulsion jet and 150-165 main jet.

VELOCITY STACKS *

72mm. (2.834)
10mm. radius
20mm. (.787)
10mm. (.393)
Polish inside of funnel
50mm. (1.968)
51.8mm. (2.039)
60mm. (2.362)
* NOTE: Not for Street use

(Fabricate from Aluminum)

Carburetor modifications

especially critical area on this engine, where care must be exercised during grinding, is the water jacket directly above the exhaust ports. Smooth and polish all port areas after grinding.

Mill the head 3.0 mm. (0.1182″), then flycut the combustion chambers to maintain a piston crown-to-cylinder head clearance of 0.73 mm. (0.0285″).

When tightening the head bolts, first pre-tighten to 22 ft. lbs., then turn an additional 90°. Start the engine, allow it to warm up to operating temperature, then let it cool down and turn the head bolts an additional 20°. If the car is used on the street, tighten an additional 20° after 1,000 miles with a cold engine, or after one or two competition meets.

Grind the intake and exhaust manifolds to match the ports and gaskets, then smooth and polish the inside runners.

Modify the carburetor according to the illustration, then re-jet as follows:

	Stage I & II	Stage III (with velocity stack)
Main jet	155	160–165
Air correction	150	150

To adjust the float level, use a different shim under the needle valve; never bend the float arm. To check the level:

1. Remove the air cleaner.
2. Start the engine and allow it to idle for 30 seconds, then turn off the ignition without touching the gas pedal.
3. Loosen the fuel lines and remove the top of the float chamber and the float.
4. Measure between the gasket surface and the fuel level, alongside the carburetor barrel, using a depth gauge—the proper level is 24.5± 1 mm. (0.9653± 0.039″).

Modify the air cleaner as illustrated. Since the preheater tube no longer operates after this modification, it may be necessary to add 2–4% isopropyl alcohol to the fuel to prevent carburetor icing under some weather conditions.

Modify the exhaust system as illustrated. For Stage I tune, the stock tailpipe can be used; for Stages II and III, a 6 1/2 foot long by 2″ diameter extension is recommended. This "straight" pipe must be so arranged to exit just behind the rear of the door.

Use copper spark plug wires, lock the ignition advance, and install a double contact breaker spring. It is also a good idea to exchange the fiber shims for steel washers (in the distributor).

When assembling the distributor, make sure there is at least 0.004″ axial shaft play, measured with a feeler gauge under the drive gear. Set the ignition timing to 20° BTDC for a start, then work from there.

For maximum vibration damper life, do not exceed 6,300 rpm. The torsional vibra-

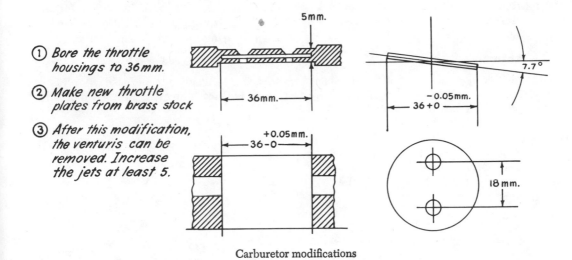

① Bore the throttle housings to 36mm.

② Make new throttle plates from brass stock

③ After this modification, the venturis can be removed. Increase the jets at least 5.

5mm.

36mm.

7.7°

−0.05mm.
36 +0

+0.05mm.
36 −0

18 mm.

Carburetor modifications

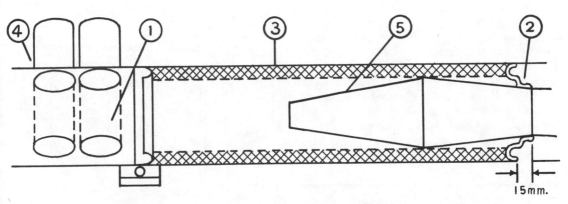

15mm.

1· Remove the exhaust tubes from the inside.

2· Cut the inlet pipe at the weld and remove 110mm. (4.33 in.) of the pipe leading into the cone so the taper starts at 15mm. (.590 in.) before the inlet end of the muffer.

3· Remove the glass wool and perforated sheet tube.

4· Weld reinforcing gussets to the outlet pipes.

5· Existing cone with 80 holes moved outward 4.33 in.

Exhaust system modifications

tion damper should be inspected at regular intervals. If necessary, replace the rubber disc and the damper spring (1.125″).

Handling

There are so many opinions as to how to set up a SAAB suspension that no one procedure can be specifically prescribed. See the V4 section on handling for specific parts numbers.

Springs

The SAAB can be made to handle quite a bit better by lowering the entire car. The best way to accomplish this is to cut the coil springs 1–1/2—3 turns each. Never heat the springs in order to collapse them, as this is an unsafe practice. Coil springs are under considerable compression when installed, and can be dangerous if removed without proper precautions. Always use a good coil spring compressor, especially on the front coils. It is easier to remove the rear coils by first removing the limit straps and shocks, then lowering the rear axle far enough to release most of the compression.

Shock Absorbers

Many different shock absorbers and shock absorber combinations can be, and have been, used. The best all-around answer to the problem is to install Koni adjustable shock absorbers at all four wheels. These shock absorbers have a wide variety of adjustment combinations, which the driver can use to advantage by tailoring the handling to each specific course.

Wheels and Tires

The greatest single handling improvement can be achieved by using wider tread tires, in conjunction with wider reinforced rims. The choice of racing tires is quite wide, and care should be exercised so as not to select a tire too large in diameter for the available power. Depending on track conditions, any number of tire types and tread patterns can be successful. Racing tire distributors are probably the best source of information as to the type of tire that has been proven most successful at local tracks and, of course, a look at what the competition is using also may be a help.

Part II—V4 Models

Power

The V4 engine responds to modification in much the same way as does any four-stroke engine—increased power with slightly reduced reliability and tractability. Procedures are listed in this chapter can be performed either entirely, or in part, depending on the stage of tune desired for the particular competition. Remember, any of these modifications tend to increase the exhaust emissions above the minimum levels established for each year car; therefore the car should not be driven on the street if at all possible.

ENGINE BLOCK

It is not necessary to mill the block to increase compression, simply file or sand the decks lightly to remove any burrs, then lightly chamfer all machined surfaces. Have the block "hot tanked" before beginning assembly, because metal chips and dust often lodge in inaccessible places. These

chips, if allowed to remain, will eventually circulate through the lubrication system and cause bearing and crankshaft damage.

CYLINDER HEADS

Mill the heads to increase compression ratio. Do not, however, remove more than

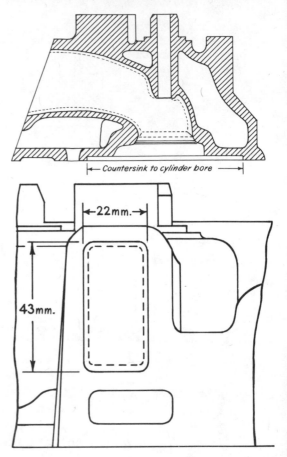

← Countersink to cylinder bore →

The intake ports are opened up as illustrated. The dotted lines show the original size and shape of the ports. If more than 0.040″ is milled from the heads or block, the intake manifold must be machined to match. If the block is milled 2.5 mm. (0.0985″) the seating surfaces must be milled 1.5 mm. (0.0591″) to match. Cut valve seat width to 0.0472-0.0623″ for intake valves, 0.0632-0.0787″ for exhaust valves.

0.040″ from each head or the intake manifold will have to be machined to mate properly with the heads. Porting and polishing results in better gas flow, thus more power. If the 1 3/4″ exhaust system is to be used (which it should for maximum power), machine the exhaust ports to 1 3/4″ as per the illustration. Machine the flange that goes between the head and exhaust pipe to 1 3/4″ as well, then enlarge the bolt holes and use gasket No. 707712.

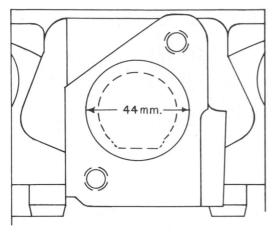

Open up the exhaust ports to 44 mm. (1.732″), as well as the manifold flange. Use gasket No. 707712, after enlarging the bolt holes.

Oversize Valves

The ports must be modified if oversize valves are to be used. Machine the intake ports "funnel shaped" with the top port diameter, directly below the seat, opened out to 1.575″. The ports should be machined to 1.250″ in diameter about 1/4″ below the seat, then all sharp corners should be removed and the ports polished.

Machine the exhaust port "funnel shaped" with the top port diameter, directly below the seat, opened out to 1.275″. The port should be machined to 1.150″ in diameter about 1/4″ below the seat, then all sharp corners should be removed and the ports polished.

POLISH

SMOOTH

1.6-2.0 mm.

1.2-1.6 mm.

RADIUS .4-.5 mm.

Valves should be polished to remove all roughness. Radius the bottom edge to achieve a seating surface of 0.0157-0.0197″ from the outer edge. Cut the seats as described in the text.

The valve guides *must* be knurled to obtain proper stem-to-guide clearance (very light thumb press fit), then the seats must be ground. Grind the intake seats so that the width is 0.050″; the exhaust seat width must be wider to accommodate the increased temperatures in that area—0.065″.

The oversize valves must be machined and polished as per the illustration, then they must be adjusted as follows (depending on camshaft used):

3/4 race cam:	0.016H	(intake)
	0.018H	(exhaust)
Full race cam:	0.018H	(intake)
	0.020H	(exhaust)
Track grind cam:	0.020H	(intake)
	0.024H	(exhaust)

Use intake valve part No. 11000, exhaust valve part No. 11010.

Valve Train

The pushrods need no modification, nor should any be attempted. The valve springs should be replaced with part No. 11250, and aluminum retainers, part No. 11300, used.

For best results, install full-floating Teflon valve guide seals. These seals are available from SAAB under competition part No. 11020. To install these seals, a special tool (part No. 11021) is required. The valve guide must be machined as well, to provide sufficient clearance between the spring retainer and the new seal when the valve is fully open. Cut the guide down to 0.425″ from the spring seat to obtain this clearance.

The stock valve lifters should be discarded and lighter competition lifters, part No. 12100, installed.

Carburetor

If the car is used in events where major modifications are not permitted, use an early Solex (part No. 786638) single-barrel unit; this carburetor does not have exhaust emission settings. Remove the venturi from this carburetor and install 195–200 main jet for best results.

For more performance, use a Weber two-barrel 28/36 DCD carburetor (part No. 15000). A special two-barrel manifold is available from SAAB under part No. 14001. This particular carburetor and manifold is also available in a complete Stage I tuning kit, along with a chromed air filter, vented oil cap, and necessary linkage and gaskets.

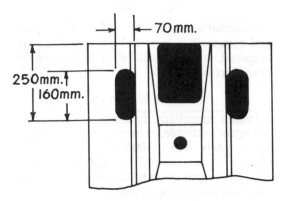

The exhaust pipe openings in the floor pan must be enlarged to accommodate the larger diameter exhaust pipe. All dimensions are in mm.

petition encountered, and even individual courses, the following list of modifications should serve only as a guide to better handling. This list shows what the factory does to its rally cars—the owner can decide which modifications to include in his own car.

CHASSIS

The chassis is lightened as much as possible, while making sure the car retains its structural soundness. The entire chassis floor is spot welded closer than on a standard SAAB, and all undercoating is removed to save weight.

SUSPENSION

The springs in the front are replaced with rally springs (No. 40100) and Ferodo 2430 pads are used on the front discs. The rear axle (No. 40200) is more thoroughly welded at all points, especially at the center bushing, shock absorber mounts, and control arm attaching points. In addition, the axle tube is made of heavier gauge tubing. The rear control arms and the tubes that attach the control arms to the chassis are made of heavier stock as well, and the control arms are more thoroughly welded. Heavy-duty shock absorbers are used on the rear.

It would be most impractical for the average enthusiast to make up a set of special rear control arms and a heavier axle tube; therefore it is recommended that these two items be bought from SAAB. Their cost is low compared to the effort of making new parts from scratch.

FRONT END

Modifications to the front end are concerned mainly with reinforcing the points where fracture is most likely to occur. Reinforcing plates are added to both the inside and outside sections of the upper shock mountings, and extra welding is done in these areas. Plates are welded on the outside of the spring towers where they attach to the floor pan, and plates are welded around the holes where the upper A-arms go through the inner fender panels.

The A-arm beams are reinforced underneath (the ones that hold the rubber bumpers) and reinforcement is added behind the upper spring supports (No. 730062) where they are attached to the chassis. The front spring support (No. 730062) is made of heavier stock and is more thoroughly welded than on standard cars, and channel-type reinforcement is added where the inner fender panels attach to the outer fenders above the spring towers. Plates are welded around the holes where the steering arms come through, and heavy gauge washers are added where the rubber bumpers (No. 707601) attach to the spring brackets. Plates also are added where the upper and lower A-arms attach to the chassis.

REAR FLOOR PAN

Reinforcement plates are welded to the floor pan where the rear axle control arms attach to the chassis, and a plate is added where the center axle bushing attaches to the chassis.

NOTE: *Cars are available from SAAB built to the above specifications. These cars are built for competition only, thus do not have a warranty. Also, the drive train and engine is standard to meet the emission laws, and the engine must be modified separately. Price for the car is approximately $2,800.*

SAAB High-Performance Parts

The following list is compiled from the latest information available. Although list prices are noted, it must be kept in mind that SAAB prices are subject to change, and that this list cannot be construed to be official in any way. Any inquiries should be sent to the local SAAB dealer, or: SAAB Competition Department, 100 Waterfront Street, New Haven, Conn. 06506, phone 203-469-2331 extension 293.

11000 42 mm. oversize intake valve $4.49
Enlargement of intake port is required by machining. Modification should only be performed by a professional machine shop. Valve guides must be knurled to insure proper valve stem clearance and life.

11010 35 mm. oversize exhaust valve $7.28 ea.
Enlargement of exhaust port is required by machining. Modification should only be performed by a professional machine shop. Valve guides must be knurled to insure valve stem clearance and life.

11020 full floating teflon $7.80
      valve guide seals (set of 8)
Machining of the valve guide is required by using cutting tool 11021. The metal housing which holds the spring loaded teflon seal is then press fitted over the guide. Oil leaking past poor valve guide seals pollutes the air fuel/mixture and gives poor combustion and carbon build up. These seals prevent oil seepage and power loss especially in higher rpm ranges.

11021 valve guide seal cutting tool $10.40
Tool required to machine valve guides before installing full floating teflon valve guide seals. Requires a 1/2" drill to perform the necessary work.

11250 valve springs (set of 8) $12.16
Heavier than stock springs. When used with retainers 11300, and lifters 12100, engine rpm redline may be increased to 7,000.

11300 aluminum spring retainers $7.50
Each retainer weighs half the weight of a standard retainer. Multiplied by eight means considerably less weight on the valve train and less chance of valve float at high rpm.

12000 3/4 race camshaft $71.50
Excellent camshaft for street use. Has excellent torque characteristics thruout entire rpm range. 11250 springs, 11300 retainers and 12100 lifters recommended.

12001 full race camshaft $78.00
May be used as a camshaft for street use. However, has rough idle and torque is in higher rpm range. Starts developing good power at 2,200 rpm. Good street camshaft for the lighter weight Sonett. 11250 springs, 11300 retainers, 12100 lifters recommended.

12002 track camshaft $84.50
Should be used for all out competition only, such as oval tracks and road racing. Power starts at 3,200 rpm. 11250 springs, 11300 retainers, 12100 lifters must be used to receive full benefit of right rpm torque.

12100 lightweight lifters $14.00
Standard lifter weighs 104 grams. These specially designed lifters weigh only 74 grams and have less power robbing friction in lifter bore than standard lifter. One piece cast unit.

12125 steel balance shaft gear $48.67
This gear should be installed on engines for all out competition. Replaces fibre balance shaft gear which tends to have excessive back lash after running for extended periods at high rpm.

13150 chrome moly bolts (set of 8) $10.50
Any engine being run in excess of 6,000 rpm must use these specially designed bolts if a blown engine is not desired. These bolts come complete with locknut and are very inexpensive insurance for keeping an engine together.

14000 2-barrel intake manifold $84.20
Aluminum manifold which accepts the Weber 2-barrel carburetor. Fits all SAAB 95 and 96 V4's. Because of height clearance problems this manifold cannot be used on Sonett V4's.

14001 2-barrel intake manifold $52.33
A new intake manifold designed to fit all SAAB V4 engines. Comes complete with carburetor mounting studs and spacer plate which allows the full installation of power brake hose and PCV valves on '69 and later SAAB V4's. No machining is necessary and either the 40 DFI or 28/36 DCD Weber may be used.

14200 high pressure oil pump $27.30
Recommended for all engines to be used in competition. Has constant pressure of 70 psi.

14500 Stage I tuning kit $123.50
Kit includes 14001 manifold, 28/36 DCD Weber carburetor, chrome air filter, vented oil cap, and necessary throttle linkage to complete full installation. Increases SAE horsepower rating from 73 to 90. Gas mileage of 24 to 26 mpg may be expected.

15000 28/36 DCD Weber carburetor $68.75
A progressive linkage which allows the use of one barrel at cruising speeds and the use of both barrels at full acceleration makes this a very good carburetor for increased performance while highway driving. Gas mileage figures average 24 to 26 mpg at cruising speeds.

15001 40 DFI Weber carburetor $78.00
Twin 40 mm. chokes and direct linkage. Best carburetor for competition purposes. Will clear the Sonett hood when used with intake manifold 14001. No air filters are available for this carburetor yet.

15050 chrome air filter assembly $5.25
Complete assembly with washable. filter element and necessary hardware to attach filter to 28/36 DCD carburetor only,

16000 2 cycle 74 mm. pistons $33.00
These pistons complete with rings increase the SAAB 2-cycle displacement to 940 cc. A special copper head gasket must be made to use this type of piston.

16001 74 mm. piston rings $2.29 ea.
Use with piston 16000. Two per piston.

16005 1,500 cc. V4 $62.40 ea.
      high compression piston
Specially designed piston for the 1,500 cc. V4 engine to increase compression ratio to 11.2:1. Complete with lightweight wrist pin and rings. No machining of block or cylinder heads nec-

essary. Used in all SAAB 1,500 cc. factory prepared rally cars.

16010   V4 stroker crankshaft $110.00
Increases stroke of V4 by 5/16″. Displacement increased to 1,700 cc. No machine work necessary to install. 1,700 cc. piston and rod assemblys must be used with this crankshaft as wrist pin height in piston is different.

16011   1,700 cc. piston $39.00 ea.
            and rod assembly
Comes complete with rings and must be used with 16010 crankshaft in early type open block V4 engines using 1/2″ spark plugs. No machining necessary to install. Increases compression ratio to 10:1.

16012   .040″ oversize 1,700 cc. piston $40.00 ea.
Comes complete with rings and must be used with 16010 crankshaft in early type open block V4 engines using 1/2″ reach spark plugs. Boring of the engine to .040″ oversize is necessary. Increases displacement to 1,730 cc. and compression ratio to 10.3:1.

16020   1,700 cc. piston & rod assembly $35.00 ea.
Comes complete with rings and must be used with 16010 crankshaft in late model blue engines using 3/4″ reach spark plugs. No machining necessary to install. Increases compression ratio to 10:1.

17400   V4 engine oil cooler kit $52.00
Light alloy cooler with hardware and instructions included to make a complete installation. Recommended for all V4 engines to be used in competition or when considerable high speed driving is done in hot climates. Fits all SAAB 96, 95 and Sonetts.

20100   capacitive discharge $44.95
            ignition system
Fits all SAAB engines 2 cycle, V4 or 99. Especially good for solving plug fouling problems on 2 cycle engines. The distributor points are used as a breaker switch only, and has no high amperage as in a standard ignition; therefore, no point burning. Test results on a V4 after 18,000 miles proved, points like new, spark plugs extremely good and two mpg better mileage experienced throughout the test. Guaranteed for one full year by the manufacturer.

20110   ignition wire $.96 per ft.
Wire has special silicon covering which is unaffected by gas, oil, or heat. This same wire is standard equipment on all Indy twin cam Ford engines.

20150   AG-12 Autolite spark plugs $1.25
Should be used for high speed highway driving on late V4 engines equipped with AG-22 spark plugs.

20151   AG-901 racing spark plugs $1.25
Should be used on all modified V4 engines using AG-22 spark plugs as standard equipment.

20152   AE-901 racing spark plugs $1.25
Should be used on all modified V4 engines

using AE-22 spark plugs as standard equipment.

20200   European rectangular $40.00
            headlight kit
Fits SAAB 95 and 96 from 1969 on and gives a much wider and lower frontal appearance. Kit includes all necessary parts to perform a complete change including different grille assembly. No drilling or special tools required. Now comes with brighter than standard 45/60 watt bulbs. *These are not legal in the United States* as they are not sealed beam units. Very good lighting for off road races and rallys.

30050   gearbox side support kit $5.75
Kit comes with all necessary hardware to perform a complete installation. A must for all SAABS in competition. When accelerating thru turns the power train tries to roll sideways, due to torque load, which is very hard on engine and gearbox mounts. The shift column u-joint is also misaligned during a power train roll which creates hard shifting. This kit substantially decreases the power train roll.

30100   close ratio gear set $125.00
Comparing these gears to the standard gearbox first and second are higher, third is the same and fourth is slightly lower. Gears are straighter cut for strength and will have slightly more noise than a standard gearbox. Using a 4.88:1 ring and pinion these are excellent gears for highway driving. The 5.43:1 ring and pinion and these gears are excellent for autocross and gymkhana use. However, rpm's are much higher in fourth gear while highway cruising.

30101   gearbox bearing kit $11.60
If close ratio gears 30100 are installed into earlier gearbox these bearings and circlips are needed to install.

30200   6.00:1 ring and pinion $140.00
Specially designed for rallys and off road racing. Teeth of ring and pinion are much wider than standard and much stronger. Only ring and pinion used on Swedish rally cars.

30203   4.67:1 ring and pinion $72.28
Highest speed ring and pinion available.

30210   nylon tie straps $7.10 per 50
                                                    $13.50 per 100
U-joint boot tie straps. Takes only seconds to install. Saves time and headaches for the mechanic. Sold only in packs of 50 and 100.

30300   competition pressure plate $35.70
Special pressure plate with heavy duty springs and fully balanced. A must for good clutch life with modified engines.

40002   competition disc brake pads $15.00
Harder racing pad which fits all V4 95, 96 and Sonetts.

40090   rally swing arm bushings $1.68 ea.
Used in front upper swing arms. Thicker rubber in bushing to give better dampening and hold the front end in alignment during rough road driving.

40091   rally swing arm bushings $1.68 ea.
(upper swing arm)
Used in front upper swing arms. Thicker rubber in bushing to give better dampening and hold the front end in alignment during rough road driving.

40100   special rally front springs $10.50 ea.
Recommended for all racing and rallying. Standard equipment on all 1970 Orange competition cars sold. Recommended for areas of U.S. where rough roads are common. Also can be used on air conditioned cars because of extra weight on front end.

40110   rally rear spring $7.25
For use on rallys or in areas of U.S. where rough roads are common. May also be used for SAABs with heavy trunk loads or pulling trailers with heavy tongue weight.

40150   rally shock absorbers (front) $28.10 ea.
Specially designed gas filled shocks for all rough terrain type driving. Used on all Swedish factory rally cars and in Baja. The only shock found to withstand the beating at Baja. Fits all V4 SAAB 95 and 96.

40151   rally shock absorbers (rear) $30.45 ea.
Specially designed gas filled shocks for all rough terrain. Used on all Swedish factory rally cars and in Baja. The only shock found to withstand the beating of Baja. Fits SAAB 96 only.

40200   heavy duty rear axle $130.00
Axle tube is made of heavier gauge tubing and more thoroughly welded at attaching points. Standard equipment on all 1970 Orange competition cars sold.

40700   4 1/2″ wide competition wheel
Discontinued. Use Sonett part number 741207.

50101   rally protection plate $150.00
Full protection aluminum skid plate with spring steel reinforcement. Use on all 95 and 96 V4's using standard exhaust system. Has special steel plate to protect front muffler and exhaust pipe as well as oil pan. Comes complete with mounting brackets.

50102   rally protection plate $126.00
Engine protection skid plate. Made from aluminum with spring steel reinforcement. Comes complete with mounting brackets.

10500   120 HP V4 engine assembly $995.00
Completely new, not rebuilt, 1,700 cc. high compression V4 engines. Highly tuned for top performance yet mild enough for city driving. Engine: 1,700 cc. displacement; 10:1 compression ratio; high pressure oil pump; 3/4 race camshaft; fully modified valve train; chrome moly rod bolts; modified water distribution pipe; 2-barrel manifold assembly; 28/36 DCD carburetor; chrome air filter unit. This engine does not conform to smog emission regulations. Engine is warranted against defects in material and workmanship for 60 days. The Competition Department is not responsible for any components damaged due to improper installation. Please specify, when ordering, whether engine is to be installed in 96, 95 or Sonett. No air filter available for Sonett as hood clearance is a problem. Recommended rpm redline of 6,600. In order to insure new 1,700 cc. V4 engines SAAB does not accept the 1,500 cc. V4 engine in exchange as they do not use the 1,500 cc. V4 engine.

Appendix

Specifications—1960–64 SAAB Models

General Specifications

	SAAB 95	SAAB 96	GT-750
Overall length, including bumpers	13 ft. 6 in. (4120 mm.)	13 ft. 2 in. (4015 mm.)	13 ft. 2 in. (4015 mm.)
Overall width	5 ft. 2 in. (1570 mm.)	5 ft. 2 in. (1570 mm.)	5 ft. 2 in. (1570 mm.)
Overall height, empty	4 ft. 10 in. (1470 mm.)	4 ft. 10 in. (1475 mm.)	4 ft. 10 in. (1475 mm.)
Road clearance (2 people front)	7.5 in. (190 mm.)	7.5 in. (190 mm.)	7.5 in. (190 mm.)
Track, front and rear	4 ft. (1220 mm.)	4 ft. (1220 mm.)	4 ft. (1220 mm.)
Wheelbase	8 ft. 2 in. (2490 mm.)	8 ft. 2 in. (2488 mm.)	8 ft. 2 in. (2488 mm.)
Turning radius	18 ft. (5.5 m.)	18 ft. (5.5 m.)	18 ft. (5.5 m.)
Empty weight, incl. fuel, water, tools and spare tire	1985 lbs. (900 kg.)	1810 lbs. (820 kg.)	1895 lbs. (860 kg.)
Weight distribution Empty, front	54%	58%	57.5%
Fully loaded, incl. pass. and lug., front	48%	48%	49%
Number of seats	7	5	2+2
Available lug. space	39 cu. ft. (1.1 m)	13 cu. ft. (0.37 m)	13 cu. ft. (0.37 m)
With full pass. load	none		
Loading deck with 5 pass.	39×37 in. (1000×950 mm.)	39×37 in. (1000×950 mm.)	39×37 in. (1000×950 mm.)
Loading deck with 2 pass.	63×37 in. (1600×950 mm.)		
Height of lug. space	31½ in. (800 mm.)	18 in. (460 mm.)	18 in. (460 mm.)

Engine

GENERAL DATA	850 cc.	750 cc (GT)
Piston displacement	51.9 cu. in. (841 cc.)	46 cu. in. (748 cc.)
Brake horsepower DIN	38 at 4250 rpm.	45 at 4800 rpm.
SAE	42 at 5000 rpm.	48 at 5000 rpm.
Torque DIN	59 ft. lb. at 3000 rpm. (8.2 mkg at 3000 rpm.)	61 ft. lb. at 3500 rpm. (8.5 mkg at 3500 rpm.)
Bore	2.76 in. (70 mm.)	2.6 in. (66 mm.)
Stroke	2.87 in. (73 mm.)	2.87 in. (73 mm.)
Compress. ratio, nom.	7.3:1	9.3:1
Firing order	1—2—3	1—2—3

DIMENSIONS AND TOLERANCES (in mm.)		
Bore, standard		
Class A	69.987—69.994	65.994—66.001
AB	69.994—70.001	66.001—66.008
B	70.001—70.008	66.008—66.015
C	70.036—70.046	66.043—66.053
Bore, oversizes (OD)		
OD 0.5 A	70.501—70.508	66.508—66.515
0.5 B	70.508—70.515	66.515—66.522
1.0 A	71.001—71.008	67.008—67.015
1.0 B	71.008—71.015	67.015—67.022
Piston diameter, standard. Measure at 90° to piston pin. Measure at indicated distance from edge of skirt.	20	15
Class A	69.930—69.937	65.907—65.914
AB	69.937—69.944	65.914—65.921
B	69.944—69.951	65.921—65.928
C	69.979—69.986	65.956—65.963
Piston diameter, oversizes (OD)		
OD 0.5 A	70.444—70.451	66.421—66.428
0.5 B	70.451—70.458	66.428—66.435
1.0 A	70.944—70.951	66.921—66.928
1.0 B	70.951—70.958	66.928—66.935

	850 cc.	750 cc. (GT)
Piston clearance	0.050—0.067	0.080—0.097
Max. permiss. clearance betw. piston and cyl.	0.15	0.18
Out-of-round, piston Difference betw. measure. at 90° to pin and in line with pin	0.08—0.10	0.08—0.10
Meas. at indicated dist. from edge of skirt	20	15
Width of piston rings	2.478—2.490	2.478—2.490
Piston ring gap	0.25—0.50	0.25—0.50
Ring clear. in groove		
Upper	0.07—0.12	0.07—0.12
Center	0.07—0.12	0.06—0.10
Lower	0.05—0.09	0.05—0.09
Piston pin diameter	18	18
Connect. rod side clear. Guided at piston		
At crankpin	—	2.05—2.14
At piston pin	—	0.10—0.40
Guided at crankshaft		
At crankpin	0.08—0.12	0.08—0.12
At piston pin	4	4
Connecting rod bearing radial clear.	0.015—0.020	0.015—0.020
Piston pin radial clear.		Should be easy fit with thumb pressure, pin rotatable with two fingers.
Crankshaft lateral throw, maximum	0.05	0.05
Compress. in new engine (at temp. of 175°F (80°C) with open throttle and full starter rpm)		
psi.	112±7	138±7
kg./sq. cm.	7.9±0.5	9.8±0.5

Clutch

STANDARD

SPECIFICATIONS

Type	dry single plate
Clutch pedal free movement at tip of pedal	3/4—1 in. (20—25 mm.)
Clearance release plate flywheel	1 in. (26 mm.)
Pressure plate springs	
Length, uncompressed	1.95 in. (49.5 mm.)
compressed	1.16 in. (29.4 mm.)
Tension when compressed	108—115 lbs. (49—52 kg.)
Minimum permissible tension	100 lbs. (45 kg.)
Dimensions of clutch facing	7x5x0.14 in. (180x125x3.5 mm.)
New disc	
Thickness, unloaded	0,36—0,37 in. (9,1—9,4—mm.)
loaded with 350 kp	0,33—0,34 in. (8,3—8,7 mm.)
Clutch pressure	294—312 kp.

SPECIAL TOOLS

Description	Part No.
Clutch lever spacers	784065
Clutch centering tool	784064

SAXOMAT

SPECIFICATIONS

Clutch	Saxomat
Release bearing clearance at approx. 2,000 rpm	0.08—0.12 in. (2—3 mm.)
Release bearing clearance at approx. 2,000 rpm measured at linkage lever	0.35—0.50 in. (9—13 mm.)
Gear lever contact gap (1/4 turn of socket nut)	0.006—0.008 in. (0.15—0.20 mm.).

New disc

Thickness, unloaded	0,33—0,34 in. (8,3—8,7 mm.)
loaded with 350 kp	0,30—0,35 in. (7,6—8,0 mm.)
Gear lever's point gap	0,006—0,008 in. (0,15—0,20 mm.)

Adjustment can be done by turning the sleeve nut 1/4 turn.

SPECIAL TOOLS

Description	Part No.
Clutch centering tool	784064

Transmission

SPECIFICATIONS

Oil required	4 pints (2 liters)
Type of oil	
SAAB 95 and 96	SAE 90 EP
SAAB GT-750	SAE 80-EP

Overall transmission ratios	SAAB 96 3-speed	SAAB 95 4-speed	GT-750 4-speed
1st gear	16.7:1	19.3:1	18.3:1
2nd gear	8.5:1	11.4:1	10.7:1
3rd gear	5.1:1	7.0:1	6.6:1
4th gear	—	4.5:1	4.3:1
Reverse	21.0:1	17.6:1	16.7:1
Ratio, ring gear and pinion	5.43:1	5.43:1	5.1:1
No. of teeth, pinion/ring gear	7:38	7:38	7:36

Road speed in m.p.h. at 1,000 rpm engine speed

	SAAB 96 3-speed	SAAB 96 4-speed	SAAB 95 4-speed	GT-750 4-speed
1st gear	4.3	3.7	3.8	3.8
2nd gear	8.4	6.3	6.4	6.6
3rd gear	14.0	10.3	10.4	10.7
4th gear	—	15.7	15.9	16.1
Reverse	3.4	4.1	4.1	4.6

Road speed in km/h at 1,000 rpm engine speed

	SAAB 96 3-speed	SAAB 96 4-speed	SAAB 95 4-speed	GT-750 4-speed
1st gear	6.9	5.9	6.0	6.1
2nd gear	13.4	10.0	10.3	10.5
3rd gear	22.4	16.4	16.8	17.1
4th gear	—	25.1	25.5	26.0
Reverse	5.4	6.5	6.6	6.7

Pinion/ring gear adjustment: specified dimension ± 0.002 in. (0.05 mm.). Ring gear lash: specified dimension ± 0.002 in. (0.05 mm.).

MATCHED GEARSETS

3-speed	4-speed
3rd speed drive gear	3rd speed drive gear
3rd speed gear wheel	3rd speed gear wheel
2nd speed drive gear	4th speed drive gear
2nd speed gear wheel	4th speed gear wheel
Crown wheel	Crown wheel
Pinion shaft	Pinion shaft
Syncromesh	Syncromesh

Fuel System

GENERAL DATA

Fuel tank capacity	
SAAB 95	11.5 gal. (43 liters)
SAAB 96 and GT-750	10.5 gal. (40 liters)
Fuel pump, all models	S.U. part No. AUA 79 or 89
Contact gap	0.03 in. (0.75 mm.)
Pump capacity	8 gph. (30 1/hour)
Del. head at (15 1/h— 1 1—4 min.) capacity	12—34 in. (320—850 mm.)
Del. head at zero capacity	20—43 in. (500—1100 mm.)

CARBURETORS

SOLEX (Normal Settings)

	40 AI or 40 BI	44 PII
Main jet system		
Choke tube	1.1 in. (28 mm.)	1.3 in. (32 mm.)

Main jet,		
SAAB 95 and 96 (850 cc.)	135	
SAAB GT-750 (750 cc.)	150	150
Emulsion tube jet	250	300
Emulsion tube	1	19
Idling system		
Idling air jet	100	140
Idling fuel jet	45	50
Cold starter system		
Starter air jet	3.5	
Starter fuel jet	190	
Needle valve	2.0	2.5
Float weight	0.75 oz.	0.35 oz.
	(21 gr.)	(10 gr.)

Float level with 23 1/2 in.
(600 mm.) fuel column (nor- 0.78 in ±0.04 0.78 in ±0.04
mal pump pressure)   (21 mm. ± 1)   (20 mm. ± 1)
Volume control screw   1 1/2—2 turns 2 1/2—2 turns

ZENITH (Normal Settings)	*34 VNN*
Main jet system	
Choke tube	1.2 in.
Main jet	107
Compensating jet	110
Main air jet	200
Idling system, Fuel jet	50
Idling air bleed (drilled in barrel)	140
Air (richness) regulating screw, opening	1 1/2—2 turns
Needle, valve 0.08 in. (2 mm.) seat washer	2.0
Throttle opening with closed strangler flap	0.040—.045 in.
	(1.1—1.2 mm.)
Fuel level with float chamber removed	
Float in position	1.02 in. (25.5 mm.)
Float removed	1.18 in. (30 mm.)
Fuel level with float chamber	
assembled and fitted	0.83 in. (21 mm.)
Float weight	0.22—0.24 oz.
	(6.2—6.8 gr.)

Exhaust System

GENERAL DATA
Exhaust pipe bore

SAAB 95 and 96	1.34 in.
	(34 mm.)
SAAB GT-750 Super	2.01 in.
	(51 mm.)

Cooling System

SPECIFICATIONS
Capacity of cooling system

Excluding heater system	1.82 gal.
	(6.9 liters)
Including heater system	2.03 gal.
	(7.7 liters)
Thermostat temp. range (185° F [85° C])	181°—199° F.
	(83°—93° C.)
Thermostat temp. range (170° F [75° C])	163°—181° F.
	(73°—83° C.)
Radiator pressure cap opens at	3.5—4.5 psi
	(0.25—0.30 kg/cm²)

TABLES
Freezing point in the table below is the point at which ice
crystals start to form in the cooling system. The use of alcohol
as antifreeze is not recommended since alcohol evaporates at
relatively low temperatures. Both glycol and alcohol may
damage the paintwork and should be handled carefully.

Water — ethylene glycol mixtures

% of ethylene glycol by vol.	Freezing point ° C.	° F.	Boiling point ° C.	° F.	Spec. gravity
10	— 4	25	101	214	1.012
20	—10	14	102	216	1.027
30	—17	2	103	217	1.041
40	—26	—15	104	219	1.055
50	—39	—38	106	223	1.068
60	—56	—68	109	228	1.076

Data for various quantities of glycol in the system

Quarts (liters) of glycol in system	Approx. % by volume	Freezing point ° C.	° F.	Boiling point ° C.	° F.	Specific gravity
1 (1.1)	13	— 6	21	101	214	1.017
2 (2.1)	25	—14	7	103	217	1.034
3 (2.91)	38	—24	—11	104	219	1.055
4 (3.81)	50	—39	—38	106	223	1.070

Front Axle and Suspension

SPECIFICATIONS

Front shock absorbers, length, compressed	9 3/4 in.
	(250 mm.)
extended	14 1/2 in.
	(370 mm.)
stroke, installed	3 1/4 in.
	(82 mm.)
Front coil springs, number of turns	11
Wire diam.	0.46 in.
	(11.7 mm.)
Front coil springs, length	15 in.
	(380 mm.)
Maximum spring extension, front	5 1/2 in.
	(140 mm.)
Front wheel alignment, no load	
Kingpin inclination	7 ± 1°
Caster	2 ± 1/2°
Camber	3/4 ± 1/4°
Toe-in at wheel rim	0.08 ± 0.04 in.
	(2 ± 1 mm.)
Turning angles	
Outer wheel	20°
Inner wheel	22 1/2 ± 1 1/2°

TORQUES

Castle nut, front wheel hub	1450—1700 in. lbs.
	125—145 ft. lbs.
	(17—20 kpm.)

SPECIAL TOOLS
The following SAAB special tools are required for work on
the front axle and suspension.

Description	Part No.
Rule for measuring toe-in	784001
Hub puller	784002
Tie rod end extractor	784004
Wrench for axle shaft seal nut, front wheel hub	784020
Drift for front wheel bearing	784075
Coil spring compressor	784081
Coil spring, clamp, for disassembly and assembly	784082
Press tool, upper rubber bushing spring arm	784133
Press tool, lower rubber bushing spring arm	784134

Rear Axle and Suspension

SPECIFICATIONS	SAAB 95	SAAB 96 and GT-750
Max. spring expansion	6 3/4 in.	6 3/4 in.
	(170 mm.)	(170 mm.)
Rear coil springs, length	13 1/2 in.	13 1/2 in.
	(342 mm.)	(342 mm.)
Rear coil springs, No. of turns	9	9
Rear coil springs, wire diam.	0.45 in.	0.43 in.
	(11.4 mm.)	(11 mm.)
Shock absorbers, type	Arm, hydraulic	Telescopic, hydraulic
Shock absorbers, stroke	4 1/4 in.	4 1/4 in.
	(106 mm.)	(106 mm.)

REAR WHEEL ALIGNMENT

Chamber	0° ± 1°
Toe-in, both wheels together	0° ± 1°
measured rim-to-rim	0 ± 7mm. (0.28 in.)
Toe-in for each wheel must not exceed	0° ± 3/4°
Maximum difference in wheelbase, left and right	0.6 in.
(front wheels pointing straight forward)	(15 mm.)

TORQUES
Crown nut, rear wheel hub: 9—10 kpm, 780—870 in. lbs.,
65—72 ft. lbs.

SPECIAL TOOLS
The following SAAB special tools are supplied for work on the rear axle and suspension.

Description	Tool No.
Hub puller	784002
Driver, ball bearing	784032
Driver, ball bearing	784033
Socket wrench, grease nipple	784036
Driver and extractor, bushing	784073
Driver and holder, bushing	784076

Steering and Column Gearshift

SPECIFICATIONS

Steering gear adjusments	
Pinion side clearance	.004—.008 in.
	(0.1—0.2 mm.)
Rack radial clearance, max.	.012 in.
	(0.3 mm.)
Steering ratio, mean	14:1
Wheel motion, full lock to full lock	2 1/4 turns
Tie-rod ends	
Distance between wrench flat and locknut, max.	1.5 in.
	(40 mm.)
Permissible diff. in distance between left and right-hand ends, max.	.08 in.
	(2 mm).

TORQUE SETTINGS
Nut, tie-rod end: 3.5—5 kgm., 300—440 in. lbs., 25—36 ft. lbs.

SPECIAL TOOLS
The following special tools are required for work on the steering and column gear shift.

Description	Tool No.
Ratchet wrench, inner ball joint	784071
Tool for driving off tie-rod ends	784004
Disassembly tool for taper pin in interm. shaft	784083

Brakes

GENERAL	Types I and II	Type III
Make	Lockheed	Lockheed
Type, front	Two leading shoe	self adjusting
rear	One leading shoe	One leading shoe
Footbrakes	Hydraulic	two—circuit type
Handbrake	Mechanical	Mechanical

DIMENSIONS, etc.	Type I	Type II	Type III
Brake drum, front	9 in.	9 in.	9 in.
	(228.6 mm.)	(228.6 mm.)	(228.6 mm.)
rear	8 in.	8 in.	8 in.
	(203.2 mm.)	(203.2 mm.)	(203.2 mm.)
Master cylinder	7/8 in.	3/4 in.	3/4 in.
Wheel cylinder, front			
SAAB 95 & 96	7/8 in.	0.8 in.	0.8 in.
rear SAAB 95 & 96	7/8 in.	3/4 in.	3/4 in.
GT-750			
rear, GT-750	3/4 in.	3/4 in.	3/4 in.
Brake shoes, front	9 in. x	9 in. x	9 in. x
	1 3/4 in.	1 3/4 in.	1 3/4 in.
rear	8 in. x	8 in. x	8 in. x
	1 1/2 in.	1 1/2 in.	1 1/2 in.
Brake hoses, front	10 1/2 in.	10 1/2 in.	10 1/2 in.
rear	15 1/2 in.	8 1/2 in.	8 1/2 in.
Brake tube, reservoir	5 1/6 in.	Hose	Hose
—master cylinder	Bundy	3/16 in.	3/16 in.
Other brake tubes	3/16 in. Bundy	Bundy	Bundy
Brake fluid	Lockheed Super Heavy Duty Brake Fluid, specification SAE 70 R 3 or equivalent		
Clear. betw. master-cyl. piston and push-rod, min.	0.0315 in. (0.8 mm.)	0.0315 in. (0.8 mm.)	0.02-0.05 in. (0.6-1.2 mm.)
Correct clear. at brake pedal top	0.2-0.4 in. (5-10 mm.)	0.2-0.4 in. (5-10 mm.)	0.12-0.24 in. (3-6 mm.)

Adjustment machining of brake drums permitted to diam. (max.):

Front	9.059 in.
	(230.1 mm.)
Rear	8.059 in.
	(204.7 mm.)
Max. total indicated radial brake-drum throw	.006 in.
	(0.15 mm.)

TORQUES

Castle nut,	
front wheel hub	17—20 kgm., 1400—1700 in. lbs.
	122—144 ft. lbs.
rear wheel hub	9—10 kgm., 800—850 in. lbs.
	65—72 ft. lbs.

SPECIAL TOOLS
The following special SAAB tool will be required for work on the brakes.

Description	Part No.
Puller	784002

Controls

Distance from brake/clutch pedal pad to toeboard	
Max. pedal travel, approx.	6 1/2 in.
	(160 mm.)
Free movement, clutch pedal, at pedal top	3/4—1 in.
	(20—25 mm.)
Free movement, brake pedal, at pedal top up to model 1963	3/16—3/8 in.
	(5—10 mm.)
at pedal top from model 1964	0.12—0.24 in.
	(3—6 mm.)
Total travel, accelerator pedal	2 in.
	(50 mm.)

Wheels and Tires

WHEELS

Type	wide base
Size	4J x 15 in.
Depth of drop center	1.77 in.
	(45 mm.)
Permissible out-of-round, rim	0.1 in.
	(2.5 mm.)
Permissible out-of-round, rim	0.1 in.
	(2.5 mm.)

TIRES

Size, SAAB 96, tubeless	5.00 x 15 in.
SAAB 95, tubeless	5.60 x 15 in.

Tire pressures, SAAB 96	Front	Rear
Light load	25 psi. (1.8 kg./cm)	22 psi. (1.6 kg./cm)
Full load	25 psi. (1.8 kg./cm)	25 psi. (1.8 kg./cm)
Tire pressures, SAAB 95		
Light load	24 psi. (1.7 kg./cm)	24 psi. (1.7 kg./cm)
Full load	25 psi. (1.8 kg./cm)	28 psi. (2.0 kg./cm)

Size, GT-750, with tube	155 x 15 in.
Tire pressures: Front	22—24 psi.
	(1.5—1.7 kg./cm)
Rear	21—23 psi.
	(1.4—1.6 kg./cm)

WHEEL BOLTS

Wrench size	3/4 in. (19.05 mm.)
Thread	SAE 9/16 in.—12 UNC—2

TORQUE SETTINGS

Wheel bolts	8—10 kgm.
	670—850 in. lbs.
	58—72 ft. lbs.

Electrical

BATTERY

Voltage	12 V
Capacity	54 Ah

GENERATOR, BOSCH

Type	LJ/GEG 160/12/2500+W30R4
Rated output	160 W
Rated voltage	12 V
Rated speed	2500 rpm
Max. permissible load	20 A
Direction of rotation	Clockwise
Brush spring pressure	450—600

CHARGING RELAY BOSCH
Up to model 1963

Type designation	RS/TBA 160/12/1
Cut-in voltage	12.4—13.1 V
Voltage setting when idling	14.3—15.3 V
Voltage setting when loaded with 15 A	13.5—14.5 V
Return current relay breaks at	3—9 A
Max. effect	240 W

From model 1964

Type designation	RS/VA 200/12/A2
Cut-in voltage	12.3—13.3 V
Voltage setting when idling	13.8—14.8 V
Voltage setting when loaded with 25 A	13.3—14.3 V
Return current relay breaks at	2—7,5 A
Max. effect warm regulator	300 W
Max. effect cold regulator (2—3 minutes from starting)	420 W

STARTER MOTOR, BOSCH

Type designation SAAB 95 and SAAB 96 To chassis No. 1120 and 112499 respectively	CD/0,5/12AR12
From chassis No. 1121 and 112500 respectively	AL/EDD 0,5/12R4
Type designation SAAB GT-750	AL/EDD 0,5/12R4 previously CDD 0,5/12R8
Number of teeth on pinion	9
Number of teeth on ring gear	97
Brush spring pressure	550—700 gr.

DISTRIBUTOR, BOSCH

	SAAB 95 and 96	SAAB 95 and 96	SAAB GT-750
Type	VJ3 BR8T	VJU3 BR1T and VJU3 BR2T	VJ3 BR7T
Capacitor	LMKO 1 Z30Z	LMKO 1 Z42Z	LMKO Z30Z
Ignition setting			
Basic setting	10° B.T.D.C.	7° B.T.D.C.	2° B.T.D.C.
At 3000 rpm	20° B.T.D.C.	17° B.T.D.C. (Vacuum hose disconnected)	22° B.T.D.C.
Order of firing	1—2—3	1—2—3	1—2—3
Breaker point gap	0.3—0.4 mm.	0.3—0.4 mm.	0.3—0.4 mm.
Dwell angle	77°—83°	77°—83°	80°—84°
Contact pressure	400—500 g.	400—500 g.	1100—1200 g.
Direction of rotation	Clockwise	Clockwise	Clockwise
Shaft end play	0.1—0.2 mm.	0.1—0.2 mm.	0.1—0.2 mm.

IGNITION COIL, BOSCH

Type designation combined		
With ignition switch	ZS/KZ 1/12 A	ZS/KZ 2/12 A
Without ignition switch	TK 12 A4	TK 12 AJ0
Serial resistance		ZWJ 11 Z4Z
Model 1964 Type	K12	

SPARK PLUGS, BOSCH

Normal driving	M 225 T1	M 240 T1
Hard driving	M 240 T1	M 270 T16
Spark gap clear.		
normal ignition cables	0.7 mm.	0.7 mm.
with resistance	0.8 mm.	0.8 mm.
Thread	18 mm.	18 mm.
Tightening torque	4.5 kpm	4.5 kpm

BULBS

	All cars	Philips No.	Watts
Sealed Beam USA	2 pcs.		50/40
Head light asymmetric	2 pcs.	12620	45/40
Turn ind./parking lights front	2 pcs.	1034	25/7 or 32/4 CP
Turn ind. stop lights, rear	2 pcs.	1073	25 W 32 CP
Tail light	2 pcs.	12821	5
Number plate lights	2 pcs.	12844	5

	SAAB 95	SAAB 96	GT 750	Philips No.	Watt
Courtesy light	2 pcs	1 pc	1 pc	12844	5 W
Warning and instru. model 1960—63	3+2 pcs	3+2 pcs	4+2 pcs	12913	2 W
Warning and instru. model 1964	—	10 pcs	—	12829	2 W
Warning and fuel gauge model 1964	5 pcs	—	—	12829	2 W
Remaining instru. lights model 1964	4 pcs	—	—	12913	2 W
Back-up light	—	—	2	1034	25 W
Luggage compart.	—	1	—	12929	4 W
FUSES	10+2 pcs	10+2 pcs	10+2+ 4 pcs		8A

FLASHER RELAY

Type, Lucas	FL5 12V 42 W
Hella	91 PSt 2x32 Cp 12 V

HORN, HELLA

Type	B 31—12 V

FUEL GAUGE TANK UNIT, VDO

Type, SAAB 95	VDO K 22.000
SAAB 96	VDO 20.228
GT-750	VDO 625

WINDSHIELD WIPER MOTOR

Type, Bosch	WS/GA 12/14
SWF, LHD cars	SWA 1105/66b
SWF, RHD cars	SWA 1105/66r

HEATER FAN MOTOR

Type, Bosch	KM/RCC 25/12—2500 R 5
Electrolux	KS 3442/240

WINDSHIELD WASHER MOTOR, BOSCH (GT 750 only)

Type	WS/SPE 2/12/1

Instruments

SPEEDOMETER DRIVE RATIOS

Model	Ratio Ring gear/ pinion	Dynamic radius of road wheel in.	mm.	Speedometer Rev. per km. covered	Rev. per mile covered
95	38:7	12.2	(310)	643	1035
96	38:7	12.0	(305)	654	1052
GT 750	36:7	11.7	(298)	634	1020
GT 750 (3-speed)°	34:7	11.7	(298)	599	964

° Earliest version of GT-750, with 3-speed transmission.

Body

SPECIFICATIONS

Basic body dimensions	SAAB 95	SAAB 96 GT-750
Overall length	13 ft. 4 in. (4060 mm.)	12 ft. 7 in. (3830 mm.)
Greatest width	5 ft. 2 in. (1565 mm.)	5 ft. 2 in. (1565 mm.)
Greatest height	4 ft. 1 in. (1265 mm.)	4 ft. 1 in. (1240 mm.)
Weight of body assembly fully fitted	661 lbs. (300 kg)	568 lbs. (258 kg)
Weight of excg. doors, fenders and rear compartment lid	507 lbs. (230 kg)	423 lbs. (192 kg)

SPECIAL TOOLS

Description	Part No.
Alignment tool, body diagonal measurement	784077
Alignment tool, installation of power unit	784078

Wrench Torques for Bolts Not Specifically Covered

Size (in.)	kg. m.	Wrench torques in. lbs.	ft. lbs.
1/4	0.7— 1.0	61—87	5—7
5/16	1.5— 2.5	130—220	10—18
3/8	2.5— 4.0	220—350	18—28
7/16	4.0— 7.0	350—600	28—50
1/2	7.0—10.0	600—850	50—72
9/16	10.0—14.0	850—1200	72—100
5/8	14.0—20.0	1200—1700	100—145

Specifications—1965–68 SAAB Models (two-stroke)

General Specifications

	SAAB 95				SAAB 96				SAAB Sport	Monte Carlo 850
	Model 1965	Model 1966	Model 1967	Model 1968	Model 1965	Model 1966	Model 1967	Model 1968	Model 1965	Model 1966
Overall length, including bumpers	14 ft. 0 in. (4270 mm.)		14 ft. 0 in. (4270 mm.)		13 ft. 8 in. (4170 mm.)	13 ft. 8 in. (4170 mm.)			13 ft. 8 in. (4170 mm.)	
Overall width	5 ft. 2 in. (1580 mm.)		5 ft. 2 in. (1580 mm.)		5 ft. 2 in. (1580 mm.)	5 ft. 2 in. (1580 mm.)			5 ft. 2 in. (1580 mm.)	
Overall height, empty	4 ft. 10 in. (1470 mm.)		4 ft. 10 in. (1470 mm.)		4 ft. 10 in. (1475 mm.)	4 ft. 10 in. (1475 mm.)			4 ft. 10 in. (1475 mm.)	
Ground clearance (2 people front)	7.5 in. (190 mm.)		7.5 in. (190 mm.)		7.5 in. (190 mm.)	7.5 in. (190 mm.)			7.5 in. (190 mm.)	
Track, front and rear	4 ft. 0 in. (1220 mm.)		4 ft. 0 in. (1220 mm.)		4 ft. 0 in. (1220 mm.)	4 ft. 0 in. (1220 mm.)			4 ft. 0 in. (1220 mm.)	
Wheelbase	8 ft. 2 in. (2498 mm.)		8 ft. 2 in. (2498 mm.)		8 ft. 2 in. (2498 mm.)	8 ft. 2 in. (2498 mm.)			8 ft. 2 in. (2498 mm.)	
Turning radius	17 ft. 6 in. (5.3 m.)		17 ft. 5 in. (5.3 m.)		17 ft. 6 in. (5.3 m.)	17 ft. 5 in. (5.3 m.)			17 ft. 6 in. (5.3 m.)	
Empty weight, incl. fuel, water, tools and spare tire	1930 lbs. (880 kg.)	1930 lbs. (880 kg.)	1980 lbs. (900 kg.)	2.010 lbs. (920 kg.)	1780 lbs. (810 kg.)	1775 lbs. 805 kg.	1,805 lbs. (820 kg.)	1,850 lbs. (840 kg.)	1965 lbs. (890 kg.)	1905 lbs. (865 kg.)
Total weight, incl. passengers and luggage	3300 lbs. (1500 kg.)	3300 lbs. (1500 kg.)	3300 lbs. (1500 kg.)	3.300 lbs. (1.500 kg.)	2750 lbs. (1250 kg.)	2750 lbs. (1250 kg.)	2750 lbs. (1250 kg.)	2.875 lbs. (1.300 kg.)	2750 lbs. (1250 kg.)	
Weight distribution — Empty	front 53%		front 53%		front 58%		front 85%		front 58%	
Fully loaded, incl. passengers and luggage	front 40%		front 40%		front 48%		front 48%		front 50%	
Number of seats	7		7		5		5		2+2	
Available luggage space	39 cu. ft. (1.1 m.)		39 cu. ft. (1.1 m.)		13 cu. ft. (0.37 m.)		13 cu. ft. (0.37 m.)		13 cu. ft. (0.37 m.)	
Loading area with driver + 4 passengers	39.4x37.4 in. (1000x950 mm.)		39.4x37.4 in. (1000x950 mm.)		39.4x37.4 in. (1000x950 mm.)		39.4x37.4 in. (1000x950 mm.)		39.4x37.4 in. (1000x950 mm.)	
Loading area with driver + 1 passenger	63x37.4 in. (1600x950 mm.)		63x37.4 in. (1600x950 mm.)							
Trunk height	31.4 in. (800 mm.)		31.4 in. (800 mm.)		18.1 in. (460 mm.)		18.1 in. (460 mm.)		18.1 in. (460 mm.)	

Engine

General Data	SAAB 95 and 96 Model 1965	SAAB Sport 1965 and Monte Carlo 850 1966	SAAB 95 and 96 from Model 1966
Cubic capacity	51.9 cu. in. (841 cc.)	51.9 cu. in. (841 cc.)	
Brake horsepower, DIN	40 at 4250 rpm	55 at 5000 rpm	42 at 4250 rpm
Torque, DIN	60 ft. lbs. (8.35 kgm) at 3000 rpm	68 ft. lbs. (9.3 kgm) at 3800 rpm	62 ft. lbs. 8,4 kpm at 3100 rpm
Bore	2.76 in. (70 mm.)	2.76 in. (70 mm.)	
Stroke	2.87 in. (73 mm.)	2.87 in. (73 mm.)	
Compression ratio	8.1:1	9:1	8.5:1
Order of firing	1—2—3	1—2—3	

Dimensions and Tolerances (in mm.)

Bore, standard		
Class A	69.987—69.994	69.987—69.994
AB	69.994—70.001	69.994—70.001
B	70.001—70.008	70.001—70.008
C	70.036—70.046	70.036—70.046
Bore, oversizes (OD)		
OD 0.5 A	70.501—70.508	70.501—70.508
B	70.508—70.515	70.508—70.515
1.0 A	71.001—71.008	71.001—71.008
B	71.008—71.015	71.008—71.015

The letters OD are stamped into the oversize pistons and into the cylinder block.

Piston diameter, standard		
Class A	69.927—69.939	69.895—69.902
AB	69.934—69.946	69.902—69.909
B	69.941—69.953	69.909—69.916
C	69.976—69.988	69.944—69.951
Piston diameter, oversizes (OD)		
OD 0.5 A	70.444—70.451	70.409—70.416
B	70.451—70.458	70.416—70.423
1.0 A	70.944—70.951	70.909—70.916
B	70.951—70.958	70.916—70.923

Measuring the piston diameter: Measure at an angle of 90° to piston pin. Distance from lower edge of piston when measuring

measuring	0.8 in. (20 mm.)	0.6 in. (15 mm.)
Piston clearance	0.048—0.067 mm.	0.035—0.099 mm.

Max. permis. clear. betw. piston and cyl., limit of

wearing	0.0059 in. (0.15 mm.)	0.0059 in. (0.15 mm.)

Out-of-round piston: Difference in meas. at 90° in line with pin

	0.03—0.04 in. (0.08—0.10 mm.)	0.03—0.04 in. (0.08—0.10 mm.)

Distance from lower edge of piston when

measuring	0.8 in. (20 mm.)	0.6 in. (15 mm.)

Width of piston ring

95 and 96	2.478—2.490	

Width of piston rings,

upper		2.478—2.490
lower		1.978—1.990

	SAAB 95, 96	SAAB Sport Monte Carlo 850
Piston-ring gap	0.01—0.02 in. (0.25—0.50 mm.)	0.01—0.02 in. (0.25—0.50 mm.)
Piston-ring clear. in groove		
Upper ring	0.0027—0.0047 in. (0.07—0.12 mm.)	0.0035—0.0043 in. (0.08—0.11 mm.)
Center ring	0.0027—0.0047 in. (0.07—0.12 mm.)	0.0027—0.0040 in. (0.07—0.10 mm.)
Lower ring	0.002—0.0035 in. (0.05—0.09 mm.)	0.0024—0.0035 in. (0.06—0.09 mm.)
Diameter of piston pin	0.75 in. (18 mm.)	0.75 in. (18 mm.)
Axial clear. of connecting rod		
At crankpin	0.807—0.913 in. (2.05—2.32 mm.)	0.807—0.913 in. (2.05—2.32 mm.)

At piston pin	0.004—0.016 in. (0.1—0.4 mm.)	0.004—0.016 in. (0.1—0.4 mm.)
Radial clear. of connect. rod bearing	0.0004—0.0006 in. (0.010—0.016 mm.)	0.0004—0.0006 in. (0.010—0.016 mm.)

Radial clear. of piston pin bearing — Should fit with light thumb pressure. Pin easily rotable with 2 fingers.

Max. lateral throw of crankshaft	0.02 in. (0.05 mm.)	0.02 in. (0.05 mm.)

Compress. in new engine (measured at engine temp. of 175°F or 80°C with throttle wide open and full starter rpm)

	cyl. 1 and 3, 121±7.1 psi, (8.5±0.5 kg/cm²) 114±7,1 psi cyl. 2 (8.0± (8.0±0,5 kg/cm²) model 1966, all cyl. 128±7.1 psi (9.0±0.5 kg/cm²)	all cyl. 128±7.1 psi (9.0±0.5 kg/cm²)

Torque Specifications

Unit	Bolts Quant.	Size	Wrench torque kgm	in. lbs.	ft. lbs.
Spark plugs					
Conventional	3	M 18	4.5	390	32
Bosch MGV 260 T31S	3	M 18	2	175	14
Cylinder head	12	7/16 in.	3[1]	275[1]	22[1]
Crankcase halves 95 and 96	9	5/16 in.	2.5	220	18
	8	3/8 in.	4	340	29
Crankcase halves SAAB Sport	8	5/16 in.	2.5	220	18
	8	3/8 in.	4	340	29
Flywheel bolts	8	5/16 in.	3	275	22
Crankshaft pulley	1	1/2 in.	5	440	36

Note! Angle tightening of cylinder head bolts should be used.

[1] After tightening to a torque of 3 kgm (= 275 in. lbs. or 22 ft. lbs.), turn bolt through 90°. When the engine has warmed up, turn another 20°. After 1,200 miles (2,000 km.) driving, another 20°. (See text for details.)

Fuel System

General Data

Fuel tank capacity		
SAAB 95	11.5 gal. (43 liters)	
SAAB 96 and Sport	10.5 gal. (40 liters)	
Fuel pump, all models	Pierburg PE 15201; alt. PE 15522	

Pressure above pump at

zero capacity and starter rpm	SAAB 95, 96	SAAB Sport
	2.1—3.5 psi (0.15—0.25 kg/cm²)	2.1—4.3 psi (0.15—0.30 kg/cm²)

STANDARD SOLEX

CARBURETORS	Model 1965	From Model 1966
Normal setting and type	Solex 40 B1	34 W2 (Y)
Main system		
Choke tube	1.1 in. (28 mm.)	1.1 in. (28 mm.)
Main jet	140	Carb. 1 (middle) 135; carb. 2 (outer) 120
Holder, Main jet		A
Emulsion jet	250	220
Emulsion tube	1	21
Idling system		
Fuel jet		55
Idling rpm	600— 750 rpm	600— 750 rpm
Idling air jet	100	
Idling fuel jet	40	35 only carb. 1 (middle)
Cold-starting system		
Starter air jet	3.5	3.5 ⎫ only
Starter fuel jet	190	170 ⎬ carb. 1 ⎭ (middle)
Needle valve	1.5	1.2
Weight of float	0.75 oz. (21 g.)	0.2 oz. (5.1 g.)
Float level, float chamber filled when idling	0.83±0.04 in. (21±1 mm.)	
Float level, meas. at 1500 mm. fuel column, with level tube 784210		0.93 in.±0.04 (23.5±1 mm.)
Float level, meas. at 1500 mm. fuel column, (float removed) with a vernier gauge at choke tube		1.04 in±0.04 (26.5±1 mm.)

STANDARD ZENITH

Normal setting and type	Zenith 34 VNN
Main System	
Choke tube	1.2 in. (30 mm.)
Main jet	105
Compensating jet	105
Emulsion jet	200
Idling system	
Idling rpm	600— 750 rpm
Air jet	50
Fuel jet	45
Air duct (drilled in barrel)	140
Volume screw set for the highest idling rpm	
Needle valve (with 0.08 in. = 2 mm. washer)	1.5
Throttle opening with closed choke flap	0.043— 0.047 in. (1.1— 1.2 mm.)
Float level, (float chamber filled when idling) measured with float chamber removed	
Float in position	1.0 in.± 0.04 in. (25.5±1 mm.)
Float removed	1.18 in.± 0.04 in. (30.0±1 mm.)
(Fuel level with float chamber fitted)	0.83 in. (21.0 mm.)
Weight of float	0.22— 0.24 oz. (6.2—6.8 g.)

SPORT AND MONTE CARLO 850 SOLEX

	Model 1965	From Model 1966
Normal setting and type	34W	34 W 2 (Z)
Choke tube	1.1 in. (28 mm.)	1.1 in. (28 mm.)
Main jet	120	120
Holder marked, Main jet	A	A
Emulsion jet	200	200
Emulsion tube	21	21
Low speed system		
Fuel jet	60	55
Idling system		
Idling rpm	600— 750 rpm	600— 750 rpm
Fuel jet	35	Carb. 1 (middle) 35
Cold-starting system		
Fuel jet	170	170 ⎫ only
Air jet	3.5	3.5 ⎬ carb. 1 ⎭ (middle)
Needle valve	1.5	1.2
Float weight	0.2 oz. (5.7 g.)	0.2 oz. (5.7 g.)
Float level, meas. at 1500 mm. fuel column, with level tube 784210	0.84 in. ±0.04 in. (21.5±1 mm.)	0.93 in.±0.04 (23.5±1 mm.)
Float level, (float chamber filled when idling) meas. (float removed) with a vernier gauge at choke tube	0.97 in. ±0.04 in. (24.5± 1 mm.)	1.04 in.±0.04 (26.5±1 mm.)

Exhaust System

GENERAL DATA

Inside diameter of exhaust pipe	
SAAB 95 and 96	1.34 in. (34 mm.)
SAAB Sport, twin exhaust pipe	1.34 in. (34 mm.)

Cooling System

SPECIFICATIONS

Capacity of cooling system	
Excl. heater system	1.51 gal. (5.7 liters)
Inc. heater system	1.72 gal. (6.5 liters)
Thermostat opening temperature range	180—200° F (81—92° C)
Radiator pressure cap opens at	3.4—4.25 psi (0.25—0.30 kg/cm)

TABLES

The freezing point in the table below is the temperature at which ice crystals begin to form in the cooling system. The use of alcohol as antifreeze is not recommended, since it evaporates at relatively low temperatures. Both glycol and alcohol are injurious to paintwork and must therefore be handled with care.

Amount of glycol in the cooling and heating system

Quarts of glycol in system	Approx. % by volume	Freezing point °C.	°F.	Boiling point °C.	°F	Specific gravity
1	15	− 7	19	101	214	1.020
2	31	±18	± 0	102	216	1.035
3	46	−33	−27	105	221	1.053

Electrical System

BATTERY	SAAB 95, 96 Monte Carlo 850 to Model 1966	SAAB 95, 96 from Model 1967
Voltage	12 V	12 V
Capacity	34 Ah	44 Ah

GENERATOR, BOSCH	SAAB 95, 96 Sport Model 1965	Monte Carlo 850 Model 1966 SAAB 95, 96, 1967

Gear ratio gen.— eng.	1.6:1	
Type	EG(R)14V25A31	K1⟷14V 35A 20
Rated voltage	12 V	12 V
Max. permiss. contin. ld.	25 A	35 A
Direct. of rotation	Clockwise	Clockwise and counter-clock.
Brush-spring press.	450—600 g. (16—21 oz.)	

VOLTAGE REGULATOR, BOSCH   *Monte Carlo 850 1966*

Type	AD 1 14 V (radio suppressed) AD 1 14 V (not suppressed) *SAAB 95, 96 Sport Model*

CHARGING REGULATOR, BOSCH   1965

Type	VA 14V 25 A or RS/VA 200/12/A2
Cut-in voltage	12.4—13.1 V
Voltage set. idling	13.5—14.5 V
Voltage set. with 25 A load	13.3—14.3 V
Reverse current relay breaks at	2—7.5 A
Max. output of warm reg.	300 W
Max. output of cold reg. (2—3 min. after start.)	420 W

STARTER MOTOR, BOSCH   *All Models*

Type	AL/EDD 0.5/12 R 4 or DD(R)12V 0,5 PS
No. of teeth on pinion	9
No. of teeth on ring gear	97
Brush-spring press.	800—900 g. (19—25 oz.)

DISTRIBUTOR, BOSCH	SAAB 95, 96 *Model* 1965	SAAB 95, 96 *From Model* 1966	*Sport Model* 1965	*Monte Carlo 850 From Model* 1966
Type	JFU3(R) or VJU3 BR2T	JFU3 0 231 144 003VJ3 BR11T	JF3(R) or	JFU3 0 231 144 004
Capacitor	LMKO 1 Z42	LMKO 1 Z42	LMKO 1 Z 30	LMKO 1 Z42
Ignition setting Basic	7° BTDC	10° BTDC	10° BTDC	10° BTDC
At 3000 rpm	17° BTDC (Vac. hose discon.)	15° BTDC (Vac. hose discon.)	20° BTDC	20° BTDC (Vac. hose discon.)
Order of firing	1—2—3	1—2—3	1—2—3	1—2—3
Breaker gap	0.012—0.016 in. 0.3—0.4 mm.	0.014—0.018 in. 0.35—0.45 mm.	0.014—0.018 in. 0.35—0.45 mm.	0.014—0.018 in. 0.35—0.45 mm.
Dwell angle	80—84°	75—82°	75—82°	75—82°
Contact press.	14—19 oz. 400—530 g.	18—22 oz. 500—630 g.	14—19 oz. 400—530 g.	18—22 oz. 500—630 g.
Direct. of rotat.	Clockwise	Clockwise	Clockwise	Clockwise
Axial play, distr. shaft	0.004—0.008 in. (0.1—0.2 mm.)	0.004—0.008 in. (0.1—0.2 mm.)	0.004—0.008 in. (0.1—0.2 mm.)	0.004—0.008 in. (0.1—0.2 mm.)

IGNITION COIL, BOSCH

Type	K 12	KW 12 V	KW 12 V	KW 12 V
Series resist.		Vitrom	Mallory Scott 4320196	Vitrom

SPARK PLUGS	SAAB 95, 96 *Model* 1965, 1966	*Sport Model 1965 Monte Carlo 850 Model 1966*
Easy driv.	Bosch M 175 T1	
Normal driv.	Bosch M 240 T1	
Hard driv.	Bosch M 225 T1	Bosch MGV 260 T31S

Normal and hard driv.   Bosch MGV 260 T31 S

	Side electrode	Side electrode	Surface gap	Side electrode
Type				
Electrode gap with resist. ignit. cable	0.032 in. (0.8 mm.)	0.032 in. (0.8 mm.)	New 0.028 in. (0.7 mm.) max. 0.047 in. (1.2 mm.)	(0.55—0.60 mm.)
Thread	0.75 in. (18 mm.)	(18 mm.)	(18 mm.)	(18 mm.)
Tightening torque	32 ft. lbs. (4.5 kpm)	32 ft. lbs. (4.5 kpm)	14 ft. lbs. (2 kpm)	32 ft. lbs. (4.5 kpm)

BULBS	*All Models*	*Philips No.*	*Watts*
Headlamps, asymmetric	2	12620	45/40 W
Parking lights and flashers, front	2	1034	25/5 W or 32/4 Cp
Stop lights and flashers, rear	4	1073	25 W or 32 CP
Tail lights	2	12821	5 W
License plate lights	2	12844	5 W

	SAAB 95	SAAB 96	*Sport*	*Philips No.*	*Watts*
Dome light	2	1	1	12844	5 W
Long-range and fog light			2	12247	45 W
Instru. lights, warning lamps	5	10	10	12829	2 W
Other instru. lights	4		2	12913	2 W
Back-up lights			2	1034	32 W
Trunk light		1	1	12929	4 W
Fuses	12	12	12		8 A

FLASHER UNIT

Type: Lucas	FL5 12V 42 W
Hella	91 PSt 2x32 Cp 12 V

HORN, HELLA

Type	B 32/5 — 12 V

FUEL GAUGE TANK UNIT

Type: SAAB 95	Veglia 67—8011
SAAB 96	VDO 20.228
SAAB Sport	VDO 625

HEATER FAN MOTOR

Type: Electrolux	KS 3430/220 12 V

WINDSHIELD WIPER MOTOR

Type: SWF	SWA 400. 438 C
from model 1967 Lucas	Lucas DL 3 A

WINDSHIELD WASHER

Sport, Monte Carlo 850—1966	Dahlberg
From Model 1968 (all models)	Meab

Clutch

FICHTEL & SACHS

	SAAB 95, 96	*Sport, Monte Carlo 850*
Type	single dry plate	single dry plate
Clearance release bearing-clutch meas. at slave cylinder	0.16 in. (4 mm.)	0.16 in. (4 mm.)
Clearance bet. release plate and flywheel	1.02±0.02 in. (26±0.5 mm.)	1.02±0.02 in. (26±0.5 mm.)
Pressure-plate springs Length uncompressed	1.95 in. (49.5 mm.)	1.15 in. (49.5 mm.)
Length compressed	1.16 in. (29.4 mm.)	1.16 in. (29.4 mm.)
Tension, compressed	108—115 lbs. (49—52 kg)	108—115 lb. (49—52 kg)

Min. permiss. tension compressed	100 lb. (45 kg)	100 lbs. (45 kg)
Inner springs (Sport only)		
Length uncompressed		1.95 in. (49.5 mm.)
Length compressed		1.03 in. (26.2 mm.)
Tension, compressed		35—40 lbs. (16—18 kg)
Min. permiss. tension compressed		33 lbs. (15 kg)
Dimens. of clutch facing	7x5x0.14 in. (180x125x 3.5 mm.)	(180x125x 3.5 mm.)
New clutch disc		
Thickness, unloaded	0.358—0.370 in. (9.1—9.4 mm.)	0.358—0.370 in. (9.1—9.4 mm.)
loaded with 770 lbs. (350 kg)	0.327—0.343 in. (8.3—8.7 mm.)	0.327—0.343 in. (8.3—8.7 mm.)
Max. throw clutch disc	0.024 in. (0.6 mm.)	0.024 in. (0.6 mm.)
Engagement pressure	648—688 lbs. (294—312 kg)	860—926 lbs. (390—420 kg)

SAXOMAT

Release bearing clear. at approx. 2000 rpm	0.08—0.12 in. (2—3 mm.)
Release bearing clear. at approx. 2000 rpm, meas. at pull-rod	0.35—0.51 in. (9—13 mm.)
New clutch disc Thickness, unloaded	0.327—0.343 in. (8.3—8.7 mm.)
loaded with 770 lbs. (350 kg)	0.299—0.315 in. (7.6—8.0 mm.)
Gearshift lever contact gap	0.006—0.008 in. (0.15—0.20 mm.) or back off sleeve nut 1/4 turn

HYDRAULIC

	Master Cylinder	Slave Cylinder
Make and type	Girling 5/8 in.	Girling D2
Cylinder diameter	5/8 in.	3/4 in.
Max. permissible stroke	1.38 in. (35 mm.)	
Hose connection	3/8 in. UNF-24	3/8 in. UNF-24
Hose length bet. master and slave cyl.	14 in. (355.6 mm.)	
Distance from clutch-pedal foot plate to toe-board (max. pedal stroke)	approx. 6.3 in. (160 mm.)	
Clearance, release bearing-clutch meas. at slave cyl.	0.16 in. (4 mm.)	

Transmission

SPECIFICATIONS

Oil capacity	approx. 1.4 quarts (1.4 liters)
Type of oil	SAE 80 EP

Gear ratios, total	SAAB 96 3-speed	SAAB 95, 96 4-speed	Sport 1965	Monte Carlo 850 1966
1st gear	16.7:1	19.3:1	18.3:1	17.0:1
2nd gear	8.5:1	11.4:1	10.8:1	10.2:1
3rd gear	5.1:1	7.0:1	6.6:1	6.3:1
4th gear	—	4.5:1	4.3:1	4.1:1
Reverse	21.0:1	17.6:1	16.7:1	15.5:1

Dif. gear ratio, pinion: ring gear	5.43:1	5.43:1	5.14:1	4.88:1
No. of teeth, pinion: ring gear	7:38	7:38	7:36	8:39

Road speed in mph at 1000 rpm engine speed	SAAB 96 3-speed	SAAB 96 4-speed	SAAB 95 4-speed	Sport 1965	Monte Carlo 850 1966
1st gear	4.3	3.7	3.7	3.8	4.2
2nd gear	8.4	6.2	6.3	6.5	6.9
3rd gear	14.0	10.2	10.4	10.7	11.1
4th gear	—	15.6	15.8	16.2	17.2
Reverse	3.4	4.0	4.0	4.2	4.5

Gear ratios, total SAAB 95 and 96, model 1966:

1st gear	18.9:1
2nd gear	11.3:1
3rd gear	7.0:1
4th gear	4.5:1
Reverse	17.3:1
Dif. gear ratio, pinion/ring gear	5.43:1
No. of teeth, pinion: ring gear	7:38

Road speed at 1000 rpm engine speed	SAAB 95 from model 1966	SAAB 96 from model 1966
1st gear	3.8 mph (6.2 km/h)	3.7 mph (6.0 km/h)
2nd gear	6.4 mph (10.3 km/h)	6.3 mph (10.0 km/h)
3rd gear	10.3 mph (16.6 km/h)	10.0 mph (16.1 km/h)
4th gear	16.0 mph (25.7 km/h)	15.6 mph (24.9 km/h)
Reverse	4.2 mph (6.7 km/h)	4.1 mph (6.5 km/h)

Pinion/ring-gear adjustment: specified dimension ±0.002 in. (0.05 mm.). Ring-gear backlash: specified dimension ±0.002 in. (0.05 mm.).

MATCHED GEARSETS

3-speed	4-speed
3rd speed gear	3rd speed gear
Pinion shaft 3rd gear	Pinion shaft 3rd gear
2nd speed gear	4th speed gear
Pinion shaft 2nd gear	Pinion shaft 4th gear
Ring gear	Ring gear
Pinion shaft	Pinion shaft
Synchromesh	Synchromesh

TIGHTENING TORQUES

Application	Bolts No.	Size	kpm	in. lbs.	ft. lbs.
Transmis. case end cover	6	5/16"	2.5	220	18
Differential bearings	4	3/8"	4	340	29
Ring gear bolts	12	5/16"	2.5	220	18
Pinion-shaft nut. First tightening			12	1050	87
Then slacken and retighten	1	7/8"	6	530	44
Nut, primary shaft	1	3/4"	5	425	36
Nut, countershaft	1	9/16"	8	700	60

Brakes

GENERAL	SAAB 95, 96 Model 1965, 1966	Sport Model 1965 Monte Carlo 850 Model 1966	SAAB 95, 96 Model 1967
Make	Lockheed	Lockheed	Lockheed
Type, front	Two lead. shoe, self-adjust.	Disc brake	Disc brake
rear	One lead. shoe	One lead. shoe	One lead. shoe
Footbrake	Hydraulic two-circuit type	Hydraulic two-circuit type	Hydraulic two-circuit type
Handbrake	Mechanical	Mechanical	Mechanical

DIMENSIONS, ETC.

Brake, front drum	9 in. (228.6 mm.)		
disc		10 3/4 in. (273 mm.)	10 1/2 in. (266.70 mm.)
Brake, rear drum	8 in. (203.2 mm.)	8 in. (203.2 mm.)	8 in. (203.2 mm.)
Master cylinder	3/4 in.	3/4 in.	3/4 in.
Wheel cylinder, front	0.8 in.	2 in.	2 in.
rear	3/4 in.	3/4 in.	SAAB 96 5/8 in. SAAB 95 3/4 in.
Brake shoes, front	9 in. x 1 3/4 in.		
rear	8 in. x 1 1/2 in.	8 in. x 1 1/2 in.	8 in. x 1 1/2 in.
Brake hoses, front, length of	10 1/2 in.	10 in.	8 1/2 in.
rear, length of	SAAB 96 8 1/2 in. SAAB 95 6 1/2 in.	8 1/2 in.	SAAB 96 8 1/2 in. SAAB 95 6 1/2 in.
Other brake lines	3/16 in. Bundy tube	3/16 in. Bundy tube	3/16 in. Bundy tube
Clearance between master-cylinder piston and push-rod	0.024— 0.047 in. (0.6— 1.2 mm.)	0.024— 0.047 in. (0.6— 1.2 mm.)	0.024— 0.047 in. (0.6— 1.2 mm.)
Same clearance at tip of brake pedal	0.12— 0.24 in. (3— 6 mm.)	0.12— 0.24 in. (3— 6 mm.)	0.12— 0.24 in. (3— 6 mm.)

Distance from brake-pedal
footplate to toe-board Max stroke approx. 6.3 in. (160 mm.) all versions.

Brake fluid Satisfying the requirements of spec. SAE 70 R 3, e.g. Lockheed Super Heavy Duty Brake Fluid. For Sport and Monte Carlo 850: Lockheed HD 328 Brake Fluid.

Adjustment machining of brake drums permitted
to max. dia.
  Front 9.059 in. (230.1 mm.)
  Rear 8.059 in. (204.7 mm.)
Max. total indicated radial brake-drum
throw 0.006 in. (0.15 mm.)
Max. total indicated axial brake drum
throw 0.08 in (0.2 mm.)
Centerless grinding of brake linings, front 0.010—0.012 in.
(0.25—0.30 mm.)
              rear 0.020—0.022 in.
(0.50—0.56 mm.)
less than the drum

Tightening torques
  Castle nut,
    front wheel hub 1500 in. lb., 130 ft. lb., 18 kgm.
    rear wheel hub 800 in. lb., 65 ft. lb., 9 kgm.

Suspension and Wheel Alignment

WHEEL ALIGNMENT
Front wheel alignment, no load
  Kingpin inclination 7° ± 1
  Caster 2° ± 1/2
  Camber 3/4° ± 1/4
  Toe-in at wheel rim 0.09 in. ± 0.04 (2 mm. ± 1)
Turning angles
  Outside wheels 20°
  Inside wheels 22 1/2° ± 1 1/2

STEERING GEAR
Steering-gear adjustment
  Pinion axial clearance 0.004—0.008 in. (0.1—0.2 mm.)
  Radial clearance of rack max. 0.012 in. (0.3 mm.)
  Steering, ratio 14:1

Wheel travel between limit positions 2 1/4 turns
Tie-rod ends
  Distance between wrench flat and
    lock nut Max. 1.5 in. (40 mm.)
      The following is valid for certain cars of model 1968: The distance between end of thread and locknut must not exceed 1.2 in. (30 mm.).
  Permissible difference between lefthand
    and righthand dimension Max. 0.08 in. (2 mm.)

TIGHTENING TORQUE
Nut, tie-rod end:
  3.5—5 kgm, 300—440 in. lbs., 25—36 ft. lbs.

FRONT COIL SPRING
Max. spring expansion, front 5 1/2 in.
(140 mm.)
Front coil springs, length 15.4 in.
(391 mm.)
Front coil springs, number of coils 11
Wire diameter 0.46 in.
(11.7 mm.)

REAR COIL SPRING	SAAB 95	SAAB 96 and Sport
Max. spring expansion	6 3/4 in. (170 mm.)	6 3/4 in. (170 mm.)
Rear coil springs, length	13 1/2 in. (342 mm.)	13 1/2 in. (342 mm.)
No. of coils	9	9
Wire diameter	0.45 in. (11.4 mm.)	0.43 in. (11.0 mm.)

REAR WHEEL ALIGNMENT
Camber 0° ± 1
Toe-in (toe-out) 0° ± 1
  Both wheels together or measured
    rim-to-rim 0 ± 0.28 in. (7 mm.)
Toe-in (toe-out) per wheel must not exceed 0° ± 3/4
Max. dif. wheelbase, left and right
  (front wheels pointing straight ahead) 0.6 in. (15 mm.)

FRONT SHOCK ABSORBERS
Type Telescopic, hydraulic
Length 9 3/4 in. (250 mm.)
  Extended 14 1/2 in. (390 mm.)
Stroke, fitted 3 1/4 in. (82 mm.)

REAR SHOCK ABSORBERS	SAAB 95	SAAB 96, Sport Monte Carlo 850
Type	Arm, hydraulic	Telescopic, hydraulic
Length between center hole and shoulder for washer		10 in. (255 mm.)
Extended		16 7/16 in. (417 mm.)
Stroke	4 1/4 in. (106 mm.)	4 1/4 in. (106 mm.)

Wheels and Tires

WHEELS
Type wide base
Size 4J x 15 in.
Depth of drop center 1.77 in. (45 mm.)
Permissible out-of-round of rim 0.06 in. (1.5 mm.)
Permissible rim runout 0.06 in. (1.5 mm.)

TIRES
Size, SAAB 96, tubeless 5.20 x 15 in.
     SAAB 95, tubeless 5.60 x 15 in.
     SAAB Sport, with tube 155 x 15 in.
     Alt. dim. Sport and Monte Carlo 850 6.25—15 GP

Tire pressures	Front	Rear
SAAB 96		
Light load	26 psi (1.8 kg/cm.)	23 psi (1.6 kg/cm.)
Full load	26 psi (1.8 kg/cm.)	26 psi (1.8 kg/cm.)
SAAB 95		
Light load	24 psi (1.7 kg/cm.)	24 psi (1.7 kg/cm.)
Full load	26 psi (1.8 kg/cm.)	30 psi (2.1 kg/cm.)

	Up to Model 1966	From Model 1967
Sport dim. 155x 15 in.		
Light load	21 psi (1.5 kg/cm.)	20 psi (1.4 kg/cm.)
Full load	24 psi (1.7 kg/cm.)	24 psi (1.7 kg/cm.)
Sport dim. 6.25—15 GP		
Light load	20 psi (1.4 kg/cm.)	18 psi (1.3 kg/cm.)
Full load	20 psi (1.4 kg/cm.)	20 psi (1.4 kg/cm.)

WHEEL BOLTS	Up to Model 1966	From Model 1967
Width across flats	3/4 in. (19.05 mm.)	3/4 in. (19.05 mm.)
Thread SAAB 95 and 96	UNC 9/16 in.	UNC 9/16 in.
Thread SAAB Sport	UNC 5/8 in.	UNC 9/16 in.

TIGHTENING TORQUES
Castle nut,	
front wheel hub	1500 in. lbs., 130 ft. lbs. (18 kgm.)
rear wheel hub	850 in. lbs., 70 ft. lbs. (9.5 kgm.)
Wheel bolts	670—850 in. lbs., 58—72 ft. lbs. (8—10 kgm.)

Body

SPECIFICATIONS

	SAAB 95	SAAB 96, Sport, Monte Carlo 850
Body dimensions		
Overall length	13 ft. 7 in. (4160 mm.)	12 ft. 10 in. (3930 mm.)
Overall width	5 ft. 2 in. (1585 mm.)	5 ft. 2 in. (1585 mm.)
Overall height	4 ft. 1 1/2 in. (1256 mm.)	4 ft. 1 in. (1240 mm.)
Weight of body, total excl. hood, doors, fenders and luggage compart. cover	646 lbs. (293 kg) 496 lbs. (225 kg)	555 lbs. (252 kg) 415 lbs. (188 kg)

Instruments

SPEEDOMETER DRIVE RATIO

Model	Ratio ring gear: pinion	Dynamic radius of road wheel in.	Dynamic radius of road wheel mm.	Speedometer Rev. per kilometer covered	Rev. per mile covered
95	7:38	12.2	310	649	1035
96 3-speed and 4-speed	7:38	12.0	305	645	1052
Sport, 1965	7:36	11.8	300	625	1006
Monte Carlo 1966	8:39	11.8	300	585	942

Specifications—1967–70 SAAB Models (V4)

General Specifications— 1967–68

	SAAB 95	SAAB 96	Monte Carlo
Overall length, including bumpers	14 ft. 0 in. (4270 mm.)	13 ft. 8 in. (4170 mm.)	13 ft. 8 in. (4170 mm.)
Overall width	5 ft. 2 in. (1580 mm.)	5 ft. 2 in. (1580 mm.)	5 ft. 2 in. (1580 mm.)
Overall height, unloaded	4 ft. 10 in. (1470 mm.)	4 ft. 10 in. (1475 mm.)	4 ft. 10 in. (1475 mm.)

Ground clearance (2 people front)	5.1 in. (130 mm.)	5.1 in. (130 mm.)	5.1 in. (130 mm.)
Track, front and rear	4 ft. 0 in. (1220 mm.)	4 ft. 0 in. (1220 mm.)	4 ft. 0 in. (1220 mm.)
Wheelbase	8 ft. 2 in. (2498 mm.)	8 ft. 2 in. (2498 mm.)	8 ft. 2 in. (2498 mm.)
Turning radius	17 ft. 5 in. (5.3 m.)	17 ft. 5 in. (5.3 m.)	17 ft. 5 in. (5.3 m.)
Empty weight, incl. fuel, water, tools and spare tire	2080 lbs. (945 kg.)	1940 lbs. (880 kg.)	2000 lbs. (910 kg.)
Total weight, incl. permiss. pass. and lug.	3370 lbs. (1530 kg.)	2880 lbs. (1300 kg.)	2880 lbs. (1300 kg.)
Weight distribution Empty, front	57%	62%	61%
Fully loaded, incl. pass. and lug., front	44%	52%	51%
Number of seats	7	5	2+2
Available lug. space	39 cu. ft. (1.1 m.)	13 cu. ft. (0.37 m.)	13 cu. ft. (0.37 m.)
Loading area with driver + 4 pass.	39.4 x 37.4 in. (1000 x 950 mm.)	39.4 x 37.4 in. (1000 x 950 mm.)	39.4 x 37.4 in. (1000 x 950 mm.)
Loading area with driver + 1 pass.	63 x 37.4 in. (1600 x 950 mm.)		
Trunk height	31.4 in. (800 mm.)	18.1 in. (460 mm.)	18.1 in. (460 mm.)

General Specifications—1969

	SAAB 95	SAAB 96
Overall length, including bumpers	14 ft. 1 in. (4300 mm.)	13 ft. 9 in. (4200 mm.)
Overall width	5 ft. 2 in. (1580 mm.)	5 ft. 2 in. (1580 mm.)
Overall height, unloaded	4 ft. 10 in. (1470 mm.)	4 ft. 10 in. (1475 mm.)
Ground clear. (2 people front)	5.1 in. (130 mm.)	5.1 in. (130 mm.)
Track, front and rear	4 ft. 0 in. (1220 mm.)	4 ft. 0 in. (1220 mm.)
Wheelbase	8 ft. 2 in. (2498 mm.)	8 ft. 2 in. (2498 mm.)
Turning radius	17 ft. 9 in. (5.4 m.)	17 ft. 9 in. (5.4 m.)
Empty weight, incl. fuel, water, tools and spare tire	2160 lbs. (980 kg.)	2000 lbs. (910 kg.)
Total weight, incl. permissible passengers and luggage	3370 lbs. (1530 kg.)	2880 lbs. (1300 kg.)
Weight distribution Empty, front	57%	62%
Fully loaded, incl. pass. and lug., front	44%	52%
Number of seats	7	5
Available lug. space	39 cu. ft.. (1.1 m³)	13 cu. ft. (0.37 m³)
Loading area with driver+4 pass.	39.4x37.4 in. (1000x 950 mm.)	39.4x37.4 in. (1000x 950 mm.)
driver+1 pass.	63x37.4 in. (1600x 950 mm.)	
Trunk height	31.4 in. (800 mm.)	18.1 in. (460 mm.)

General Specifications—1970

	SAAB 95	SAAB 96
Overall length, including bumpers	14 ft. 1 in.	13 ft. 9 in.
	(4300 mm.)	(4200 mm.)
Overall width	5 ft. 2 in.	5 ft. 2 in.
	(1580 mm.)	(1580 mm.)
Overall height, unloaded	4 ft. 10 in.	4 ft. 10 in.
	(1490 mm.)	(1490 mm.)
Ground clear. (2 people front)	5.1 in.	5.1 in.
	(130 mm.)	(130 mm.)
Track, front and rear	4 ft. 0 in.	4 ft. 0 in.
	(1220 mm.)	(1220 mm.)
Wheelbase	8 ft. 2 in.	8 ft. 2 in.
	(2498 mm.)	(2498 mm.)
Turning radius	17 ft. 6 in.	17 ft. 6 in.
	(5.4 m.)	(5.4 m.)
Empty weight, incl. fuel, water, tools and spare tire	2150 lbs.	2000 lbs.
	(975 kg.)	(905 kg.)
Total weight, incl. permiss. pass. and lug.	3395 lbs.	2990 lbs.
	(1540 kg.)	(1350 kg.)
Weight distribution		
Curb weight incl. driver	front 57%	front 61%
Total weight	front 45%	front 51%
Max. roof load	220 lbs.	220 lbs.
	(100 kg.)	(100 kg.)
Max. trailer weight	2000 lbs.	2000 lbs.
	(910 kg.)	(910 kg.)
Number of seats	7	5
Available lug. space	39 cu. ft.	13 cu. ft.
	(1.1m)	(0.37 m.)
Loading area with driver+4 pass.	39.4x37.4 in.	39.4x37.4 in.
	(1000x 950 mm.)	(1000x 950 mm.)
driver+1 pass.	63x37.4 in.	60.5x37.4 in.
	(1600x 950 mm.)	(1540x 950 mm.)
Trunk height	31.4 in.	18.1 in.
	(800 mm.)	(460 mm.)

Engine

GENERAL DATA

Engine, type V4	4 stroke, 4 cylinders
Power DIN at 4700 rpm	65 bhp
Max. torque at 2500 rpm	85 ft. lbs. (11.7 kpm.)
Compression ratio, nominal	9.0:1
Number of cylinders	4
Cylinder bore	3.54 in. (90 mm.)
Stroke	2.32 in. (58.86 mm.)
Cylinder displacement	91.4 cu. in. (1498 cc.)
Firing order	1—3—4—2
Placement of cylinders (from front)	
Right-hand side	1—2
Left-hand side	3—4
Idling speed	800—900 rpm
Engine suspension	3-point
Weight, incl. electr. equip. and carb.	265 lbs. (120 kg.)

CYLINDER BLOCK

Type	60° V, block and crankcase one piece cast
Material	Cast iron of a special alloy
Number of main bearings	3
Cylinder blocks bores for camshaft bushings	
Front	44.65—44.68 mm.
Center	44.27—44.30 mm.
Rear	43.89—43.92 mm.
Cylinder block bores for balance shaft bushings	
Front	54.420—54.445 mm.
Rear	57.620—57.645 mm.
Cylinder bore	
Standard	90.030—90.040 mm.
Oversize 0.02 in. (0.5 mm.)	90.530—90.540 mm.
Oversize 0.04 in (1.0 mm.)	91.030—91.040 mm.
Diameter main bearing bore: Red	60.62—60.63 mm.
Blue	60.63—60.64 mm.
Thrust bearing width	22.61—22.66 mm.

PISTONS

Material	Aluminum
Number of rings, each piston	2 compress. and 1 oil control (tripartite)
Permissible diff. in weight (piston and connect. rod) in one engine	0.46 oz. (13 g.)
Piston-ring groove width	
Upper	2.030—2.055 mm.
Center	3.030—3.056 mm.
Lower	5.017—5.042 mm.
Piston diameter: (Piston is out-of-round and spherical)	
Standard	89.978—90.002 mm.
Oversize 0.5	90.478—90.502 mm.
Oversize 1.0	90.978—91.002 mm.
Piston clearance	0.0011—0.0024 in.
	0.03—0.06 mm.
Piston, removal	From upper side of block
Position of the piston	Notch turned forward

Piston and connecting rod must not be separated. Therefore, only piston with connecting rod mounted is available as a spare part.

PISTON RINGS

Upper compression ring	
Thickness	1.978—1.990 mm.
Width	0.15 in. max. (max. 3.76 mm.)
Piston-ring clearance in groove	0.0394—0.077 mm.
Gap in position	0.250—0.500 mm.
Lower compress. ring	
Thickness	2.978—2.990 mm.
Width	0.15 in. max. (max. 3.76 mm.)
Piston ring play (in groove)	0.040—0.078 in.
Gap in position	0.250—0.500 mm.
Oil control ring (tripartite)	
Thickness (total)	4.839—4.991 mm.
Width (segment)	3.430—3.580 mm.
Piston ring play in groove (total)	0.026—0.203 mm.
Gap in position (segment)	0.380—1.400 mm.

CONNECTING RODS

Bore diam. in big-end	
Red	56.820—56.830 mm.
Blue	56.830—56.840 mm.
Vertical inner diam. of fitted con-rod bearing inserts	
Standard blue	54.004—54.034 mm.
red	54.014—54.044 mm.
Undersize 0.05	53.943—53.983 mm.
0.25	53.760—53.800 mm.
0.50	53.506—53.546 mm.
0.75	53.252—53.292 mm.
1.00	52.998—53.038 mm.
Diam. of crankpins	
Standard blue	53.99 —53.98 mm.
red	54.00 —53.99 mm.
Undersize 0.05	53.929—53.919 mm.
0.25	53.476—53.736 mm.
0.50	53.492—53.482 mm.
0.75	53.238—53.228 mm.
1.00	52.984—52.974 mm.
Journal clear. in main bear.	
Standard	0.014—0.054 mm.
Undersize	0.014—0.064 mm.

CRANKSHAFT

Crankpin diameter	see above
Number of main bearings	3
Main bearing diam.	
Standard red	57.000—56.990 mm.
blue	56.990—56.980 mm.
Undersize 0.05	56.929—56.919 mm.
0.25	56.746—56.736 mm.
0.50	56.492—56.482 mm.
0.75	56.238—56.228 mm.
1.00	55.984—55.974 mm.
Vertical inner diam. of fitted main bearing inserts	
Standard blue	57.004—57.020 mm.
red	57.014—57.030 mm.
Undersize 0.25	56.760—56.776 mm.
0.50	56.506—56.522 mm.
0.75	56.252—56.268 mm.
1.00	55.998—56.014 mm.
Clear. betw. insert and crank pin	
Standard	0.012—0.048 mm.
Undersize	0.014—0.058 mm.
Thrust journal length (center main bearing)	26.44—26.39 mm.
Crankshaft end-play	0.102—0.203 mm.
Thrust (axial) bearing insert width	26.29—26.24 mm.

BALANCE SHAFT

Number of bearings	2
Clear. in bushing: Front	0.02—0.08 mm.
Rear	0.03—0.07 mm.
Balance shaft end-play	0.05—0.15 mm.
Inner diam. of bushings: Front	50.85—50.88 mm.
Rear	54.03—54.05 mm.
Bear. diam. of balance shaft: Front	50.83—50.80 mm.
Rear	54.00—53.98 mm.
Backlash, new drive gear	0.05—0.14 mm.
Backlash, wear limit	0.40 mm.

CAMSHAFT

Number of bearings	3
Insert diameter, Front	41.516—41.542 mm.
Center	41.135—41.161 mm.
Rear	40.754—40.780 mm.
Bearing clearance, All	0.077—0.0025 mm.
Inner diam. of bushings, Front	41.587—41.593 mm.
Center	41.186—41.212 mm.
Rear	40.805—40.831 mm.
Camshaft end-play	0.025—0.076 mm.
Spacer thickness, Red	4.064—4.089 mm.
Blue	4.089—4.114 mm.
Camshaft drive	gear pinion
Number of teeth on pinion	34
Number of teeth on camshaft gear	68
Backlash, new drive gear	0.05—0.20 mm.
Backlash, wear limit	0.40 mm.
Cam lift	0.256 in. (6.490 mm.)
Cam heel-to-toe dimension	34.201—33.998 mm.

VALVE MECHANISM

Angle of seat (cylinder head) intake and exhaust	45°	
Seat width, intake and exhaust	0.059—0.070 in. (1.5—1.7 mm.)	
Stem diameter		
Intake: Standard	8.043—8.025 mm.	
Oversize	8.243—8.225 mm.	
	8.443—8.425 mm.	
	8.643—8.625 mm.	
	8.843—8.825 mm.	
Exhaust: Standard	8.017—7.999 mm.	
Oversize	8.217—8.199 mm.	
	8.417—8.399 mm.	
	8.617—8.599 mm.	
	8.817—8.799 mm.	
		Monte Carlo
Stem bore in cyl. head intake and exhaust	8.063—8.088 mm.	
Clearance betw. stem and guide, Intake	0.020—0.063 mm.	
Exhaust	0.046—0.089 mm.	
Disc diam. Intake	1.46 in. (37 mm.)	
Exhaust	1.26 in. (32 mm.)	
Valve lift	0.38 in. (9.7 mm.)	
Valve clearance, cold engine		
Intake	0.014 in. (0.35 mm.)	
Exhaust	0.016 in. (0.40 mm.)	
Free length of springs	1.78 in. (45.2 mm.)	1.85 in. (47.0 mm.)
Fully compressed	1.13 in. (28.6 mm.)	1.06 in. (27.0 mm.)
Load for compression to 1.59 in. (40.26 mm.)	17.8—21.5 kp (39—47 lbs.)	27.0—30.0 kp (59—66 lbs.)
Valve tappet diam.	22.202—22.190 mm.	
Clear. betw. tappet and bore	0.023—0.060 mm.	

VALVE TIMING (meas. at valve play of 0.425 mm.)

Intake, Opens	21° BTDC
Closes	82° ATDC
Exhaust, Opens	63° BTDC
Closes	40° ATDC

LUBRICATION SYSTEM

Type	Circulation system lub. under pressure Oil pump of rotor type
Pressure lubricated bearings	Camshaft, crankshaft, balance shaft, connecting rods, rocker arms
Splash lubrication	Piston pins and cylinder walls
Transmission gear, lubrication	Oil spray

Oil filter, type	Full-flow type
Crankcase ventilation, semi enclosed	from the oil cap via crankcase to the air filter
Crankcase ventilation, totally enclosed	From air filter via crankcase and NOVO-valve to inlet manifold

Oil

Summer	SAE 20 W 20
	Multi-grade SAE 10 W 30
	Multi-grade SAE 10 W 40
Winter (below 14°F—10°C)	SAE 10 W
	Multi-grade SAE 10 W 30
	Multi-grade SAE 10 W 40
At extremely cold weather (constant temp. below —4°F (—20°C)	SAE 5 W 20

NOTE! This oil must not be used at temperatures above 32°F (0°C).

Oil pan cap. incl. oil filter	3.3 quarts (3.3 liters)
Oil pan cap. excl. oil filter	3.0 quarts (3 liters)
Oil pump relief valve opens at	47—55.5 psi (3.3—3.9 kp/cm²)
Oil press. warning light operates at	4.3—8.5 psi (0.3—0.6 kp/cm²)
Draining plug, thread	M 14x1.5 (width across flats 0.75 in. = 19 mm.)

Oil pump

Clearance rotor to housing	0.012 in. (0.3 mm.)
Clearance rotor to sealing surface	0.004 in. (0.1 mm.)

WRENCH TORQUES

Bolt Joints	kpm	ft. lbs.
Main bearing cap bolts	10	72
Connecting rod nuts	3,5	25
Crankshaft gear bolt	5,0	36
Flywheel retaining bolts, crankshaft	7,0	50
Camshaft thrust plate, block	2,0	15
Bolt — camshaft gear	5,0	36
Cylinder head to block (to be tightened in 3 stages)	5,5	40
	7,0	50
	9,5	68
Inlet manifold up to and incl. chassis No. 95/66.249, 96/524.379. To be tightened in 2 stages.		
Stage 1 Bolts	0.4—0.8	2.9—5.8
2 Bolts	2.2—2.9	16—21
Stage 1 Nuts	0.3—0.5	2.2—3.6
2 Nuts	1.5—1.8	11—13
From chassis No. 95/66.250, 96/524.380		
Stage 1 Bolts	0.4—0.8	2.9—5.8
2 Bolts	2.1—2.5	15—18
Stage 1 Nuts	0.4—0.8	2.9—5.8
2 Nuts	2.1—2.5	15—18
Intermediate plate to block	2.0	15
Transmission cover	2.0	15
Water pump to transmission cover	1.0	7
Pulley to balance shaft	5.0	36
Oil pump to block	1.5	11
Oil pan to block	0.5	4
Thermostat housing to induction manifold	2.0	15
Valve cover to cylinder head	0.5	4
Rocker shaft bracket	4.5	32

Oil filter half a turn after contact between gasket and engine block.

Fuel System

CARBURETORS

MODEL 1967—1968

Engine equipped with SaFree exhaust emission control device.

Type: Solex with automatic choke	28-32 PDSIT-7	32 PDSIT-4	32 PDSIT-4
Main jet	125	127.5	127.5
Choke tube	25.5	25.5	25.5
Emulsion jet	110	95	100
Idling jet, fuel	50	50	42.5
air (drilling)	1.5	1.5	1.5
	1.5	1.5	1.5
Float valve			
Float weight	7.3 g.	7.3 g.	7.3 g.
Acceleration jet	50	50	50

Acceleration
pump cap.   0.6±0.12 (cu. in.) 10±2 cm³/10 strokes
Idling speed   800— 900 rpm
Fast idling
  stage I   1100—1300 rpm
  stage II   1700—1900 rpm
  stage III   2700—2900 rpm
Float level when
  idling   Nom. 0.59±0.04 in. (15±1 mm.)
                                         from gasket level

MODEL 1969
Engine equipped with SaFree Exhaust Emission Control Device.

Type	FoMoCo C8GH —9510—G	C8GH—9510 —H (USA)
Choke	Automatic	Automatic
Main jet	140	135
Float valve	2.0	2.0
Acceleration pump cap.	0.27—0.4 cu. in. (4.5—6.5 cm)/10 strokes	
Idling speed	800—900 rpm	900 rpm
Fast idling third step	1800 rpm	1900—2100 rpm
Float level, fully closed float valve	1.08 in. (27.5 mm.)	1.080±0.010 in. (27.5±0.25 mm.)
Float level, fully open float valve	1.34 in. (34.0 mm.)	1.420±0.010 in. (36±0.25 mm.)

MODEL 1970

Type	See above	70 TW—9510 —AA (USA)
Choke		Automatic
Main jet		135
Float valve		2.0
Idling speed		900 rpm
Rapid idling speed with headlights lower beam on third step		1700—1900 rpm
Float level, fully closed float valve		1.080±0.010 in. (27.5±0.25 mm.)
Float level, fully open float valve		1.420±0.010 in. (36±0.25 mm.)

FUEL PUMP
Type   Membrane pump driven by
                         eccentric on camshaft
Feeding pressure   3.4—4.3 psi (0,24—0,30 kp/cm²)
                         at 4000 crankshaft rpm

FUEL TANK
Capacity: SAAB 96 and Monte Carlo   10.5 gal. (40 liters)
          SAAB 95   11.5 gal. (43 liters)
Fuel transmitter
  Type, SAAB 95 to chassis No. 57.023   Veglia 67-8011
  Type, SAAB 95 from 57.024   VDO 38/20
  Type, SAAB 96 to chassis No. 475.599   VDO 20.228
  Type, SAAB 96 from 475.600   VDO 38/228

Exhaust System

Exhaust pipe, internal diameter   1.34 in. (34 mm.)

Cooling System

Type   overpressure
Capacity incl. heater
  Model 1969   7.2 quarts (6.8 liters)
  Model 1969 USA   7.5 quarts (7.1 liters)
  Model 1967—68   7.9 quarts (7.5 liters)
Thermostat opening range   181°F. (83°C.), previous
                                        type 189°F. (87°C.)
  Max. opening   0.28 in. (7 mm.)
Radiator pressure cap opens at   2.2—4.3 psi
                                      (0.25—0.30 kp/cm)
Fanbelt, designation   9.5 x 1025 La.

Freezing points for glycol mixtures

Volume % glycol	Freezing Point °F.	°C.
10	25	−4
20	14	−10
30	1	−17
40	−15	−26
50	−38	−39

Electrical System

BATTERY
Voltage   12 V
Capacity   44 Ah

ALTERNATOR, BOSCH
Type   K 1 ←→ 14V 35 A 20   0 120 400 565
Rated voltage   14 V
Rated rpm   2000
Max. permiss. contin. load   35 A
Direction of rotation   Clockwise and counter-clockwise
Brush-spring pressure   10.5—14 oz. (300—400 g.)

CHARGING REGULATOR, BOSCH
Type   Bosch AD   1 14 V
                                 (not radio suppressed)

STARTER MOTOR, BOSCH	Model 1967-68	Model 1969-70
Type	EF (R) 12V 0,8 PS 0 001 208 029	GF 12V 1,0 PS 0 001 311 024
Number of teeth on pinion	9	
Number of teeth on ring gear	138	
Brush-spring pressure	40.5—46 oz. 1150—1800 g.)	
Output	0.8 hp	1.0 hp

DISTRIBUTOR, BOSCH
Type   JFUR 4
  Previous designation: 0 231 146 044 or
                         0 231 146 024
  Latest designation: 0 231 146 033 or
                         0 231 146 073   1 231 146 084
Capacitor   1 237 330 091
Ignition setting
  Basic setting with
    test lamp   6°, BTDC
  Basic setting with
    stroboscope at
    500 rpm with
    disconnected vac. hose   6°, BTDC
        NOTE: 1° on balance shaft pulley corre-
        sponds to approx. 0.05 in. (1.2 mm.) on
        circumference of pulley.
Order of firing, cyl. 1 is
  the furthermost right-
  hand one   1—3—4—2
Breaker gap   0.016 in. (0.4 mm.)
Dwell angle   50±2°
Contact pressure   14—19 oz.
                          (400—530 g.)
Direction of rotation   clockwise

IGNITION COIL, BOSCH
Type   K 12
Performances at a primary
  voltage of 12 V
  4,000 sparks/minute
  (1,000 distributor
  rev.) Spark length
  min.   0.55 in. (14 mm.)
  16,000 sparks/minute
  (4,000 distributor
  rev.) Spark length
  min.   0.24 in. (6 mm.)
Primary-winding resis. (bet.
  connect. 1 and 15)   3.1—3.6 ohms

SPARK PLUGS

Black or Silver Painted Engine	Blue Engine
Up to chassis No. 95/55.766, 96/487.638	As from chassis No. 95/55.767, 96/487.639
For USA up to chassis No. 95/54.854, 96/482.197	For USA as from chassis No. 95/54.855, 96/482.198

Auto-Lite		AE-22	AG-22		
Auto-Lite interference					
suppressed		AER-22			
Bosch		W 225 T35	W 200 T30		
Champion		L 82 Y	N-9Y		
NGK		B-7 H	BP 7E		
Electrode gap		0.024—0.028 in. (0.6—0.7 mm.)			
Tightening torque		22—29 ft. lbs. (3.0—4.0 kpm.)			

BULBS

	Qty.				
	SAAB 95	SAAB 96	Monte Carlo	Cap	Effect
Headlights					
Sealed Beam	2	2	2		50/40 W
Asymmetric	2	2	2	P 45 T	45/40 W
Parking light and dir. ind.					
light, front	2	2	2	BAY 15 D	21/5 W
Stop light and dir. ind.					
light, rear	4	4	4	BA 15 S	21 W
Tail	2	2	2	BA 15 S	5 W
License plate	2	2	2	S 8,5	5 W
Back-up	—	—	2	BAY 15 D	21/5 W
Dome	2	1	1	S 8,5	5 W
Fog and spot			2	BA 20 S	45 W
Temp., fuel gauge, speedom.			4	BA 7 S	2 W
Lighting, clock			1	BA 9 S	4 W
Lighting, tachometer			1	BA 9 S	2 W
Control lamps	9	11	6	BA 7 S	2 W
Other instr. lamps	2			BA 9 S	2 W
Trunk		1	1	BA 9 S	4 W
Fuses	12	12	12		8 A

As FROM MODEL 1969

Headlights, Sealed Beam	2	2			50/40 W
Asymmetric	2	2		P 45 T	45/40 W
Parking light, front	2	2		BA 15 S	5 W
Dir. ind., front	2	2		BA 15 S	21 W
Parking and dir.				US No. 1073	
ind., front (USA)	2	2		BAY 15 D	5/21 W
Dir. ind., rear	2	2		BA 15 S	21 W
Tail	2	2		BA 15 S	5 W
Stop	2	2		BA 15 S	21 W
License plate	3	2		S 8,5	5 W
Control and instrument	11	11		BA 7 S	2 W
Dome	2	1		S 8,5	5 W
Trunk		1		BA 9 S	4 W
Back-up	2			BA 15 S	21 W
Side position (USA)	2			BA 9 S Mini.	4 W
Tachometer (USA)		2		BA 9 S Mini.	2 W

FLASHER UNIT		
Type: Lucas		FL 5 12 V 42 W
Hella		91 PSt 2x32 Cp 12 V

HORN, HELLA	
Type	B 32/5—12 V

HEATER FAN MOTOR	
Type: Electrolux	KS 3430/220 12 V

WINDSHIELD WIPER MOTOR	
Type: Lucas up to and incl. model 1969	DL 3 A
Lucas as from model 1970	15 W

WINDSHIELD WASHER	
Monte Carlo model 1967	Dahlberg
Windshield washer from model 1968 (all models)	Meab

Transmission

Oil capacity	1.4 quarts (1.4 liters)
Type of oil	EP-oil SAE 80
Gear ratios, total	
1st gear	17.0:1
2nd gear	10.2:1
3rd gear	6.3:1
4th gear	4.1:1
Reverse	15.5:1
Differential gear ratio, pinion: ring gear	4.88:1
Number of teeth, pinion: ring gear	8:39

Road speed in mph at 1000 rpm engine speed

	SAAB 95	SAAB 96	Monte Carlo
Tire dimension	5.60 x 15 in.	5.20 x 15 in.	155 x 15 in.
1st gear	4.2 mph (6.8 km/h)	4.2 mph (6.7 km/h)	4.2 mph (6.7 km/h)
2nd gear	7.1 mph (11.4 km/h)	7.0 mph (11.2 km/h)	6.9 mph (11.1 km/h)
3rd gear	11.5 mph (18.5 km/h)	11.3 mph (18.2 km/h)	11.2 mph (18.0 km/h)
4th gear	17.7 mph (28.4 km/h)	17.2 mph (27.8 km/h)	17.1 mph (27.6 km/h)
Reverse	4.7 mph (7.5 km/h)	4.7 mph (7.4 km/h)	4.5 mph (7.3 km/h)

Pinion/ring-gear adjustment: specified dimension ±0.002 in. (0.05 mm.). Ring-gear backlash: specified dimension ±0.002 in. (0.05 mm.).

MATCHED GEAR SETS

3rd speed gear	Ring gear
Pinion shaft 3rd gear	Pinion shaft
4th speed gear	Synchromesh
Pinion shaft 4th gear	

TIGHTENING TORQUES, TRANSMISSION

	Bolts		Tightening Torques	
Bolt	Quant.	Size	kpm	ft. lbs.
Transmiss. case end cover	6	5/16 in.	2.5	18
Differential bearings	4	3/8 in.	4	29
Ring gear bolts	12	5/16 in.	2.5	18
Pinion-shaft nut. First tightening, then slacken and retighten	1	7/8 in.	12	87
			6	44
Nut, primary shaft	1	3/4 in.	5	36
Nut, countershaft	1	9/16 in.	8	60

Clutch

FICHTEL & SACHS

Type	single dry plate
Clearance, release bearing — clutch meas. at slave cylinder	0.16 in. (4 mm.)
Clearance bet. release plate and flywheel	approx. 1 in. (26 mm.)
Pressure-plate springs	
Length compressed	0.96 (24.5 mm.)
Tension compressed	134—147 lbs. (61—67 kp.)
Dimensions of clutch facing	5—6.5 in. (127x190.5 mm.)
New clutch disc thickness, unloaded	0.33±0.04 in. (8.4±0.1 mm.)
loaded with 825 lbs. (375 kg)	0.28±0.01 in. (7.2±0.3 mm.)
Max. throw clutch disc	0.024 in. (0.6 mm.)
Engagement pressure	750—935 lbs. (340—425 kp.)

CLUTCH OPERATION, HYDRAULIC
UP TO MODEL 1968

	Master cylinder	Slave cylinder
Make and type	Girling	Girling 3/4 in.
	5/8 in.	
Cylinder diameter	5/8 in.	3/4 in.
Max. permissible stroke	1.38 in. (35 mm.)	
Hose connection	3/8 in. UNF-24	3/8 in. UNF-24
Hose length bet. master and slave cyl.	14 in. (355.6 mm.)	

Distance from clutch-pedal
 foot plate to lower part
 of dash panel (max.
 pedal stroke)   approx. 6.3 in. (ca 160 mm.)
Clearance, release bearing—
 clutch meas. at slave
 cylinder   0.16 in. (4 mm.)

As from Model 1969

Make and type	Lockeed	Girling
	5/8 in.	3/4 in.
Cylinder diameter	5/8 in.	3/4 in.
Stroke	1.22 in.	
	(31 mm.)	
Hose connection	7/16 in.—	7/16 in.—
	20 UNF-2B	20 UNF-2B

Hose length bet. master and
 slave cyl.   15.3 in.
                                        (388.6 mm.)
Distance from clutch—pedal
 foot plate to lower part of
 dash panel (max. pedal
 stroke)   5.1 in.
                                        (130 mm.)
Clearance, release bearing—
 clutch measured at slave
 cylinder   0.16 in.
                                        (4 mm.)

Brakes

General
Make   Lockheed
Type, front   Disc brake
  rear   One leading shoe
Footbrake, up to and incl. model 1968   Hydraulic, diagonal
                                        twocircuit type
  from model 1969   Hydraulic, diagonal
                                        twocircuit type
                                        with vacuum servo
Handbrake   Mechanical

Dimensions, Etc.
Brake front, disc   10 1/2 in. (266.70 mm.)
  rear, drum   8 in. (203.2 mm.)
Master cylinder, models 1967, 1968   3/4 in.
  from model 1969   13/16 in.
Wheel cylinder, front   2 in.
  rear   SAAB 96, Monte Carlo: 5/8 in.
                    SAAB 95 up to and incl. model
                                        1969: 3/4 in.
                    SAAB 95 as from model
                                        1970: 5/8 in.
Brake shoes, rear   8x1 1/2 in.
Brake hoses, front, length of   8 1/2 in.
  rear, length of   SAAB 96 and Monte Carlo
                    8 1/2 in., SAAB 95 6 1/2 in.
Other brake lines   3/16 in. Bunday tube
Clearance between master-cylinder
 piston and pushrod   0.024—0.047 in.
                                        (0.6—1.2 mm.)
Same clearance at tip of brake pedal   0.12—0.24 in.
                                        (3—6 mm.)
Distance, brake-pedal footplate
 to lower part of dash panel
 max. stroke approx.   6.3 in. (160 mm.)
Brake fluid   Satisfying the requirements
                                of spec. SAE 70 R 3, e.g.
                                Lockheed Super Heavy
                                Duty Brake Fluid.
Adjustment machining of brake drums
 permitted to max. diam., rear   8.06 in. (204.7 mm.)
Max. total indicated radial
 brake-drum throw   0.006 in. (0.15 mm.)
Max. total indicated axial
 brake disc throw   0.08 in. (0.2 mm.)
Centerless grinding of brake
 linings   Thickness of rear brake lining:
                                0.020—0.022 in. (0.50—0.56
                                mm.) less than that of the drum

Torques
Castle nut, front wheel hub   18 kpm., 130 ft. lbs.
              rear wheel hub   9 kpm., 65 ft. lbs.

Vacuum Servo (from Model 1969)
Make   Lockheed
Type   4258—193

Suspension and Wheel Alignment

Wheel Alignment
Front wheel alignment, no load
  Kingpin inclination   7±1°
  Caster   2±1/2°
  Camber   3/4±1/4°
Toe-in at wheel rim   0.08±0.04 in. (2±1 mm.)
Turning angles
  Outside wheels   20°
  Inside wheels   22 1/2±1 1/2°

Steering Gear	Up to and incl. model 1968	From Model 1969
Steering-gear adjustment		
Pinion axial clearance	0.004—0.008 in.	max. 0.005 in.
	(0.1—0.2 mm.)	(0.12 mm.)
Radial clearance of rack	max. 0.012 in.	max. 0.01 in.
	(0.3 mm.)	(0.25 mm.)
Steering ratio, steering wheel/road wheels average	14:1	15.5:1
Wheel travel betw. limit positions	2 1/4 turns	2.7 turns
Tie-rod ends		
Distance betw. wrench flat (end of thread) and locknut	max. 1.5 in.	max. 1.2 in.
	(40 mm.)	(30 mm.)
Permiss. dif. betw. lefthand and right-hand dimen.	max. 0.08 in.	max. 0.08 in.
	(2 mm.)	(2 mm.)

The following is valid for certain cars of
model 1968. The distance between end
of thread and locknut must not exceed
1.2 in. (30 mm.).

Tightening Torque
Nut, tie-rod end   3.5—5 kpm., 25—36 ft. lbs.

Rear Wheel Alignment
Camber   0±1°
Toe-in (toe-out) both wheels
 together or meas. rim-to-rim   0±0.28 in. (7 mm.)
Toe-in (toe-out) per wheel
 must not exceed   0±3/4°
Max. dif. in wheelbase, left and (front
 wheels pointing straight ahead)   0.6 in. (15 mm.)

Front Shock Absorbers
Type   Telescopic, hydraulic
Length   9 3/4 in. (250 mm.)
                       Extended 15 3/8 in. (390 mm.)
                                3 1/4 in. (82 mm.)
                   From Model 1968, 3 1/3 in. (85 mm.)

Rear Shock Absorbers	SAAB 95	SAAB 96, Monte Carlo
Type	Arm, hydraulic	Telescopic, hydraulic
Length betw. center hole and shoulder for washer		10 in. (255 mm.)
Extended		16 7/16 in. (417 mm.)
Stroke	4 1/4 in. (106 mm.)	4 1/4 in. (106 mm.)

Front coil spring	Model 1967	Model 1968-70
Max. expansion,	5 1/2 in. (140 mm.)	5 1/2 in. (140 mm.)
length	15.4 in. (391 mm.)	15.9 in. (405 mm.)
number of coils	11	10 1/2
Wire diameter	0.46 in. (11.7 mm.)	0.48 in. (12 mm.)

	SAAB 95	SAAB 96, Monte Carlo
Rear coil spring		
Max. expansion	6 3/4 in. (170 mm.)	6 3/4 in. (170 mm.)
Length	13 1/2 in. (342 mm.)	13 1/2 in. (342 mm.)
Number of coils	9	9
Wire diameter	0.45 in. (11.4 mm.)	0.43 in. (11.0 mm.)

WHEEL BOLTS

Width across flats	3/4 in. (19.05 mm.)	3/4 in. (19.05 mm.)
Thread SAAB 95 and 96	UNC 9/16 in.	UNC 9/16 in.
Thread Monte Carlo	UNC 5/8 in.	UNC 9/16 in.

TIGHTENING TORQUES

Castle nut,
Front wheel hub	18 kpm	130 ft. lbs.
Rear wheel hub	9 kpm	65 ft. lbs.
Wheel bolts	8—10 kpm	58—72 ft. lbs.

WHEELS

Type   wide base disc (from model 1969 with safety rim)

Size	4Jx15 in.
Depth of drop center	1.77 in. (45 mm.)
Permiss. out-of-round of rim	0.06 in. (1.5 mm.)
Permiss. rim runout	0.06 in. (1.5 mm.)

TIRES, SAAB 95 AND 96

Size, SAAB 96	520x15 in. or 5.60x15 in. or 155SR 15 in.
SAAB 95	5.60x15 in. or 155SR 15 in.

Tire pressure
Lightly loaded, front and rear	24 psi (1.7 kp/cm)
Fully loaded, front and rear	27 psi (1.9 kp/cm)

At full load the rear tires of the SAAB V4 station wagon should be inflated to 30 psi (2.1 kp/cm).

TIRES, MONTE CARLO

Size, Monte Carlo, with tube   155x15 in.

Tire Pressure	Front	Rear
Light load	21 psi (1.5 kp/cm²)	20 psi (1.4 kp/cm²)
Full load	24 psi (1.7 kp/cm²)	24 psi (1.7 kp/cm²)

For fast driving, the tire pressure should be 24 psi (1.7 kp/cm² both front and rear, irrespective of load.

Body

SPECIFICATIONS	SAAB 95	SAAB 96, Monte Carlo
Body dimensions		
Overall length	13 ft. 7 in. (4160 mm.)	12 ft. 10 in. (3930 mm.)
width	5 ft. 2 in. (1585 mm.)	5 ft. 2 in. (1585 mm.)
height	4 ft. 1 1/2 in. (1256 mm.)	4 ft. 1 in. (1240 mm.)
Weight of body, total excl. hood, doors, fenders, lug. compart. cover	646 lbs. (293 kg.) 496 lbs. (225 kg.)	555 lbs. (252 kg.) 415 lbs. (188 kg.)

Instruments

SPEEDOMETER DRIVE RATIO

Model	Ratio ring gear: pinion	Dynamic radius of road wheel in.	mm.	Speedometer Rev. per kilometer covered	Rev. per mile covered
95	8:39	12.2	310	565	910
96	8:39	11.8	305	575	926
Monte Carlo	8:39	11.8	300	585	942

Specifications—SAAB Sonett II (two-stroke)

General Specifications

Overall length, including bumpers	12 ft. 4 in. (3770 mm.)
Overall width	4 ft. 11 in. (1500 mm.)
Overall height with driver	3 ft. 10 in. (1160 mm.)
Ground clearance at curb weight	5 in. (125 mm.)
Track, front and rear	4 ft. (1220 mm.)
Wheelbase	7 ft. 1 in. (2149 mm.)
Turning circle diameter	31 ft. 6 in. (9.6 m.)
Curb weight incl. fuel, water, tools and spare tire	1.630 lbs. (740 kg.)
Weight distribution fully loaded	front 60%

Engine

GENERAL DATA

Cubic capacity	51.9 cu. in. (841 cc.)
Brake horsepower, DIN	60 at 5200 rpm
Torque, DIN	69.4 ft. lbs. (9.6 kpm.) at 4000 rpm
Bore	2.76 in. (70 mm.)
Stroke	2.87 in. (73 mm.)
Compression ratio	9:1
Order of firing	1—2—3

DIMENSIONS AND TOLERANCES (in mm.)

Bore, standard	
Class A	69.987—69.994
AB	69.994—70.001
B	70.001—70.008
C	70.036—70.046
Bore, oversizes (OD)	
0.5 A	70.501—70.508
B	70.508—70.515
1.0 A	71.001—71.008
B	71.008—71.015

The letters OD are stamped into the oversize pistons and into the cylinder block

Piston diameter, standard	
Class A	69.895—69.902
AB	69.902—69.909
B	69.909—69.916
C	69.944—69.951
Piston diameter, oversizes (OD)	
0.5 A	70.409—70.416
B	70.416—70.423
1.0 A	70.909—70.916
B	70.916—70.923

Measuring the piston dia. meas. at an angle of 90° to piston pin

Distance from lower edge of piston when meas.	0.6 in. (15 mm.)
Piston clearance	0.085—0.099 mm.
Max. permiss. clear. bet. piston and cylinder, limit of wearing	0.0059 in. (0.15 mm.)

Out-of-round, piston
	in.	mm.
Dif. in meas. at 90° to pin and in line with pin	0.03—0.04	0.08—0.10

Dist. from lower edge of piston when meas.	0.6 in. (15 mm.)
With of piston rings, upper	2.478—2.490 mm.
Width of piston ring, lower	1.978—1.990 mm.
Piston-ring gap	0.01—0.02 in. (0.25—0.50 mm.)

Piston-ring clear. in groove

Upper	0.0035–0.0043 in.	(0.08–0.11 mm.)
Center	0.0027–0.0040 in.	(0.07–0.10 mm.)
Lower	0.0024–0.0035 in.	(0.06–0.09 mm.)

Diameter of piston pin   0.75 in. (18 mm.)
Axial clear. of connecting rod

At crankpin	0.807–0.913 in.	(2.05–2.32 mm.)
At piston pin	0.004–0.016 in.	(0.1 –0.4 mm.)

Radial clear. of connecting rod
 bearing   0.0004–0.0006 in. (0.010–0.016 mm.)
Radial clear. of piston pin
 bearing   Should fit with light thumb
                                  pressure. Pin easily rotable
                                       with 2 fingers
Max. lateral throw of crankshaft   0.02 in. (0.05 mm.)
Compression in new engine (measured
 at engine temp. of 175°F or 80°C
 with throttle wide open and full
 starter rpm)   all cyl. 128±7.1 psi
                                        (9.0±0.5 kp/cm²)

WRENCH TORQUES

		Bolts		Wrench torque		
Unit	Quant.	Size	Kpm.	in. lbs.	ft. lbs.
Spark plugs	3	M 18	4.5	390	32
Cylinder head	12	7/16 in.	3¹	275¹	22¹
Crankcase halves	8	5/16 in.	2.5	220	18
	8	3/8 in.	4	340	29
Flywheel bolts	8	5/16 in.	3	275	22
Crankshaft pulley	1	1/2 in.	5	440	36

   Note: Angle tightening of cylinder head bolts.
   ¹ After tightening to a torque of 3 kpm (= 275
   in. lbs. or 22 ft. lbs.), turn bolt through 90°.
   When the engine has warmed up, turn
   through another 20°. After 1200 miles (2000
   km) driving, another 20°.

Fuel System

Fuel tank capacity	15.8 gals (60 litres)
Fuel pumps	Bendix 480534

CARBURETOR

Type Solex	3–40 DHW sidedraft
Choke tube	33
Main jet, cyl. 1 and 3	122.5
cyl. 2	130
Emulsion jet	240
Bypass fuel jet	65
Bypass air jet	100
Idling fuel jet (only carburetor, cyl. 2)	45
Idling air jet (only carburetor, cyl. 2)	100
Float, return fuel chamber	7.3 g.
Float value, return fuel chamber	2.0 g.

Exhaust System

GENERAL DATA
Inside dia. of exhaust pipe   1.34 in. (34 mm.)

Cooling System

SPECIFICATION

Capacity of cooling system incl. heater system	1.72 U.S. gal. (6.5 liters)
Thermostat opening temp.	180°F. (82°C)
Radiator press. cap opens at	3.4–4.25 psi (0.25–0.30 kp/cm²)

TABLES
The freezing point in the table below is the temperature at
which ice crystals begin to form in the cooling system. The
use of alcohol as anti-freeze is not recommended, since it
evaporates at relatively low temperatures. Both glycol and
alcohol are injurious to paintwork and must therefore be
handled with care.

Amount of glycol in the cooling and heating system

Quarts of glycol in system	Approx. % by volume	Freezing point °C.	Freezing point °F.	Boiling point °C.	Boiling point °F.	Specific gravity
1	15	−7	19	101	214	1.020
2	31	−18	±0	102	216	1.035
3	46	−33	−27	105	221	1.053

Electrical System

BATTERY

Voltage	12 V
Capacity	44 Ah

GENERATOR, BOSCH

Gear ratio generator–engine	1.68:1
Type	K1 ⟷ 14V 35A 20
Rated voltage	12 V
Max. permissible continuous load	35 A
Direction of rotation	Clockwise and counter-clockwise

CHARGING REGULATOR, BOSCH

Type	BOSCH ADN 1 14V
Cut-in voltage	12.4–13.1 V
Voltage setting when idling	13.5–14.5 V
Voltage setting with a load of 25 A	13.3–14.3 V
Reverse current relay breaks at	2–7.5 A
Max. output of warm regulator	300 W
Max. output of cold regulator (2-3 min. after start.)	420 W

STARTER MOTOR, BOSCH

Type	AL/EDD 0.5/12 R 4
Number of teeth on pinion	9
Number of teeth on ring gear	97
Brush-spring pressure	800–900 g. (19–25 oz.)

DISTRIBUTOR, BOSCH

Type	JF3(R)
Capacitor	LMKO 1 Z 30
Ignition setting	
Basic setting	10° BTDC
At 3000 rpm.	20° BTDC
Order of firing	1–2–3
Breaker gap	0.35–0.45 mm. (0.014–0.018 in.)
Dwell angle	75°–82°
Contact pressure	400–530 g. (14–19 oz.)
Direction of rotation	Clockwise
Axial play, distr. shaft	(0.1–0.2 mm.) 0.004–0.008 in.

IGNITION COIL, BOSCH

Type	KW 12V
Series resistance	Vitron

SPARK PLUGS

Type	Side electrode Bosch MGV 260 T31S
Electrode gap with resist. ignit. cable (starting electrode)	0.022–0.024 in. (0.55–0.60 mm.)
Thread	0.75 in. (18 mm.)
Tightening torque	32 ft. lbs. (4.5 kpm.)

BULBS

	Philips Number No.	Watts
Headlights, sealed beam	2	
Parking lights, front	2 12819	6W
Flasher, front	2 1073	25W
Stop lights and flashers, rear	4 1073	25W
Tail lights	2 12821	5W
License plate lights	2 12844	5W
Map reading light	1 12844	5W
Temp. and fuel gauges, Speedometer and control lights	9 12829	2W
Other instrument lights	2 12913	2W
Back-up lights	2 1034	32 Cp
Clock, lighting	1 12929	4W
Fuses	12	8 Amps.

FLASHER UNIT

Type: Lucas	FL5 12V 42 W
Hella	91 PSt 2x32 Cp 12 V

Horn, Hella
Type   B 32/5—12 V

Fuel Gauge Tank Unit
Type   VDO 625

Heater Fan Motor
Type: Electrolux   KS 3430/220 12 V

Windshield Wiper Motor
Type: Lucas   LUCAS DL 3 A

Windshield Washer   Dahlberg

Tightening Torques

Application	Bolts No.	Size	Tightening torques kpm	in. lbs.	ft. lbs.
Transmiss. case end cover	6	5/16 in.	2.5	220	18
Differential bearings	4	3/8 in.	4	340	29
Ring gear bolts	12	5/16 in.	2.5	220	18
Pinion-shaft nut. First tightening	1	7/8 in.	12	1050	87
Then slacken and retighten			6	530	44
Nut, primary shaft	1	3/4 in.	5	425	36
Nut, countershaft	1	9/16 in.	8	700	60

Clutch

Fichtel & Sachs

Type	Single dry plate
Clearance bet. release plate and flywheel	1.02±0.02 in. (26±0.5 mm.)
Pressure-plate springs	
Length uncompressed	1.95 in. (49.5 mm.)
Length compressed	1.16 in. (29.4 mm.)
Tension, compressed	108—115 lbs. (49—52 kp.)
Min. permiss. tension compressed	100 lbs. (45 kp.)
Inner springs	
Length uncompressed	1.95 in. (49.5 mm.)
Length compressed	1.03 in. (26.2 mm.)
Tension, compressed	35—40 lbs. (16—18 kp.)
Min. permiss. tension compressed	33 lbs. (15 kp.)
Dimensions of clutch facing	(180x125x3.5 mm.)
New clutch disc	
Thickness, unloaded	0.358—0.370 in. (9.1—9.4 mm.)
loaded with 770 lbs. (350 kp.)	0.327—0.343 in. (8.3-8.7 mm.)
Max. throw clutch disc	0.024 in. (0.6 mm.)
Engagement pressure	860—926 lbs. (390—420 kp.)

Transmission

Specifications

Oil capacity	1.4 quarts (1.4 liters)
Type of oil	SAE 80 EP
Gear ratios, total	
1st gear	17.0:1
2nd gear	10.2:1
3rd gear	6.3:1
4th gear	4.1:1
Reverse	15.5:1
Differential gear ratio, pinion ring gear	4.88:1
No. of teeth, pinion: ring gear	8:39
Road speed in mph at 1000 rpm engine speed	
1st gear	4.2
2nd gear	6.9
3rd gear	11.1
4th gear	17.2
Reverse	4.5

        Pinion/ring-gear adjustment: specified dimension ±0.002 in. (0.05 mm.). Ring-gear backlash: specified dimension ±0.002 in. (0.05 mm.).

Matched Gearsets
4-speed

3rd speed gear	Ring gear
Pinion shaft 3rd gear	Pinion shaft
4th speed gear	Synchromesh
Pinion shaft 4th gear	

Brake System

General

Make	Lockheed
Type, front	Disc brake
rear	One leading shoe
Footbrake	Hydraulic two-circuit type
Handbrake	Mechanical

Dimensions, Etc.:

Brake front, disc	10 1/2 in. (266,70 mm.)
rear, drum	8 in. (203,2 mm.)
Master cylinder	3/4 in.
Wheel cylinder, front	2 in.
rear	5/8 in.
Brake shoes, rear	8 in. x 1 1/2in.
Brake hoses, front, length of	8 1/2 in.
rear, length of	8 1/2 in.
Other brake lines	3/16 in. Bundy tube
Clearance between master-cylinder piston and push-rod	0.024—0.047 in. (0.6—1.2 mm.)
Same clearance at tip of brake pedal	0.12—0.24 mm. (3—6 mm.)
Brake fluid	SAE 70 R3
Adjustment machining of brake drums permitted to max. dia. Rear	8.059 in. (204.7 mm.)
Max. total indicated radial brake-drum throw	0.006 in. (0.15 mm.)
Max. total indicated axial brake drum-throw	0.08 in. (0.2 mm.)
Centerless grinding of brake linings, rear	0.020—0.022 in. (0.50—0.56 mm.) less than the drum
Tightening torques	
Castle nut, front	
wheel hub	18 kpm., 1500 in. lbs., 130 ft. lbs.
rear	
wheel hub	9 kpm., 800 in. lbs., 65 ft. lbs.

Suspension, Steering, and Wheel Alignment

Wheel Alignment

Front wheel alignment, no load	
Kingpin inclination	7° ± 1
Caster	2° ± 1/2
Camber	0° ± 1/4
Toe-in at wheel rim	0.04 in. ± 0.04 (1 mm. ± 1)
Turning angles	
Outside wheels	20°
Inside wheels	22 1/2° ± 1 1/2

Steering Gear

Steering-gear adjustment	
Pinion axial clearance	0.04—0.08 in. (0.1—0.2 mm.)
Radial clearance of rack,	max. 0.012 in. (0.3 mm.)
Steering, ratio	14:1
Wheel travel between limit positions	2 1/4 turns
Tie-rod ends	
Distance between wrench flat and retaining nut	Max. 1.5 in. (40 mm.)
Permissible difference between left hand and right hand dimension	Max. 0.08 in. (2 mm.)

Tightening Torque
Nut, tie-rod end 3.5—5 kpm., 300—440 in. lbs., 25—36 ft. lbs.

Front Coil Spring
Max. expansion, front   5 1/2 in. (140 mm.)

Length | 13.3 in. (350 mm.)
Number of coils | 8
Wire diameter | 0.46 in. (11.7 mm.)

REAR COIL SPRING
Max. expansion | 6 3/4 in. (170 mm.)
Length | 11.8 in. (300 mm.)
Number of coils | 6 1/2
Wire diameter | 0.4 in. (10 mm.)

REAR WHEEL ALIGNMENT
Camber | 0° ± 1
Toe-in (toe-out) | 0° ± 1
Both wheels together or measured
rim-to-rim | 0 ±−0.28 in. (7 mm.)
Toe-in (toe-out) per wheel must not
exceed | 0° ± 3/4
Max. dif. in wheelbase, left
and right (front wheels pointing
straight ahead) | 0.6 in. (15 mm.)

FRONT SHOCK ABSORBERS
Type | Telescopic, hydraulic
Length | 9 3/4 in. (250 mm.)
Extended 14 1/2 in. (390 mm.)
Stroke, fitted | 3 1/4 in. (2 mm.)
Extended | 14 1/2 in. (390 mm.)

REAR SHOCK ABSORBERS
Type | Telescopic, hydraulic
Length between center hole and
shoulder for washer | 10 in. (255 mm.)
Extended | 16 7/16 in. (417 mm.)
Stroke | 4 1/4 in. (106 mm.)

WHEELS
Type | wide base
Size | 4J x 15 in.
Depth of drop center | 1.77 in. (45 mm.)
Permissible out-of-round of rim | 0.06 in. (1.5 mm.)
Permissible runout | 0.06 in. (1.5 mm.)

TIRES

	Front	Rear
Tire pressure, dim. 155 x 15 in.	21 psi	20 psi
	(1.5 kp/cm²)	(1.4 kp/cm²)

WHEEL BOLTS
Width across flats | 3/4 in. (19.05 mm.)
Thread | UNC 9/16 in.
TIGHTENING TORQUES
Castle nut, front
wheel hub | 18 kpm., 1500 in. lbs., 130 ft. lbs.
rear
wheel hub | 9.5 kpm., 850 in. lbs., 70 ft. lbs.
Wheel bolts | 8−10 kpm., 670−850 in. lbs., 58−72 ft. lbs.

Instruments

Model	Ratio ring gear: pinion	Dynamic radius of road wheel in.	Dynamic radius of road wheel mm.	Speedometer Rev. per kilometer covered	Rev. per mile covered
Sonett II	8:39	11.8	300	585	942

Specifications—SAAB Sonett II (V4)

General Specifications

Overall length, including bumpers | 12 ft. 4 in. (3770 mm.)
Overall width | 4 ft. 11 in. (1500 mm.)
Overall height with driver | 3 ft. 10 in. (1160 mm.)
Ground clearance at curb weight | 5 in. (125 mm.)
Track, front and rear | 4 ft. 2.5 in. (1232 mm.)

Wheelbase | 7 ft. 1 in. (2149 mm.)
Turning circle diameter | 31 ft. 6 in. (9.6 mm.)
Curb weight, incl. fuel, water, tools
and spare tire | 1.700 lbs. (775 kg.)
Weight distribution
fully loaded | front 56%

Engine

GENERAL DATA
Engine, type V4 | 4−stroke, 4 cylinders
Power DIN at 4700 rpm | 65 bhp
Max. torque at 2500 rpm | 85 ft. lbs. (11.7 kpm.)
Compression ratio, nominal | 9.0:1
Number of cylinders | 4
Cylinder bore | 3.54 in. (90 mm.)
Stroke | 2.32 in. (58.86 mm.)
Cylinder displacement | 91.4 cu. in. (1498 cc.)
Firing order | 1−3−4−2
Placement of cylinders (from front of car):
Right-hand side | 1−2
Left-hand side | 3−4
Idling speed | 900 rpm
Engine suspension | 3−point suspension
Weight, incl. electr. equip. and carb. | 265 lbs. (120 kg.)

CYLINDER BLOCK
Type | 60° V, block and crankcase one piece cast
Material | Cast iron of a special alloy
Number of main bearings | 3
Cylinder block bores for camshaft bushings
Front | 44.65−44.68 mm.
Center | 44.27−44.30 mm.
Rear | 43.89−43.92 mm.
Cylinder block bores for balance shaft bushings
Front | 54.420−54.445 mm.
Rear | 57.620−57.645 mm.
Cylinder bore
Standard | 90.030−90.040 mm.
Oversize 0.02 in. (0.5 mm.) | 90.530−90.540 mm.
Oversize 0.04 (1.0 mm.) | 91.030−91.040 mm.
Diameter main bearing bore | red 60.62−60.63 mm.
blue 60.63−60.64 mm.
Thrust bearing width | 22.61−22.66 mm.

PISTONS
Material | Aluminium
Number of rings, each piston | 2 compress. and 1 oil control (tripartite)
Permissible dif. in weight (piston
and connect. rod) in one engine | 0.46 oz. (13 g.)
Piston-ring groove width
Upper | 2.030−2.055 mm.
Center | 3.030−3.056 mm.
Lower | 5.017−5.042 mm.
Piston diameter
(Piston is out-of-round and spherical)
Standard—89.978−90.000 mm.
Oversize 0.5−90.478−90.502 mm.
Oversize 1.0−90.978−91.002 mm.
Piston clearance | 0.0011−0.0024 in. 0.03−0.06 mm.
Piston, removal | From the upper side of the cylinder block
Position of the piston | The notch forward
Piston and connecting rod must not be separated. Therefore, only piston with connecting rod mounted is available as a spare part.

PISTON RINGS
Upper compression ring
Thickness | 1.978−1.990 mm.
Width | 0.15 in. max. (max. 3.76 mm.)
Piston-ring clearance in groove | 0.0394−0.077 mm.
Gap in position | 0.250−0.500 mm.
Lower compression ring
Thickness | 2.978−2.990 mm.
Width | 0.15 in. max. (max. 3.76 mm.)
Piston ring play (in groove) | 0.040−0.078 mm.
Gap in position | 0.250−0.500 mm.

Oil control ring (tripartite):

Thckness (total)	4.839—4.991 mm.
Width (segment)	3.430—3.580 mm.
Piston ring play in groove (total)	0.026—0.203 mm.
Gap in position (Segment)	0.0380—1.400 mm.

CONNECTING RODS

Bore diam. in big-end

Red	56.820—56.830 mm.
Blue	56.830—56.840 mm.

Vertical inner diam. of fitted con-rod bearing inserts

Standard blue	54.004—54.034 mm.
Red	54.014—54.044 mm.
Undersize 0.05	53.943—53.983 mm.
0.25	53.760—53.800 mm.
0.50	53.506—53.546 mm.
0.75	53.252—53.292 mm.
1.00	52.998—53.038 mm.

Diam. of crankpins

Standard blue	53.99—53.98 mm.
Red	54.00—53.99 mm.
Undersize 0.05	53.929—53.919 mm.
0.25	53.476—53.736 mm.
0.50	53.492—53.482 mm.
0.75	53.238—53.228 mm.
1.00	52.984—52.974 mm.

Journal clear. in main bear.

Standard	0.014—0.054 mm.
Undersize	0.014—0.064 mm.

CRANKSHAFT

Crankpin diameter	see above
Number of main bearings	3

Main bearing diam.

Standard red	57.000—56.990 mm.
Blue	56.990—56.980 mm.
Undersize 0.05	56.929—56.919 mm.
0.25	56.746—56.736 mm.
0.50	56.492—56.482 mm.
0.75	56.238—56.228 mm.
1.00	55.984—55.974 mm.

Vertical inner diam. of fitted main bearing inserts

Standard blue	57.004—57.020 mm.
Red	57.014—57.030 mm.
Undersize 0.25	56.760—56.776 mm.
0.50	56.506—56.522 mm.
0.75	56.252—56.268 mm.
1.00	55.998—56.014 mm.

Clearance between insert and crank pin

Standard	0.012—0.048 mm.
Undersize	0.014—0.058 mm.
Thrust journal length (center main bearing)	26.44—26.39 mm.
Crankshaft end-play	0.102—0.203 mm.
Thrust (axial) bearing insert width	26.29—26.24 mm.

BALANCE SHAFT

Number of bearings	2

Clear. in bushing:

Front	0.02—0.08 mm.
Rear	0.03—0.07 mm.
Balance shaft end play	0.05—0.15 mm.

Inner diam. of bushings:

Front	50.85—50.88 mm.
Rear	54.03—54.05 mm.

Bear. diam. of balance shaft:

Front	50.83—50.80 mm.
Rear	54.00—53.98 mm.
Backlash, new drive gear	0.05—0.14 mm.
Backlash, wear limit	0.40 mm.

CAMSHAFT

Number of bearings	3

Insert diameter:

Front	41.516—41.542 mm.
Center	41.135—41.161 mm.
Rear	40.754—40.780 mm.
Bearing clearance, all	0.077—0.0025 mm.

Inner diam. of bushings:

Front	41.587—41.593 mm.
Center	41.186—41.212 mm.
Rear	40.805—40.831 mm.
Camshaft end-play	0.025—0.076 mm.

Spacer thickness:

Red	4.064—4.089 mm.
Blue	4.089—4.114 mm.
Camshaft drive	gear pinion
Number of teeth on pinion	34
Number of teeth on camshaft gear	68
Backlash, new drive gear	0.05—0.20 mm.
Backlash, wear limit	0.40 mm.
Cam lift	0.256 in. (6.490 mm.)
Cam heel-to-toe dimension	34.201—33.998 mm.

VALVE MECHANISM

Angle of seat (cylinder head) intake and exhaust	45°
Seat width, intake and exhaust	0.059—0.070 in. (1.5—1.7 mm.)

Stem diameter

Intake:

standard	8.043—8.025 mm.
oversize	8.243—8.225 mm.
	8.443—8.425 mm.
	8.643—8.625 mm.
	8.843—8.825 mm.

Exhaust:

standard	8.017—7.999 mm.
oversize	8.217—8.199 mm.
	8.417—8.399 mm.
	8.617—8.599 mm.
	8.817—8.799 mm.

Stem bore in cyl. head intake and exhaust	8.063—8.088 mm.
Clearance betw. stem and guide	intake 0.020—0.063 mm.
	exhaust 0.046—0.089 mm.
Disc. diam.	intake 1.46 in. (37 mm.)
	exhaust 1.26 in. (32 mm.)
Valve lift	0.38 in. (9.7 mm.)

Valve clearance, warm engine

Intake	0.0157 in. (0.40 mm.)
Exhaust	0.0157 in. (0.40 mm.)
Free length of springs	1.85 in. (47 mm.)
Fully compressed	1.06 in. (27 mm.)
Load for compression to 1.59 in. (40.26 mm.)	55—66 lbs. (27—30 kp.)
Valve tappet diam.	22.202—22.190 mm.
Clear. between tappet and bore	0.023—0.060 mm.

VALVE TIMING (meas. at valve play of 0.425 mm.)

Intake opens	21° BTDC
closes	82° ATDC
Exhaust opens	63° BTDC
closes	40° ATDC

LUBRICATION SYSTEM

Type	Circulation system lub. under pressure
	Oil pump of rotor type
Pressure lubricated bearings	Camshaft, crankshaft, balance shaft, connecting rods, rocker arms
Splash lubrication	Piston pins and cylinder walls
Transmission gear, lubrication	Oil spray
Oil filter, type	Full-flow type
Crankcase ventilation, totally enclosed	From air filter via crankcase and NOVO-valve to inlet manifold

Oil

Summer	SAE 20 W 20
	Multigrade oil SAE 10 W 30
	Multigrade oil SAE 10 W 40
Winter (below 14°F —10°C)	SAE 10 W
	Multigrade oil SAE 10 W 30
	Multigrade oil SAE 10 W 40
At extremely cold weather (i.e. at a prolonged temperature below —4°F (—20°C))	SAE 5 W 20

NOTE: SAE 5 W 20 should not be used at temperatures above +32°F (0°C)

Oil pan cap. incl. oil filter	3.3 U.S. quarts (3.3 liters)
Oil pan cap. excl. oil filter	3.0 U.S. quarts (3 liters)
Oil pump relief valve opens at	47—55.5 psi (3.3—3.9 kp/cm²)
Oil press. warning light operates at	4.3—8.5 psi (0.3—0.6 kp/cm²)
Draining plug, thread	M 14x1.5 (width across flats 0.75 in. = 19 mm.)

Oil pump

Clearance, rotor to housing	0.012 in. (0.3 mm.)
Clearance, rotor to sealing surface	0.004 in. (0.1 mm.)

Wrench Torques

Bolt	kpm	ft. lbs.
Main bearing cap bolts	10	72
Connecting rod nuts	3.5	25
Crankshaft gear bolt	5.0	36
Flywheel retaining bolts, crankshaft	7.0	50
Camshaft thrust plate, block	2.0	15
Bolt—camshaft gear	5.0	36
Cylinder head to block		
(to be tightened in 3 stages)	5.5	40
	7.0	50
	9.5	68
Induction manifold to block		
(to be tightened in 4 stages)	0.5	4
	1.5	11
	2.0	15
	2.5	18
Intermediate plate to block	2.0	15
Transmission cover	2.0	15
Water pump to transmission cover	1.0	7
Pulley to balance shaft	5.0	36
Oil pump to block	1.5	11
Oil pan to block	0.5	4
Thermostat housing to induction manifold	2.0	15
Valve cover to cylinder head	0.5	4
Rocker shaft bracket	4.5	32

Oil filter half a turn after contact between gasket and engine block

Fuel System

Sa Free Exhaust Emission

CARBURETOR

Type: Solex with automatic choke	32 PDSIT—4
Main jet	122.5
Choke tube	25.5
Emulsion jet	100
Idling jet, fuel	50
air (drilling)	1.5
Float valve	1.5
Float weight	7.3 g.
Acceleration jet	50
Acceleration pump cap.	0.6±0.12 cu. in. (10±2 cm³) /10 strokes
Idling speed	900 rpm with headlights lower beam on

Rapid idling:

stage I	1100—1300 rpm
stage II	1700—1900 rpm
stage III	2700—2900 rpm
Float level when idling	Nom. 0.59±0.04 in. (15±1 mm.) from gasket level

FUEL PUMP

Type	Diaphragm pump driven by eccentric on the camshaft
Feeding pressure	3.4—4.3 psi (0.24—0.30 kp/cm²) at 4000 crankshaft rpm
Fuel tank, capacity	15.8 U.S. gal. (60 liters)

Exhaust System

Exhaust pipe, internal diameter	1.34 in. (34 mm.)

Cooling System

Capacity incl. heater	1.9 gal. (7.2 liters)
Thermostat opening range	181°F. (83° C.)
Max. opening	0.28 in. (7 mm.)
Radiator pressure cap opens at	2.2—4.3 psi (0.25—0.30 kp/cm²)
Fanbelt, designation	9.5x1025 La.

Amount of glycol in the cooling and heating system

Glycol (quarts)	Volume % approx.	Freezing Point °F.	°C.	Boiling Point °F.	°C.	Specific Gravity
1	13	21	— 6	214	101	1,017
2	27	5	—15	216	102	1,037
3	40	—15	—26	219	104	1,055
4	53	—46	—43	225	107	1,071

Electrical System

BATTERY

Voltage	12 V
Capacity	44 Ah

Oil filter half a turn after contact between gasket and engine block

ALTERNATOR, BOSCH

Type	K 1⟷14V 35 A 20 0 120 400 657
Rated voltage	14 V
Rated rpm	2000
Max. permiss. contin. load	35 A
Direction of rotation	Clockwise and counter-clockwise
Brush-spring pressure	10.5—14 oz. (300—400 g.)

CHARGING REGULATOR, BOSCH

Type	BOSCH AD 1 14 V (not radio suppressed)

STARTER MOTOR, BOSCH

Type	EF (R) 12V 0.8 PS 0 001 208 029
Number of teeth on pinion	9
Number of teeth on ring gear	138
Brush-spring pressure	40.5—46 oz. (1150—1300 g.)
Output	0.8 hp

DISTRIBUTOR, BOSCH

Type	0 231 146 073
Capacitor	1 237 330 113
Ignition setting	
Basic setting with stroboscope at 1000 rpm with disconnected vac. hose	10° BTDC

(NOTE: 1° on the balance shaft pulley corresponds to approx. 0.05 in. (1.2 mm.) on circumference of pulley.)

Order of firing, cyl. 1 is the furthermost right-hand one	1—3—4—2
Breaker gap	0.016 in. (0.4 mm.)
Dwell angle	50±2°
Contact pressure	14—19 oz. (400—530 g.)
Direction of rotation	clockwise

IGNITION COIL, BOSCH

Type	K 12
Performances at a primary voltage of 12 V	
4,000 sparks/minute (1,000 distributor rev.). Spark length min.	0.55 in. (14 mm.)
16,000 sparks/minute (4,000 distributor rev.). Spark length min.	0.24 in. (6 mm.)
Primary-winding resist. (betw. connect. 1 and 15)	3.1—3.6 ohms

SPARK PLUGS	Grey-painted engine Up to chassis 510	Blue-painted engine From chassis 511
Auto-Lite	AE—22	AG—22
Bosch	W 225 T35	
Champion	L 82 Y	
	L 87 Y	
NGK	B—7H	

Electrode gap	0.024—0.028 in. (0.6—0.7 mm.)
Tightening torque	22—29 ft. lbs. (3.0—4.0 kpm.)

BULBS	Number	Philips No.	Watts
Headlights, Sealed Beam (USA)	2		
Parking lights, front	2	12819	6
Flasher, front	2	1073	25
Flasher and stop lights, rear	2	1073	25
Tail light	2	12821	5
License plate light	2	12844	5
Back-up light	2	12325	25
Lighting, clock	1	12929	4
Lighting, tachometer	1	12913	2
Instrument and control lights	11	12829	2
Map reading light	1	12844	5
Fuses (25 mm.)	12		8A

FLASHER UNIT

Type: Lucas	FL 5 12 V 42 W
Hella	91 PSt 2x32 Cp 12 V

HORN, HELLA

Type	B 32/5—12 V

FUEL GAUGE TANK UNIT

Type	VDO 625

Heater Fan Motor
Type: Electrolux KS 3430/220 12 V

Windshield Wiper Motor
Type: Lucas DL 3 A

Windshield Washer MEAB

Transmission

Oil capacity	approx. 1.7 quarts (1.7 liters)
Type of oil	EP—oil SAE 80
Gear ratios, total	
1st gear	16.23:1
2nd gear	9.74:1
3rd gear	6.05:1
4th gear	3.9:1
Reverse	14.8:1
Dif. gear ratio, pinion: ring gear	4.67:1
Number of teeth, pinion: ring gear	9:42

Road speed in mph at 1000 rpm engine speed, calculated running radius 11.8 in. (300 mm.)

1st gear	4.3 mph. 7.0 km/h
2nd gear	7.3 mph. 11.7 km/h
3rd gear	11.9 mph. 19.0 km/h
4th gear	18.1 mph. 29.0 km/h
Reverse	4.7 mph. 7.6 km/h

Pinion/ring-gear adjustment: specified dimension ±0.002 in. (0.05 mm.) Ring-gear backlash: specified dimension ±0.002 in. (0.05 mm.)

Matched Gearsets

3rd speed gear	Ring gear
Pinion shaft 3rd gear	Pinion shaft
4th speed gear	Synchromesh
Pinion shaft 4th gear	

Tightening Torques, Transmission

Bolt	No.	Bolts Size	Tightening torques kpm	ft. lbs.
Transmiss. case end cover	6	5/16 in.	2.5	18
Differential bearings	4	3/8 in.	4	29
Ring gear bolts	12	5/16 in.	2.5	18
Pinion-shaft nut, First tightening	1	7/8 in.	12	87
Then slacken and retighten			6	44
Nut, primary shaft	1	3/4 in.	5	36
Nut, countershaft	1	9/16 in.	8	60

Clutch

Fichtel & Sachs
Hydraulic

Type	single dry plate
Clearance, release bearing—clutch meas. at slave cylinder	0.16 in. (4 mm.)
Clearance betw. release plate and flywheel	approx. 1.71 in. (43.5 mm.)
Pressure-plate springs	
Length compressed	0.96 in. (24.5 mm.)
Tension when compressed	134—147 lbs. (61—67 kp.)
Dimensions of clutch facing	5x6.5 in. (127x190.5 mm.)
New clutch disc	
Thickness, unloaded	0.33±0.04 in. (8.4±0.1 mm.)
loaded with 825 lbs. (375 kg.)	0.28±0.01 in. (7.2±0.3 mm)
Max. throw clutch disc	0.024 in. (0.6 mm.)
Engagement pressure	750—935 lbs. (340—425 kp.)

Hydraulic:	Master Cylinder	Slave Cylinder
Make and type	Girling 5/8 in.	Girling D2
Cylinder diameter	5/8 in.	3/4 in.
Max. permissible stroke	1.38 in. (35 mm.)	
Hose connection	3/8 in. UNF—24	3/8 in. UNF—24

Hose length betw. master and slave cyl.	14 in. (355 mm.)
Distance from clutch-pedal foot plate to toe-board (max. pedal stroke)	approx. 3.55 in. (ca 90 mm.)
Clearance, release bearing—clutch meas. at slave cyl.	0.16 in. (4 mm.)

Brake System

General

Make	Lockheed
Type, front	Disc brake
rear	One leading shoe
Footbrake	Hydraulic two-circuit type
Handbrake	Mechanical

Dimensions, Etc.

Brake front, disc	10 1/2 in. (266.7 mm.)
rear, drum	8 in. (203.2 mm.)
Master cylinder	3/4 in.
Wheel cylinder, front	2 in.
rear	5/8 in.
Brake shoes, rear	8 inx1 1/2 in.
Brake hoses, front, length of	8 1/2 in.
rear, length of	8 1/2 in.
Other brake lines	3/16 in. Bundy tube
Clearance between master-cylinder piston and pushrod	0.024—0.047 in. (0.6—1.2 mm.)
Same clearance at tip of brake pedal	0.12—0.24 in. (3—6 mm.)
Brake fluid	SAE 70 R 3
Adjustment machining of brake drums permitted to max. diameter	
Rear	8.06 in. (204.7 mm.)
Max. total indicated radial brake-drum throw	0.006 in. (0.15 mm.)
Max. total indicated axial brake disc throw	0.08 in. (0.2 mm.)
Centerless grinding of brake linings	Thickness of rear brake lining: 0.020—0.22 in. (0.50—0.56 mm.) less than that of the drum
Tightening torques	
Castle nut, front wheel hub	18 kpm., 130 ft. lbs.
rear wheel hub	9 kpm., 65 ft. lbs.

Suspension, Steering, and Wheel Alignment

Wheel Alignment

Front wheel alignment, no load

Kingpin inclination	7±1°
Caster	2±1/2°
Camber	0±1/4°
Toe-in at wheel rim	0.04±0.04 in. (1±1 mm.)
Turning angles	
Outside wheels	20°
Inside wheels	22 1/2±1 1/2°

Steering Gear

Steering-gear adjustment

Pinion axial clearance	0.04—0.08 in. (0.1—0.2 mm.)
Radial clearance of rack	max. 0.012 in. (0.3 mm.)
Steering ratio, steering wheel/ road wheels average	14:1
Wheel travel between limit positions	2 1/4 turns
Tie-rod ends	
Distance between wrench flat and retaining nut	max. 1.5 in. (40 mm.)
Permissible difference between left-hand and right-hand dimension	max. 0.08 in. (2 mm.)

Tightening Torque

Nut, tie-rod end	3.5—5 kpm., 25—36 ft. lbs.

Rear Wheel Alignment

Camber	0±1°
Toe-in (toe-out)	0±1°
Both wheels together or measured rim-to-rim	0±0.28 in. (7 mm.)
Toe-in (toe-out) per wheel must not exceed	0±3/4°
Max. dif. in wheelbase, left and right (front wheels pointing straight ahead)	0.6 in. (15 mm.)

Front Shock Absorbers

Type	Telescopic, hydraulic
Length	9 3/4 in. (250 mm.) Extended 15 3/8 in. (390 mm.)
Stroke, fitted	3 1/4 in. (82 mm.)

REAR SHOCK ABSORBERS
Type	Telescopic, hydraulic
Length between center hole and shoulder for washer	10 in. (255 mm.)
Extended	16 7/16 in. (417 mm.)
Stroke	4 1/4 in. (106 mm.)

WHEELS
Type	wide base
Size	4.5 J x 15 in.
Depth of drop center	1.77 in. (45 mm.)
Permissible out-of-round of rim	0.06 in. (1.5 mm.)
Permissible runout	0.06 in. (1.5 mm.)

TIRES
Size	155x15 in.

	Front	Rear
Tire pressure	25 psi (1.8 kp/cm^2)	22 psi (1.6 kp/cm^2)

SUSPENSION WHEELS
Front coil spring
Max. expansion	5 1/2 in. (139 mm.)
Length	13.4 in. (339 mm.)
Number of coils springing	8 1/2
Wire diameter	0.47 in. (12 mm.)

Rear coil spring
Max. expansion	5.9 in. (150 mm.)
Length	12.5 in. (318 mm.)
Number of coils springing	7 1/2
Wire diameter	0.4 in. (10.0 mm.)

WHEEL BOLTS
Width across flats	3/4 in. (19.05 mm.)
Thread	UNC 9/16 in.

TIGHTENING TORQUES
Castle nut, front wheel hub	18 kpm. 130 ft. lbs.
rear wheel hub	9.5 kpm. 70 ft. lbs.
Wheel bolts	8—10 kpm. 58—72 ft. lbs.

Instruments

Speedometer drive ratio	
Ratio ring gear: pinion	9:42
Dynamic radius of road wheel	11.8 in. (300 mm.)
Speedometer	
Rev. per kilometer covered	570
Rev. per mile covered	917